Winning Résumés for Computer Personnel

Second Edition

By
Anne Hart, M.A.

©Copyright 1998 by Barron's Educational Series, Inc.

All rights reserved.
No part of this book may be reproduced
in any form, by photostat, microfilm, xerography,
or any other means, or incorporated into any
information retrieval system, electronic or
mechanical, without the written permission
of the copyright owner.

All inquiries should be addressed to:
Barron's Educational Series, Inc.
250 Wireless Boulevard
Hauppauge, New York 11788

Library of Congress Catalog Card No.: 97-30120

International Standard Book No. 0-7641-0130-7

Library of Congress Cataloging-in-Publication Data
Hart, Anne.
      Winning résumés for computer personnel / by Anne Hart. — 2nd ed.
        p.   cm.
     Includes index
     ISBN 0-7641-0130-7
     1. Résumés (Employment)   2. Electronic data processing personnel—
Vocational guidance.   3. Computer industry—Vocational guidance.
I. Title.
    HF5383.C368   1998
    808'.06665—dc21   97-30120
                                                                                            CIP

PRINTED IN THE UNITED STATES OF AMERICA
9 8 7 6 5 4 3

CONTENTS

	Introduction	iv
1	Résumés That Get You a Job	1
2	What Goes into a Résumé?	19
3	Cover and Follow-Up Letters	40
4	Organizing Skills on Paper	60
5	Edit the Résumé	87
6	Nontraditional Résumés	104
7	Retirees and Others	113
8	Which Job Is the Right Job?	126
9	Your Preferences and Type	149
10	Sample Résumés	168
11	Steering Strategies	228
12	New Opportunities with the Internet and the World Wide Web	231
	Appendices	
	A—Résumé Tracking Follow-Up Worksheet	235
	B—Computer Industry Associations	236
	C—Computer Industry Trade Periodicals	248
	Index	257

INTRODUCTION

If your current résumé isn't getting you interviews, this book will help. In this book you will learn how to write winning résumés as commercial sales tools—résumés that are powerful, competitive, and unforgettable. You will learn how to position yourself first in the eyes of future employers.

Whether you want to work in virtual reality entertainment theme parks from Singapore to Silicon Valley, donning touch-sensitive gloves and 3-D goggles; create computerized medical or architectural simulations for modeling and training; program scientific, social, or financial information; illustrate ads; design World Wide Web sites; or use a computer for word and record processing in an office, you will need to communicate how you can benefit an employer to compete for a job.

Computer companies receive the most diverse résumés in the world, because the jobs information providers perform grow more diverse daily. However, everybody working in the computer industry is doing the same job, essentially: distributing or packaging information. Employers are migrating from the "business-as-usual" processes of the past to an "information product" mindset. The impact these migration strategies are making on job hunting is awesome.

New computer careers focus on jobs in three main industries: 1) computer information science; 2) computer engineering technology; 3) computer applications and networks.

Within these three main divisions are the converging technologies tapping the Internet and intranet communications industry. Computer information science has its own niches in programming, analysis, and database technology. Computer engineering technology has network diagnostics and personal computer technology. Computer applications and networks niches include business software and systems, scientific software, and designing and administration of World Wide Web sites.

In the periphery are the telephone and telecommunications companies that are moving into immersive video, satellite technology (taking business away from the cable companies), the Internet and on-line services, and intranets (private networks within corporations or organizations that encompass electronic mail and other services).

Electronic publishing, including scrolling news or netcasting (news on computer screens with or without connection to the Internet, such as AirMedia Live), makes up a growing computer industry that changes every year.

Each of these converging industries sees your résumé in a different way. In addition, the Internet has changed forever the job market for computer personnel. It has revolutionized the way job seekers market themselves. These days your résumé may be just one page of your personal Web site. Consider whether or not your résumé should be on-line and what the format should be. Do you need a compelling video clip, or will an interactive résumé be the best way to motivate an employer to respond to you on-line?

Another challenge facing job hunters is that fewer jobs in general will be offered during the 1994 to 2005 decade. Colleges are turning out more graduates to compete for fewer positions. According to the U.S. Department of Labor, between 1994 and the year 2005, "the number of college graduates will outpace the number of available jobs by 20 percent each year." The number of older, laid-off workers returning to college is increasing as well as the number of younger college graduates—despite fewer people in their twenties in the population.

Competition for computer-related information industry jobs is increasing. It's important to target several closely related fields for flexibility as well as specialty. Pick a high-growth area within the computer industry, such as the application of computer technology to health care systems, training, artificial intelligence, or multimedia presentation graphics. The application of digital multimedia to training, communications, and entertainment will offer some of the best jobs in the computer industry in the coming decades.

Be inventive. If you are in school, seek cooperative programs where companies try out employees who are still in school by hiring them for a semester.

If you are an older worker not in school, create your own telephone marathon. Phone companies and ask for jobs—just as college fundraisers call alumni asking for donations. If the companies can't offer jobs, then ask for information and referrals.

Fundraisers know exactly how to ask for money from business owners. Fundraisers use persuasion techniques to sell benefits and ask for money in return. In this book, you will learn to use professional fundraising techniques to repackage your résumé for the computer industry (also known as the information industry). Your goal is to persuade employers to offer you an interview and, ultimately, a job.

The information industry, known as an "enabling technology," relies on the teamwork attitude. Computer companies are always seeking better ways to harness the energy, knowledge, and experience of computer users and workers. Every aspect of the computer industry is growing more interactive and user-friendly.

Look at your résumés, cover letters, interviews, and follow-up letters as windows of opportunity to free your inner voice. A résumé verifies that you have been recognized, valued, and discovered. The act of writing your résumé plugs you into your own inner energy. It's a mirror that reflects your self-esteem, because you do what you are.

Most companies still obtain résumés by advertising, employee referrals, college recruitment, employment agencies and other traditional means. Ironically, the last place an employer looks for a résumé is to the individual who contacts the company without first being asked. Therefore, by contacting organizations before they are swamped by a rush of résumés, chances are you'll stand out from the crowd.

When all résumés begin to look alike, employers may finally hire the job applicant with the most enthusiasm. Between the detailed lines of your résumé, will an employer see your positive attitude, energy, and enthusiasm?

When employers ask for "a good closer," they are talking about enthusiasm for the company and the product or service. A great résumé doesn't close the sale. Your pitch in the interview is the real closer. It summarizes in one sentence every advantage you can offer the company.

Your résumé measures how much you believe in yourself. If you really believe in what you do, you'll never have to painfully work at finding the right career. You'll value what you do so much that you'll enjoy doing the job for the salary. To be valued by others, you must first value yourself. Are you still using the word *failure* for setback?

When you write to an employer, you are really expressing the strength within yourself. Now let's look at how to present your competencies to achieve results.

1
RESUMES THAT GET YOU A JOB

TODAY'S EMPLOYERS REQUIRE TECHNICAL SKILLS OF THE MOMENT

A 1996 survey of 1,441 large and medium-size corporations found that 68 percent created new jobs in the year that ended in June of 1996, compared with 58 percent one year earlier. Only 7.1 percent of these workers lost their jobs in that time, according to the American Management Association. That's less than the 10.4 percent who lost jobs back in 1993.

For every job eliminated, a worker is hired for a new job requiring very different, usually specific, technical skills of the moment. As corporations re-engineer and restructure, more jobs are added to handle increased business.

Each year in the United States 10 million employees are terminated from their jobs. Another 10 million workers leave voluntarily. Every five years the entire work force turns over. Twenty million job seekers annually wonder how to repackage their competencies.

Who's being hired for computer-related jobs? If you are judged able to handle new technology, you are likely to be hired. Also, you must be able to fill jobs following a company's relocation. It's middle managers, who represent less than 10 percent of the U.S. workforce, who are suffering most from downsizing. In the new media, the Internet world, less supervision is required for these new technical jobs.

Nearly three middle management jobs are being cut for every one created. The management jobs are being replaced by jobs that require technical know-how of the Internet and related computer technology such as telephony, satellite TV, immersive video, and anything related to the convergence of phones, computers, and video—networking, digital interactive software, Web administration/design and engineering.

Employers hire you for a variety of reasons, but many are concerned with the clarity of your goals. Only three questions clarify goals in a résumé: 1) Where have you been? 2) How long have you been there? 3) Where are you going?

These are the same three goal-clarifying questions asked of travelers by every border crossing guard in the world. Writing a résumé is similar to crossing a boundary. Moving forward challenges you to seek a better future.

Presenting Yourself

An employer looks for familiar patterns in your résumé, patterns that are found in the company. The corporation or educational institution sees your résumé as a predictor of the organization's future. You are hired for concrete, common sense reasons. You are hired to solve problems. You are hired because you present the least possible risk to the company and the best benefits to its profit and production. An employer invests hundreds of thousands of dollars in your salary, insurance, on-the-job training, perks, and other benefits during the time you're working for the firm.

Small business entrepreneurs may see your résumé as a future spinoff of their plans for expansion. An employer might look at a carelessly written résumé and see self-rejection. Or an employer might only observe whether your skills fit the exact needs of the company at a given time.

Emphasize Your Key Abilities

Everyone in the computer industry is hired to organize. Yet the most common complaint of personnel departments is that the résumés coming in aren't organized to emphasize the applicant's most beneficial abilities. Your best abilities are often what you do well naturally. Before you begin to plan a résumé, ask yourself the following five questions:

1. What kind of mental or physical work would you do as a labor of love without being paid?
2. What job would you choose if you knew you could not get fired as long as you were doing your best?
3. What work activities offer you enough mental and physical challenges for lifelong growth?
4. Does your résumé show how you spend your time and money doing what you love to do?
5. What do you consider successful about the work experiences you've listed on your résumé?

Recognize Opportunities for Success

If the activities you enjoy most can't go on your résumé because they aren't related to your career, it indicates an opportunity you have finally recognized. Change your career. If you don't want to change your career, then change jobs within the same career. Find a position with new or different duties.

For example, if you are a medical transcriptionist doing word processing on a computer all day and don't enjoy it, perhaps you would enjoy being a manufacturer's representative selling medical records software to hospitals as you travel. You might enjoy meeting new people and talking about the efficiency and benefits of software, instead of keyboarding data.

If you would prefer a more recreational career, you might try working as a counselor at or owner/manager of a computer camp. Computer camps allow children or adults to learn about computers while vacationing in a recreational environment.

UNDERSTANDING THE ORGANIZATION'S CHARACTER AND NATURE

Are you familiar with the character of the organization you want to work for? Like people, companies have different personalities that reflect the attitudes and preferences of whomever is in charge. Comparing your personality type to the character of an organization before you apply there is known as taking the personality-centered approach to job hunting.

By matching your personality type with the character of an organization, you can create optimum productivity in any situation where you have to work with others. When the work is satisfying, you will do your best. In contrast, when you are in frequent conflict with your co-workers or bosses, you'll be more interested in looking elsewhere for a job.

Why Organizations Act As They Do

How do you find out a company's character? Ask an employer these two questions: 1) Where is the company going? 2) What is its mission or philosophy? You want to know what the company is all about.

The company may describe itself as either a benchmarking or a visioning organization. For in-depth information on benchmarking, visioning, and the character of organizations, read *The Character of Organizations,* by William Bridges (Consulting Psychologists Press, Palo Alto, 1992). Let's take a brief look at the definitions of benchmarking and visioning companies.

Benchmarking Companies

The corporate world often uses the term benchmarking. Benchmarking organizations model themselves after other companies that make something very successfully as a way to determine how things ought to be made. Benchmarkers emulate the best and most popular. An example is the company that tries to model itself after Intel (today) or IBM (a decade before the compatibles appeared in the marketplace).

Visioning Companies

Visioning companies are always looking toward the future for new possibilities, new ways of doing things. These new ways must satisfy a great need. Visioning companies seek out new ideas, new ways to think—however wild, imaginative, creative, and fantastic they seem, as long as they work. The word *visioning* is often used in the computer industry, especially in interactive multimedia and fiber optics research, to mean forward-looking, user-oriented, intuitive kind of thinking that turns ideas into new products.

Examples of visioning company products include CD-ROM machines to put your book on laser disk, Philip's Imagination Machine (CD-I technology), interactive industry magazines, and virtual reality equipment. San Francisco is a center for the interactive multimedia industry, the ultimate in visioning. For further information on interactive communications, write to San Francisco Multimedia Development, 2601 Mariposa St., San Francisco, CA 94110 (415) 553-2300 or to Ed-Tech Review, National Association for the Advancement of Computing in Education, PO Box 2966, Charlottesville, VA 22902 (804) 973-3987.

Examples of visioning ideas that the computer industry is presently developing into actual projects and business ventures include the following:

- virtual reality equipment or desktop animation software for public entertainment and for training surgeons, pilots, architects, designers, and soldiers
- hypermedia and new media publications
- robots for industrial, educational, and military security
- artificial intelligence for financial database management and predicting growth stocks
- software for fashion designers
- videotape and computers in desktop animation
- direct broadcast satellite (DBS), computers, and wireless phones
- interactive-CD for distance learning or entertainment
- fiber optics to link multimedia information highways and libraries
- electronic tracking
- media laboratories
- branching pathway fiction with alternate adventures
- computer game icon agents
- telecommunications, conferencing, and phone line-computer-satellite links
- electronic universal information libraries
- university courses by computer-to-home link-ups (distance education)

Know the Organization's Needs

A company's character defines how it communicates its needs. The organization shows you the hole that has to be filled. The character of your résumé defines how you communicate what you are about and where you are going. Visioning people need to be matched with visioning organizations. Benchmarking employees feel better when they are working with benchmarking companies.

Before you send your résumé blindly to any company, understand what kinds of help that organization needs.

Fitting in with the Group vs. Work Competency

You are hired not only for your skill competency, but also because you fit in with the group. Comfortable fit is foremost to the employer.

Comfortable fit works both ways. More people are terminated for personality conflicts than for incompetency or tardiness.

Every advertising agency on Madison Avenue knows "you don't get a second chance to make a first impression," as stated in the marketing classic, *Positioning: The Battle for Your Mind*. Positioning works the same way for job hunters in the computer industry. The company's first impression of you is your cover letter followed by your résumé.

Your résumé also reveals which part of the computer industry is right for you. It's an image of you, your personality, and your preferences.

Impulsive vs. Compulsive Organizations

Like people, companies come in impulsive and compulsive types. It's important to match a compulsive, routine-seeking job hunter who offers dependability, loyalty, service, and duty with the same type of employer.

The compulsive company emphasizes the security of and need to belong to a large, solvent firm offering steady work. Examples include: hospitals, government, schools, and the military. Other examples of compulsive companies are banks, utilities, law enforcement agencies, computer security and accounting firms, electronic systems suppliers, the electronic home response industry, home health care software suppliers, and the more traditional computer giants.

The impulsive applicant should be matched with an independent, change-oriented, and innovative employer. The impulsive company emphasizes time flexibility, creativity, achievements, analysis, communication, and a nonlinear fast track to the top. Advancement in an impulsive organization is based on ingenuity, intuition, inventiveness, and impressive profits.

Examples of impulsive computer industry organizations include cutting edge virtual reality companies, software firms dealing with the newest in CD-ROM software, educational software and video production firms, computer games manufacturers, artificial intelligence research firms, the most successful computer publications, the computer training management industry, computer human resources specialists, special effects/corporate animation/computer graphics, and simulation software design firms.

To match your résumé (and ultimately you) to either impulsive or compulsive companies, ask what magazines the company's president and your potential supervisor read. Even the computer industry has its own compulsive and impulsive publications. Try to find out whether the publications your employer reads are impulsive (like *The Futurist, Wired, New Media, Internet World, QuickTime Forum*) and scientifically oriented mass media magazines like *Omni* and *Discover;* or whether they are mainstream, business-oriented magazines such as *Forbes* and *Fortune.*

The compulsive computer industry publications follow the computer giants more than the independent company spinoffs. Impulsive periodicals follow the smaller, start-up companies, the independents, and new technology or products that compete with the giants.

How else can you tell whether the firm you select is impulsive or compulsive? Does the firm emphasize utility, the present moment, and the practical? Is the company making the computer equivalent of the safety pin? Does it look back in time to tradition in order to move forward new technology? Does it run a tight ship? It could be compulsive.

Does the organization make its tremendous profit by selling imagination? Does it sell interactive multimedia, hypertext, hypermedia, learning as entertainment, or virtual reality? Does the organization look at consumer needs and offer education as fun? Can the creative employees work flexible hours? It could be impulsive.

Knowing whether you are compulsive or impulsive in work habits helps match your résumé with a company that emphasizes your purpose in life, values, and natural abilities.

Does Your Résumé Reflect the Employer's Traditions?
When a change-oriented résumé lands on the desk of an employer looking for tradition in the most rapidly changing of businesses, you have a battle between logistics and analysis.

Consumer need for user-friendly education as entertainment technology collides with the old notion of number-crunching computers based on the universal need to count and store. The employment result pits tradition against new media that changes the way people learn and play. Every new job applicant in the computer industry struggles with change and tradition.

NETWORKING

Most people enjoy networking with others employed in coveted positions. It's draining to job hunt alone.

Professional associations use recorded telephone job referrals to increase membership and attendance at evening networking meetings. The purpose of networking is to help you feel more in control of your job search by making helpful contacts.

Networking With Your Résumé
Job hunting can be a full-time job. Always carry copies of your résumé; distributing your résumé in person while networking may result in job offers.

According to numerous firms providing career services, sending résumés to blind advertisements in the classified section of a Sunday newspaper results in 90 percent fewer hirings than making face-to-face verbal contact with an employer under relaxed conditions. It's also easier to call and ask for an informational interview to find out about a company than to cold call and ask for a job.

Hand out résumés and business cards at trade shows, conventions, conferences, seminars, computer exhibits, or fairs. Then follow up by interviewing employers for job-related information for your file on companies and employers.

Interviewing an employer in person is the best way to find out whether the character of an organization matches your personality type (and résumé format or focus).

You will probably be given the company tour and remembered. Clip any news articles you read or write about the company's newest product when each is published. Keep these in a file to help you match your technical skills to possible new job openings.

Networking That Works

Getting a foot in the door by passing your résumé to the most important people in the exhibitors' booths at software users' conventions works well. Reviewing software for publications, even the free computer user magazines and newsletters, gives you visibility in the computer industry. Article writing, product reviewing, and informational interviews are ways of networking that appeal to the marketing communications, sales, software, electronic publishing, technical communications, advertising, and public relations departments.

Article writing is a good networking strategy if you have services to sell. How-to articles publicize the abilities of computer repair technicians, technical trainers, animators, and software designers.

Public Speaking to Gain Visibility

The quickest way to get your résumé in front of an employer is to invite several employers to volunteer to speak for an hour at a computer conference. Ask your local computer industry trade journal, computer user newspaper, or a national software users' group whether you can plan a users' seminar or conference for them at their expense to showcase their products and services.

Volunteer to set up a panel of speakers or experts, a seminar, conference, event, software users' group meeting, convention, exhibit, trade show, or workshop at the expense of the national and local software users' groups, the computer trade press, or software or hardware manufacturers and distributors. The majority of software and hardware manufacturers or distributors would be glad to advertise what they have to sell to a captive audience full of potential clients, customers, or colleagues.

They might even suggest that you take a commission as an event planner for organizing and publicizing the event. If they don't, plan it anyway as a volunteer to create visibility for your résumé.

How good or bad the seminar is will reflect on you as its planner. Invite business community members with interests related to the event theme: computer graphics, desktop publishing, multimedia, educational software, management of information systems, artificial intelligence applied to the stock market, or whatever your chosen field of interest. Charge attendees a small fee to cover the cost of the room and supplies.

Open the conference to students and vendors. Let them talk, give a few demonstrations, and hand out their cards. Then give them your résumé and business card. Every job applicant needs a business card printed professionally with name, address, phone, and primary skill or area of expertise.

Volunteer yourself to speak on panels at conventions. Even if you only speak five to ten minutes about your computer education, experiences, or internships, or introduce the other panelists, it's the most visible way at an event to make important contacts with mutual interests.

Providing the Competitive Edge

Chances are if the employer enjoyed giving a speech and pitch to the audience you captured free of charge, your résumé will be flagged for the next job opening. Be sure to make a follow-up call within a week and each month thereafter for 12 to 18 months.

Sometimes the employer will give you the follow-up call to see whether you can arrange future speaking engagements, recommend potential clients, or otherwise perform a service for the company. This is the time to let the company know you appreciated its involvement in your event. Thank the speaker for the presentation, and ask for a job as soon as one opens with the firm.

Networking Through Hidden Job Markets and Resources

Professional and technical computer associations have job hotlines with tape recordings announcing job openings 24 hours a day to members, directing members to positions that may be part of a hidden job market—positions they wouldn't have seen advertised in the classified sections of daily newspapers, where most people look first for a job. Nationwide, classified daily newspaper advertisements now only list 20 percent of all job openings in any one local area.

Eighty percent of the hidden jobs are advertised in trade magazines, in the publications of professional associations, or they're placed on recorded hotlines available only to association members. Many applicants are recruited from calls put in to hidden job market hotlines accessible to members of professional computer interest organizations or technical communication societies. Jobs are also advertised in business newspapers, in chamber of commerce newsletters, or posted on on-line bulletin boards.

Job referrals are passed around on the backs of business cards or on "hot sheets" at business mixers and socials sponsored by local chambers of commerce. Jobs are also advertised in national employment publications.

Most job openings are posted on cork and electronic bulletin boards inside corporate and academic walls. There is less risk to hire from inside a company. The staffer, temporary clerk, or contingency professional has already solved problems, worked out well, and has become a familiar face. Usually it's when no one inside is available and qualified to fill a position that companies seek an employee on the outside. When corporations must go outside to hire, they frequently offer a bonus to any current employee who brings in a qualified colleague or friend to fill a job opening.

The hidden job market is a network of diverse people in different occupations serving and doing business with one another under the umbrella of a specific industry. What these people have in common is the desire to meet others who can solve their problems and who pose the least risk to employers. Employers hire the person who is the least risk to the company's financial investment in salary, insurance, training, and other benefits.

Does your résumé position and market you as the least possible financial risk to an employer?

Where and When Résumés Can Be Circulated
Most job applicants give up a search too early. Several jobs open approximately every 12 to 18 months in the average computer firm. Industrial buying patterns also cycle in 12 to 18 month periods. Companies tend to hire in cycles.

Therefore, coordinate résumé mailings with industrial buying cycles. To find out the cycles, call the purchasing department. Then compare those dates to hiring patterns by calling the personnel department.

For example, corporate desktop animation hiring peaks every February. That is the same time animated toy commercials and new Saturday morning cartoons (made the preceding February) air on television.

Communicate Your Interest in Computers
One way for those applying for jobs as content writers or communications personnel to stand out from the crowd is to write company approved freelance how-to articles or software reviews for public relations directors of computer firms or trade journals. This works well if the job you want is in marketing or technical communications, training, public relations, or corporate advertising.

This strategy is useful if you aspire to creative expression jobs like Web designer or content writer. In the new information industry that includes Internet/intranet technology, electronic publishing, virtual reality, and immsersive video, technical writers and journalists alike are called "content writers." Fiction writers for computer games and CD-ROM interactive formats are called digital storytellers.

If you're applying for an accounting job or other number-crunching or analyst position that doesn't involve writing about computers, you can still polish and illustrate your communications skills in report writing and marketing communication of results of audits. No skill goes wasted in the new media. Highlight your communications skills on your résumé regardless of whether you will be asked to write creatively or analytically.

Even if your current job is repairing computer equipment, writing articles on your experience with computers is not a waste of time. Write "how to repair or troubleshoot" articles for trade journals. This gives you visibility and opens doors when you share your technical skills, experience, and knowledge with the newspapers, magazines, and trade journals of the computer industry, or newsletters of computer user groups.

If you're selling software, hardware, Internet services, or networking and LAN/WAN skills, writing and getting published adds credibility to your mechanical skills to program, analyze, design Web sites, or repair. So keep your name in the trade and mass media papers. It's important to realize that as technologies converge—as phones, TV, and computers become one machine and one industry, and modems turn into faster satellite communications devices—showing strong communications skills, written and spoken, will be critical to your success.

Adopt a Company and Learn All About It

Writing about a company is great if your career aspirations are in corporate communications. However, freelance writing for trade journals about how a company solves its problems may backfire if you don't have professional writing and interviewing skills. If writing and publicizing a company is not your niche, then adopt a company and learn everything you can about it.

Letting a company know you have thoroughly researched it is something to communicate by phone, or during your interview, or in your cover and follow-up letters.

Keep a record of the success strategies of the company that you adopt, the financial impact the company has made on the computer industry, and the problems the company has solved. Read the trade journals.

IDENTIFYING RESUME DATABASES

Your résumé has a good chance of ending up stored in a computer database, filed under the category of work you do or the skills and training you have. If you send your résumé to a national outplacement agency or employment service that specializes in electronic résumé transfer, your résumé could make its way anywhere in the nation or even overseas if you specify that you would be willing to work anywhere.

As needed, the database of job applicants is searched, and the applicants are called for interviews. Some software firms have turned into electronic employment agencies. They refer applicants to jobs without the applicant coming in personally by sending the scanned résumé by fax or modem across the country or internationally to an employer.

Résumé Screening Services

Electronic personnel referral agencies specialize in putting résumés on computer disk for the purpose of screening them for employers too busy to interview applicants in person. Outplacement and national computer employment recruiting agencies scan your résumé onto their databases.

Your so-called confidential résumé may be placed on a database. Employment referral, outplacement, screening, and résumé consulting agencies may download your résumé from databases directly to employers all over the country (or the world) through linkage with a computerized recruiting service (and more narrowly focused databases), or corporations on mailing lists. In a national chain of agencies and outplacement services, your résumé could be accessed by any of the local branches of such services.

Once on disk, your résumé could end up in market research and advertising agencies or with employment trend forecasting businesses. Once mailed out, a résumé is like a note in a bottle floating on the sea.

It's important to realize that the purpose of most in-house corporate personnel departments is to screen résumés out. Therefore, you may get faster and better results if you send your résumé directly to the supervisor of the department you want to work for in the company of your choice.

Some colleges also keep a computerized database of teachers and technical trainers who specialize in certain types of software in use by the institution.

You don't always know whether your résumé is being handled as confidential or is being scanned onto a disk, accessible to anyone on an electronic mailing list. Most outplacement agencies will not let résumés out of their offices and do promise confidentiality. Always ask first what will happen to your résumé over time before you send it anywhere.

Résumé-Producing Software

Inexpensive commercial or public domain software is easily obtainable to create résumés for you in a variety of formats. You key in the details of your previous employment and education. A completely organized résumé is created in the style you select. Résumé-producing software ranges from programs that organize your skills and design a format to programs that can quickly turn your résumé into a Web page.

Two excellent programs are WinWay Résumé and Résumé Maker. You can change your page layout with one click and the programs help you generate the best wording. Both programs have sophisticated video screens that show what to do, give advice, and show and tell do's and don'ts. WinWay has a job finder's toolkit that supplies job hotlines in various industries, such as government, private companies, nonprofits, education, and so on. WinWay also has an Internet connection for finding job opportunities on the Web.

Résumé Maker includes contact management features for keeping track of the résumés you've sent, dates, notes, people spoken to, and so forth. It offers a "virtual interview" video feature for what to do and what not to do when job interviewing. And there's a career planner to help identify jobs and careers that match your existing abilities and personal preferences. Both programs (and there are probably many others) have prepared paragraphs for each type of letter you may need—thank you, follow up, and so on.

Interactive résumés on the Web or on disk are popular. Try putting up your résumé on a Web page if you think it's appropriate. Then link your Web site to hundreds of others, including corporations, recruiters, trade associations, unions, suppliers of the companies you like, and job banks. The more people who link to your Web site résumé for other reasons, such as similar interests, the better chance employers will see it. There are thousands of job seekers who are not putting up Web pages with their résumés, brochures, and portfolios. So if you do and if your Web site and your credentials are impressive, you may have a great competitive advantage.

However, before you send your résumé on disk, CD-ROM, or DVD, or you put it on the Web, be sure the employer you're sending it to has the software to decipher it.

The most popular way to send résumés is by fax or e-mail in plain text (or ASCII) format. When you send your résumé to employers via e-mail or on a disk, never send an attachment. Attachments can carry computer viruses, so many employers will delete any attachments, or won't read them anyway. Similarly, send portfolios or screen shots of your work on disk or CD-ROM, not as attachments. (A screen shot is a photo or graphic taken off a Web site or computer screen and captured on disk.)

Résumé Consultants

Résumé writing companies charge a fee to create your résumé and cover letter on a computer. Civil service résumés are put on a special, detailed résumé form called the Civil Service (SF 171). (For more information on SF 171 forms, see Chapter 7.) Many retiring military personnel and others applying for government jobs use these official job applications in place of personal résumés.

Many résumé-writing agencies double as job search specialists or consultants. They identify your unique capabilities and interests and put them into a résumé package. Some of these job search specialists use job search organizer software to help you set your goals. The purpose of the software and the consultants is to get you to plan your career and organize the details on software or in a workbook.

There are numerous successful national electronic résumé networks linking thousands of companies nationwide. The résumé industry itself has become computerized—all because employers want candidates matched to specific jobs. Employers are flooded with stylized, look-alike, formula-written résumés. By casting your résumé on the computerized waters, you hope a job can find you. The résumé-writing and job search assistance services electronically notify these companies of your career interests and qualifications. Each service is different and is designed to make your résumé stand out from the crowd within the electronic networking systems.

RESUME WRITING: WHAT TO DO

Control Your Job Search

What all job seekers would like most is to take control of a job search. You want to know exactly what stands between you and a career. You want to know an employer's reasons for choosing an applicant to fill an opening. You need a tool to provide the competitive edge that shows you mean business.

What you want most is to be in control. To give you more control over your job search, you prepare a résumé that offers filtered information. You may feel powerless with only a one-page résumé to represent a lifetime of training and experience.

One strategy can put you in charge of your career destination: Customize your résumé to target different employers.

Job hunting in any one of the emerging niches requires a customized résumé. Send your résumés only to employers who are looking for someone with your skills, training, experience, and habits.

How Résumés Are Slanted
Résumés are slanted (with honesty) to fit the "qualifications needed" description for each job. Act as if your qualifications will be checked and verified. You don't know when questions will come up requiring a reference or transcript check.

The systems analyst's résumé will emphasize a track record of increasingly responsible problem-solving consultant work with contract requirements. The résumé focus will be on moving company operations into "intelligent systems" that are easier to use in a change-oriented environment.

Systems analysts want to change the way the public shops, plays, and learns by teaming up with software and hardware engineers. They want to make these changes within the fastest growing industry.

Work Preferences on Your Résumé
Let's look at how work preferences guide you into a specific type of résumé and computer job. Some job titles (like hypertext writer) are so new that no one has much experience in them, so an employer must scan your résumé to find out your work preferences as indicators of whether they should hire you.

An employer sees your résumé as a business plan. Persons who state they are destined to gravitate to the top levels of computer firms as executives will have résumés that look different from systems analysts who want to solve research problems in software design by making software easier to use.

One main difference between these two résumés is that the executive's résumé will emphasize sales based on consumer needs.

The executive's goal is to profit by filling a void in the market with the best or most popular products. Those sales-oriented administrators who rise to the top of computer firms may not be the most creative, but they will have managed the best marketing staff.

Responding to Change
Your résumé shows how you respond to change. In the computer world, a résumé must reflect how you respond to changes in spur-of-the-moment job scheduling. Your biggest asset to spotlight on a résumé is that you work well under pressure—a common condition in the technostressed computer industry.[1]

---

[1] The computer industry, psychologists, and physicians treating stress symptoms of computer personnel applied the word technostressed to computer industry workers in the early 1980s. In the late 1970s, the word had been used by engineers, systems analysts, and programmers to describe mainframe computers worn out by too much number crunching.

Show that in situations where employees must find spontaneous solutions to problems and challenges, you can do the unexpected with computers and thrive on it. Résumés in this field should show that change challenges you, and that you can grow on the job and continually learn new skills.

The convergence of technologies (computer, TV, telephone) and collaboration of industries have helped job seekers find ever-narrowing niches. Nevertheless, even specialists who are hired are expected to be able to transfer their skills to new media.

Your Résumé Should State Your Profit-Making Abilities

Every company wants to know how much money you brought in for your former firm last year and how much you expect to bring in for the new employer this year.

The bottom line is profit. Leave qualifiers out of your résumé. Only state the facts using dramatic, action verbs that emphasize achievements that brought a company profit.

Profit is a hidden factor in fields such as academia, research, and human resources. In academia, if a college course is not popular, fewer students will pay to register for it, and profit for the institution will be lowered. If you are in one of these fields it's still possible to show how you and your work profited an institution—even if you can't put it in exact dollar terms.

For example, profit is hidden inside grant proposals that use direct marketing techniques to compete for what money is available from the government or from private organizations. Profit is also hidden inside fundraising events and campaigns.

Profit results from getting the public to donate money in return for a benefit. Profit is obtained by creating visibility through public relations efforts for nonprofit organizations. Public relations includes placing news stories in the media to persuade people to spend money on an organization's technology, courses, and conferences.

Beware of Conveyor-Belt Résumé Styles

It's ironic that many of today's résumés appear so similar, considering the variety of jobs that exist in the computer industry. A person applying for a job as a word-processing secretary sends in a résumé of the same size, appearance, and format as a person applying for a job as a software engineer.

The only difference is in the degree listed under the education heading and in the job experience section. After reading hundreds of résumés a week, they all begin to look alike to many interviewers. What makes your résumé stand out from the crowd?

The Power Résumé

Your résumé is a map of your presentation strategy. Find out what is important to the company you choose to receive your presentation. You want to anticipate problems or questions.

You want your résumé to be powerful; but a résumé is an original product that is an authentic expression of your inner voice. The challenge is to fit your inner voice into a company's business plan. You would like to be at ease in a job that works for you and reap benefits from the multiplying number of computer industry niches.

Research Before You Write

Before you even sit down to organize details, sort facts, and begin to write your résumé, do some detective work concerning the computer companies to which you plan to send your résumés. Find out how applicants are chosen to fill jobs.

These seven steps can help you get a job:

1. Show a company how you can solve problems. Identify employers for which you can solve problems.
2. Show a company why you will be the least possible risk if you are hired.
3. Motivate an employer. Computer firms always have their own reasons for hiring you.
4. List ten of the company's reasons why they might want to hire you.
5. Tell your prospective employer how you can serve the firm.
6. Sell your benefits as if your résumé were a personal direct mail marketing campaign.
7. Use the rule of a dozen. (Marketers have a rule of a dozen, by which they send out direct mail flyers 12 times a year to target the same potential customers.)

Impress the Reader in 20 Seconds

The person who receives your résumé will view it on average for a mere 20 seconds. Thus, the résumé is like a flash card vision of your achievements that must imprint itself on the brain of the person who skims the page. Treat it like a well-written and attractively designed advertisement. Use bold headings, plenty of white space between sections, and bullets to direct the reader's attention. The impression your résumé makes will determine the action an employer will take.

Changing Résumé Formats

A résumé format showing diversification is preferred by employers. Résumé formats do change as technology evolves. Employers today are searching less for number crunchers and more for user-friendly types—both in computers and personnel.

A strong résumé emphasizes job satisfaction through innovation and change. As your experience pushes you up the career ladder, you also need to grow laterally and learn broader applications in your specialty.

Itemize breadth and diversity in your past jobs. If you don't have relevant experience, emphasize how you can transfer your creative, technical, people, or general skills to the new job.

ASSESSING YOURSELF

Slow Down As You Write Your Résumé

Writing a résumé allows you to address your emotions and to reappraise your employment situation. As you outline your competencies (before you write your résumé), it's helpful to write down your feelings about being terminated or switching careers. Negative emotions should be worked through now, not during a job interview. Slow down as you write the final draft of your résumé. Reflect on your past job satisfaction.

Carefully writing a résumé may prevent you from sabotaging yourself in an interview. By the time you finish writing your résumé, you'll have less need to justify why you are changing jobs. You'll feel less impatient and more comfortable networking with colleagues.

Where Are You Going?

When someone asks where you are going or what your career mission is, you may respond in the manner of a visioning company or a benchmarking company. Your résumé emphasizes either visioning or benchmarking experiences, skills, training, job preferences, and career goals. Your résumé, like an organization, has a character of its own.

THE CHANGING COMPUTER INDUSTRY

Identifying Diversity

Today, new technology offers hundreds more enterprising, instructional, creative, inventive, financial, marketing, and people-oriented computer careers within niches in the computer industry that include the following fields: Internet services, Web site design and administration, virtual reality, artificial intelligence, computer security, computer law, computer medicine, software talent management, educational software design, sales management, CD-ROM, interactive software, desktop computer animation special effects for the corporate world, hypermedia (interactive communications and entertainment), multimedia communications, fiber optics design, computer presentation graphics, electronic publishing, wireless telecommunications, robotics, financial forecasting (using applied artificial intelligence software), neural networks and fuzzy logic, technical training, instructional technology and courseware design, documentation analysis, software manual writing and editing, the computer trade press magazines, the electronic and book publishing industry for journalists, computer-aided design and drafting (engineering graphics or architectural drafting), computer-aided manufacturing, numeric control, beta testing of new software for errors, software review, and desktop video for cable television and advertising agencies.

Jobs exist for database managers, managers of information systems, local area networks (LAN) and wide area networks (WAN) technicians and managers, communications technicians in utilities firms, computerized accountants, systems analysts, software designers, computer video game designers, software engineers, repair technicians, telecommunications technicians, satellite technicians and wireless telecommunications technicians, teleconferencing personnel, telecommuters, support staff—such as word processors and supervisors, data entry clericals, and computer operators.

The computer industry grows more diversified each day.

Changing Job Titles

Each year, many more job titles are invented that didn't exist the year before. New job titles and spinoffs from emerging jobs in the computer industry form every few months. Résumés reflect the traits required to succeed in each of these ever-changing jobs.

These jobs have titles such as the following: Webmaster, virtual reality designer, multimedia scriptwriter, corporate desktop animator-special effects, interactive hardware and software designer, computer security psychologist, fuzzy logic neural networks analyst, applied artificial intelligence investments planner, and system administrator (Internet services). These are only a few examples of the hundreds of new job titles created to meet the needs of continually upgraded technology. Nevertheless, new and emerging jobs still require certain traditional traits such as objectivity, punctuality, and accountability to support production and profit.

Objective, dependable people whose skills offer an employer concrete benefits are most likely to rise quickly to the top. Computers are shedding weight, and so are résumés. They are becoming more focused.

What Would You Rather Be Doing?

Hundreds of different computer industry jobs exist. Some deal with service to people, some are highly technical and oriented to machines. Still other jobs are for full-time illustrators, animators, drafters, musicians, special effects persons, virtual reality designers, and video producers.

The computer press industry hires reporters, publicists, technical writers, and software reviewers. The CD-ROM industry hires writers and instructional designers.

Do you want the flexible time schedule of a video game designer? There are sales jobs and engineering jobs, careers for the artistic, ingenious, practical, or imaginative.

There is an ever-expanding need for computer-aided software engineers, systems analysts, database managers, accountants and financial analysts, local area network managers, satellite technicians, multimedia producers, and computer specialists of every type. Programmers are less in demand now.

Would you rather be the person who designs virtual reality simulated models of the inside of the human body to train student surgeons? Perhaps you enjoy using your computer to design three-dimensional architectural models to present to architects so they can see how a neighborhood will look before building it.

Would you rather be a technical trainer? Do you teach courses in annually upgraded versions of the same word-processing software program year after year in a community college?

Does your résumé position you as an electronic publishing specialist? These examples are only a few of the hundreds of opportunities that the computer industry offers.

More than 650 small businesses exist for writers or artists using a computer full time. Such businesses include but are not limited to technical journalism about virtual reality developments, infomercial writing and production, software user manual publishing, color separation desktop publishing, hypermedia fiction writing, computer game design and illustration, desktop video scriptwriting, corporate animation, CD-ROM book production, interactive multimedia entertainment, and training materials production, design, or writing.

Due to the variety of jobs in the computer industry, what you put on paper is important, especially when your résumé is scanned onto disks and made permanent. In the next chapter, you will learn what goes into a memorable résumé.

2
WHAT GOES INTO A RESUME?

CONTENTS AND FORMAT OF A RESUME

Résumés identify you and highlight your work history in one page. A cover letter can supplement this information. The contents of a one-page résumé includes the following.

- Your name, address, home phone, work phone, or message phone.
- A concrete, specific, targeted description of your work history highlights. Leave out early job descriptions that would definitely not apply to the current job or to the computer industry. For example, skip the years you worked as a cook, hairdresser, factory assembler, babysitter, cashier, or retail sales clerk, unless the work applies to the computer industry. Include the volunteer work you did for the computer industry user groups, publications, training or tutoring, customer service, commission sales, writing, speaking, interviewing, editing, college computer and robot clubs, or anything relevant to the future job.
- All software and hardware you can use. If you have reviewed software free for trade newspapers, include that experience. Any computers and software, or machines related to spinoffs of the computer industry such as wireless telecommunications, video, or multimedia you have worked on in the past should be included. Include computer camp counseling work and any training or designing experience. Currently, computer presentation graphics, multimedia, video production, virtual reality, simulation, CD-ROM interactive software and hardware, applied artificial intelligence, neural networks/fuzzy logic, Web site design, and Internet services are burgeoning new fields with future potential. Include experience in any fields related to the convergence of technologies (TV, telephone, and computer).
- Your education and training. Include all degrees, diplomas, certificates, credentials, and special seminars that trained you in the use of specific software and hardware. If you are self-trained, include what software or hardware you use and which training manuals you have used. If you are

a self-trained computer repair technician, include how you learned your trade. It's important to mention job-related associations you belong to that present continuing education, correspondence courses, seminars, conferences, or workshops.
- Work related honors, awards, and other certificates of outstanding work evaluation.
- Professional associations you have joined for networking.
- Security clearance level.
- Civil service level, if relevant.
- Publications, articles, books authored, if relevant.

This information should fill a one-page résumé. If you are a recent graduate, military retiree, midlife career switcher, or are changing occupations at any age, include optional information, if space permits, after the primary information has been listed. The optional information may include the following.

- Your career goal.
- Computer courses taken. Your prior training might be in a nonrelated field such as the humanities, nursing, or design. Include lifelong, continuous training, conferences, convention courses, seminars, workshops—any continuing education credits or certificates given by professional associations or schools.
- A brief summary of your transferable life skills or volunteer history. Using action verbs to list transferable skills is especially recommended for military retirees entering an entirely new field and mature displaced homemakers without prior paid work experience outside the home. Action verbs include words like: designed, wrote, edited, sold, repaired, trained, managed, solved, created, illustrated, organized, publicized, researched, audited, interviewed, distributed, purchased, programmed, analyzed, presented, spoke, raised (funds), coordinated, marketed, published, and produced—to name a few. Two examples of volunteer computer experience follow.

> *Designed and wrote the church newsletter using Ventura desktop publishing software on a PC with MS Publisher and WordPerfect.*

> *Adult continuing education training received in medical terminology and transcription. Volunteered to process medical records at ABC Hospital's medical records department using medical transcription software and WordPerfect.*

If you have worked as a troubleshooter in any capacity, it shows you are interested in finding out what's broken and fixing it. If you trained anyone to use software, it shows an interest in sharing and communicating technical information to the public.

- Memberships in any organizations where you networked with computer industry personnel. Include your professional organizations, computer user groups, student chapters of national computer-related organizations, intellectual organizations, and related industry organizations. Examples include associations of trainers in the computer field, computer press associations, and computer graphic artists organizations. The Association for Computing Machinery is also an umbrella for many special interest groups. (See Appendix B at the back of this book.) Consult the *Encyclopedia of Associations* in your public or university library. This book lists thousands of associations and organizations you may join in every professional, trade, and social field imaginable. Each one of these associations has its own publication and often a job referral ser- vice, résumé databank, or recorded telephone job hotline for members.
- Foreign languages spoken, foreign software used. Bilingual skills are a plus in the computer industry. The fields of import and export of software and hardware, peripherals, and computer publishing are linked by global networking through modem, fax, and telecommunications equipment from satellites to phones.
- Diverse computer-related hobbies or hobbies that are work-related or especially creative, analytical, ingenious, or focused on problem-solving.
- Military service, if any.
- Magazines you subscribe to that show your reading preferences. Computer magazines, trade journals, scientific or creative magazines, or job-relevant publications may be listed. Don't stop at subscribing. Offer articles on a freelance basis; it's a great way to obtain informational interviews with people for whom you want to work.

Brainstorm Before You Write

Brainstorm your experiences with someone who knows you well. He or she may reveal skills you did not realize you have. For example, if you have been trained as an accountant, systems administrator, computer repair person, Web designer, software engineer, or content writer, you may not realize you have the skills to produce instructional training films to teach your skills to employees. Perhaps your speaking ability is a gift that can be transferred to making sales presentations as a manufacturer's representative for a new laptop computer. Or your hobby of creative writing may be transferred to writing computer game scripts, advertising copy for the World Wide Web, or scrolling news broadcasts on your computer screen (called narrowcasting and netcasting).

A Résumé Is Your Greatest Marketing Tool

The first paragraph of your résumé should be able to "close the sale" and get you the job in the first few seconds the employer reads it. The face-to-face interview that follows should only serve to verify the employer's decision.

How does that first paragraph on your résumé close the sale? Begin by clearly stating what benefits you will offer and how you will serve the company's needs in less than two sentences in the first paragraph. Use action verbs and keep the sentences under ten words long. Next, tell the employer exactly what you're after.

Job applicants are sometimes turned down because their résumés fall apart in front of the powerful. Employers describe a résumé that falls apart as one that looks like you don't know what you want. One way to ensure that your résumé is remembered is to send a follow-up letter to the person who interviewed you. Keep reminding the employer and interviewer of your interest.

What Never to Include in a Resume

- Leave out your age, marital status, children's ages and babysitting arrangements, marital problems, divorce information, and anything from your home life. Don't include the fact that you were just divorced or are a single parent, a victim of job discrimination, an abused spouse, or were housebound with agoraphobia for the past several years. You would be surprised at how many résumés flood into employers with this type of private information.
- Don't include your physical challenges. An employer will not hire you out of sympathy because you're disabled, homeless, a victim, a survivor, or because you're housebound and need telecommuting work. "Telecommuting/home-based computer work preferred" is all right to state on your résumé. If you are deaf, blind, invisibly disabled, or in a wheelchair and need to know whether the building is accessible or on a bus route, call ahead and discuss it with personnel before you send your résumé.
- Exclude any details that put you down. Keep negative self-talk out of your résumé. Employers are surprised by the number of résumés that start out with the statement "I dare you to hire me," or "I never worked for anyone before because I always ran my own business."
- Don't deal with past salaries and present salary demands. It's better to negotiate a job contract and salary at the final interview or when you are hired. You will have more bargaining power at that point. Salaries don't belong on résumés because they either drag you down to your former pay or price you out of the new employer's market. High salary requirements of older, experienced workers are what drives budget-cutting employers to seek younger, less experienced workers at lower pay or from overseas.
- Do not include your height, weight, or photo—unless it's requested. If you are asked to submit a photo, have it professionally taken and touched up to give a business appearance. It might end up being printed in an employee newspaper or house organ.
- Omit names of family members.

- Leave out the reference letters or names of references. If requested, you can provide letters of reference later. Some employers put names of references into a database and automatically add them to their mailing lists.
- Don't mention how you commute. If driving is the primary requirement of the job, such as a computer delivery truck driver, state only what is legally required for commercial vehicle operation.

HOW YOUR RESUME PERSUADES: THE RULE OF THE DYNAMIC DOZEN TRAITS

The most effective résumé persuades an employer that you're all of the following and more:

- affordable
- adaptable
- accurate
- accessible
- creative
- efficient
- analytical
- dependable
- decisive
- prompt
- energetic
- retrainable

YOUR RESUME STYLE

This section examines four main résumé styles. Choose the style that best displays your work history. The four styles follow.

1. chronological work history
2. abilities
3. expanded
4. creative

If you have no paid work experience, the chronological style may not fill enough space. Or if you don't want to reveal your young or old age, an abilities or creative style works better.

The unpaid volunteer may wish to use an expanded, amplified résumé to emphasize with action verbs the duties carried out in the volunteer work. A creative résumé is right for the applicant who has created many imaginative projects, such as the following.

- computer illustration and graphics
- writing computer books
- writing freelance articles
- temporary technical editing
- hourly teaching/training

Organizing Your Résumé

An employer wants only the bare bones in your résumé. There are three ways to create a terse résumé: by arranging the order yourself; by hiring a résumé writer; or by purchasing résumé-organizing software. The software arranges your facts chronologically and prints out a standardized résumé based on the software's format.

If your goal is to write the most practical one-page résumé from scratch without having to spend extra money for software or a résumé-writing service to do it for you, how will you do it? Let's discuss the four résumé styles and their usefulness.

The Chronological Work History Résumé

You list your last job first. Information is presented in a sequence. It's practical and familiar if the job you're applying for requires sequential information processing as in programming, word processing, systems analysis, troubleshooting, accounting, training, research and development, and data entry. The *chronological résumé* is based on facts presented in reverse chronological sequence.

The less experience you have in the computer industry, the more likely you will list your education first. The chronological work history résumé begins with your name, address, and phone number listed at the top of the page.

A résumé should look professionally printed. Some career consultants highly recommend using desktop publishing software to lay out your résumé so it impresses the reader and makes you unforgettable in an absolutely professional, business-like manner. To an employer, your résumé is an advertisement that started with a unique concept.

The Chronological Résumé Is an Umbrella

Chronological résumés emphasize smooth transitions—bridges from one job to the next, or one period of time to the next. To an employer, your résumé is a creative concept. It's a basic framework used like an umbrella to tie all your different facts and categories together.

Without a creative concept umbrella or a framework, all your strengths and skills would hang like a string of different beads with nothing in common, no bridge to relate the fact that came before with the fact that lies ahead.

The purpose of an umbrella or creative concept in a chronological résumé is to hold the employer's attention. To find your umbrella, look for strengths—skills, talents, experiences, or training—that tell exactly what you can do for the future employer and what you did for past employers (or teachers if you are a recent graduate). These strengths are your smooth transitions. Employers hate gaps and jumps.

What are your benefits, advantages, and features? How will you meet the employer's needs? When writing a résumé, always consider the reader. Ask yourself, "What's in my résumé for the employer?"

Separate Your Skills

Before you write the final draft of your résumé, list each of your skills in its own category. If you are writing your résumé from the beginning by hand and polishing the final draft on your computer, begin by separating your skills.

Take a pack of index cards and write down one factual strength or skill per index card so you can sort the facts in a logical order. Sort your facts and organize your cards into categories.

Color-Code Your Categories

Use a handful of colored markers and assign a different color code to each of the categories. Put a different colored dot next to each category of strengths, skills, experience, and education.

As you color-code your index cards, identify each fact or strength with its proper category. Weed out what doesn't belong in that segment. Save what you've weeded out for a different area of the résumé. Categories can also be color-coded with stick-on colored dots.

Write down the name of each category at the top of a blank sheet of paper. Take your scraps of paper or cards with notes on them and staple together all of those in the same category.

Organize your categories in chronological order showing your entire work life, school, hobby, and volunteer experience. You can tell at a glance which activities relate most to the job in question. This is why it's best to work with hard copy for the organizational stage of preparing your résumé.

Employers prefer résumés that are orderly and that show chronological facts grouped in categories without gaps. The facts will impress employers if categories are tied together in a concrete manner with the most recent experience listed first, then the most recent training.

If you are just graduating and don't have any experience, list degrees and relevant credentials first. You may also try the abilities résumé instead or use the chronological résumé but list unpaid activities, internships, or training practice in a work-like setting. Use action verbs to make the best impression. Use all action verbs to describe related job experience, whether you worked for pay or volunteered for training or an internship. See page 35 for a sample chronological résumé format.

The Abilities Résumé

Names of employers, educational history, and dates are left out of an *abilities résumé,* which is designed to emphasize your qualifications. The abilities résumé rejects any chronological order.

The abilities résumé is excellent for freelancers, consultants, and temporary workers looking to switch from freelance to corporate or educational employment. Sometimes it accompanies a portfolio or list of publications. Use it if you don't want to reveal your age or lack of corporate experience, are seeking work after retirement, if you have worked as a consultant or independent contractor, are a homemaker or a house husband, or if you want to switch from owning your own firm to working for others. However, use the abilities résumé only as a last resort if you absolutely must leave out dates, names of employers, and educational material that would prejudice an employer at first glance. Most employers overwhelmingly prefer the chronological résumé.

What If You Have Gaps?
The abilities résumé is suited for persons with gaps in their work life. Perhaps you served in the military, spent time in prison, recuperated from health problems, became a perpetual student, took time out to rear children, volunteer, travel, or write books, decided to lead the life of a fine artist, or tried your hand at acting, and now you have decided that the computer industry is right for you. You may have worked as a consultant or ran your own business for a time and then decided to moonlight part time or pull out and look for a full-time job.

At the start of creating an abilities résumé, examine your skills. They may be fragmented into related categories of talents, skills, abilities, hobbies, or interests. What you do each day shows your interests, who you are, and what you most wish you could do. The books you read generally fall into one or more categories that you prefer. Everyone has preference for tasks they do and would like to continue doing. Everyone also has a work temperament where some skills come more easily than others.

List Your Responsibilities
Your abilities, according to you, are really responsibilities to your future employer. So it's your responsibilities that would be listed on an abilities résumé. Certain responsibilities cross over to many different jobs; they are known as transferable skills. In an abilities résumé, you don't list a sequential job history. Instead, you emphasize your abilities and responsibilities in order of importance.

On an abilities résumé you're emphasizing your expertise in a field. Expertise is gained during a lifetime of increasing responsibilities. These responsibilities accumulate from many different jobs, interests, life experiences, training, service, volunteerism, freelancing, consulting, traveling, hobbies, and caregiving.

List Your Job Objectives
An abilities résumé is brief and limited to one page (just as most résumés should only be one page). It's concise and structured. Begin an abilities/responsibilities résumé with your name, address, and phone number at the top, as usual.

Below this, briefly state your specific job objective or a concrete employment goal. There should be no abstractions, ambiguity, or vagueness about your job objective.

Expertise or Involvement
Under the job objective, write the body of the résumé. The abilities résumé is only five paragraphs long. Each paragraph has a bold heading that stands out for each area of expertise.

If you don't think you have expertise in any one area, then list any involvement. To an employer involvement is expertise. Involvement suggests future expertise and present interest or preference. Most computer personnel find one area of the industry particularly appealing.

What's Your Payoff?
Ask yourself, "What's the payoff for my interest or involvement?" If you are involved in something, you'll soon become an expert if you are motivated to practice your skills. Is the involvement a labor of love or a love of the labor? Is your motivation the money you earn or the ego satisfaction? List any talents and skills you've developed. Think of the possibilities of what you're involved in now for what you'll be an expert in with continued experience.

If you have expertise in anything that can be applied to any facet of the computer industry, list it. Expertise in fashion design software sales or accounting systems database management are interests far apart but relevant to the computer industry.

If You Have No Experience
If you have no experience in any field related to the computer industry but would like volunteer experience in writing about computers and software, try writing reviews of new software and sending these brief articles to weekly and monthly computer industry newspapers and magazines. Thousands of new software programs in every category imaginable flood the market monthly.

Computer interest publications may print your reviews or articles. Some pay only in free copies of the publication. Information on new software is available from manufacturers.

Accumulate news clips of software reviews with your byline. These will impress an employer if the job for which you're applying requires expertise in technical communications or public relations. For persons seeking programming experience, try volunteering to work on computers at public or private schools or tutoring at business and technical schools.

The Function of an Abilities Résumé
The function of an abilities résumé is to outline how you turn your interests into involvement; how you turn involvement into responsibilities; and how you shape responsibilities into expertise.

Skills
Under your expertise paragraphs, group your skills by category in order of importance. List as your first skill the one that you use primarily in your present job or the skill you wish to use in your next career.

Typical headings for your skills paragraphs might be Desktop Publishing, Proofreading, Organization of Software User and Training Manuals, Support, Coordination of Documents, Documentation Analysis, and Word Processing. All of these skills show you have expertise with specific software that required training—either on the job, self-taught, or in a classroom.

Responsibilities
By grouping your skills as expertise, you tell an employer what responsibilities you handled on past jobs and what you are capable of handling in the next job. You want to show you can make a smooth transition between the software skills you used as a word processing secretary, for example, and the organizational and editorial skills you'll learn as you step up the ladder to a higher-paid job as a technical writer or editor.

You may be competing for a job against hundreds of applicants who have many years of experience as technical writers, instructional technologists, or courseware designers, as well as recent four-year college graduates with creative writing, English, journalism, education, computer information systems, and public relations degrees who have no work experience.

For example, suppose the job you want calls for someone to write/edit software user manuals so they're easy to understand. Who will the employer hire as the right person for the job? The former secretary who longs to be a technical writer, or the experienced technical writer with a programming background? Most often hired is the person who can make complex manuals easy to understand for beginners using the software for the first time.

Responsibility stands between you and the job you want. Responsibility is highlighted in the brief summary of your achievements or qualifications. The brief summary of your responsibilities is one paragraph listed under each category of skills.

What Employers Don't Like About the Abilities Résumé
For most full-time in-house jobs, the abilities résumé arouses suspicion that the person with this type of résumé may be better off as an entrepreneur or independent contractor. Suspicious staff managers complain that the abilities résumé is frequently used to disguise job hoppers who've had many jobs for short periods of time.

Temporary Work
Temporary work should be listed as such. Today the term *assignment employee* is used by many agencies. This looks better on a résumé than *temporary worker*. Make sure you're seen as a steady, loyal employee of a temporary employment service and not as a constant job changer. Many such services offer benefits to long-term workers who are sent out on many assignments over the years.

A dramatic increase in temporary desktop publishing and word-processing jobs have made temping an acceptable way of networking and presenting your computer skills until a company offers you a full-time or permanent job.

Drastic Career Change
If you feel that an abilities résumé might arouse suspicion about your work history, use the chronological résumé instead. However, when you make a drastic career change, the abilities résumé is excellent for showing a transfer of old skills to new job areas. Be sure to show how your experience in an unrelated field is relevant to the computer industry.

The Modified Abilities Résumé

The *modified abilities résumé* uses a concise chronological listing of job titles, employers, dates, and job descriptions. This abbreviated history follows your description of ability or function with the most recent employment listed first (reverse chronological order).

Military retirees switching to a totally different career field, former entrepreneurs, and mature homemakers reentering the workplace after a long absence are comfortable with modified abilities résumés. They can show their entire work histories summarized in one page of work highlights.

The Expanded Résumé

On those rare occasions when you must have a two-page résumé, use the expanded résumé to include important information. For example, suppose you are a computer scientist working on highly classified material in a government job. You apply for a university teaching position or a research and development job in the corporate world using your scientific knowledge to develop special software. All of the relevant material may not fit on a one-page résumé.

Perhaps you are a writer who has never worked outside the home but would like to attach a list of your published, computer-related articles and books when you apply for a job as a documentation analyst. A video game artist's portfolio may also use an expanded résumé/portfolio package.

The first page of an expanded résumé contains your name, address, phone number, and a brief summary of your qualifications. Names of employers and dates are included on the first page along with job titles, starting with the most recent job. Also list your training, education, degrees, and certificates in reverse chronological order. Include all the software and hardware you are familiar with and your job objective.

When describing job duties, use action verbs. Start sentences with verbs such as *programmed, designed, illustrated, animated, edited, wrote, coordinated, analyzed, managed, operated*, and so forth. Use the verb that best describes the skills you want to emphasize for each job.

The sentences should be brief—fewer than ten words each. Action verbs should be strong, dramatic, and show exactly what you did. Instead of writing, "Participated in the revision of a software manual," or "Helped coordinate the word-processing pool and the technical writers and illustrators in producing many iterations of a classified report on fire control for the military," simply state the following:

> *Dates: 1993–1994*
> *Job title: Documentation Analyst*
> *ABC Corporation*
> *123 Rex Drive*
> *Ararat, California (619) 555-1234*
> *Duties: "Revised (name of software) manuals and classified reports on fire control according to military specifications. Rewrote, edited, and proofread manuals, reports, training materials, and documents."*

Narration
A short narration can also be used to expand your job descriptions on the second page of an expanded résumé. The responsibilities always encompass more than the job describes. The work history is long and detailed in an expanded résumé. The experience is often diverse. Sometimes each succeeding job is unrelated to the one that came before.

One employer received a résumé for a computer graphic designer's job that described a woman's 31-year work history of diverse, unrelated jobs such as career counselor, programmer, computer-aided designer, corporate animator, and software manufacturer's representative. She had earned a master's degree in career counseling in the sixties, followed by an associate degree in computer science in the eighties, and a second A.S. degree in computer-aided design and animation in the nineties. A two-page résumé in this case served to emphasize how diverse skills could be combined to support the new job objective.

Disadvantages
The main disadvantage of a two-page résumé is that employers won't take the time to read it. The second page may be ignored. Many employers do not like an expansion of self-importance on a résumé. Once employed, however, employers may insist workers toot their own horn to show they have the self-esteem to turn hard work into advancement. See page 37 for a sample expanded résumé format.

The Creative Résumé
If you are applying for a highly creative job, then use a creative résumé to show how you relate your imagination to your work or to promote a company's character. For the majority of creative people in the computer industry who adapt imagination to reality, this type of résumé reveals the drive toward creative expression.

Computer industry employers that receive creative résumés fall into some of the following niches: multimedia and presentation graphics; entertainment software and video game design; virtual reality; midi-synthesizer/computer music software design; special effects; corporate animation/desktop animation; desktop video; desktop publishing (electronic publishing); graphic design (commercial art); Web site design; hardware architecture design; neural networks research; telecommunications; instructional software design; interactive fiction software production; corporate and entertainment scriptwriting; technical writing; fashion and textile design; interior or building architecture design with software; engineering graphics; computer-aided drafting; health care personnel training video production; robotics; children's programming; and applied artificial intelligence design.

Some of these niches, such as interior, textile, and fashion design, regularly use software to create their patterns and designs. The software is manufactured by computer firms but purchased by employers in the garment, textile, or interior decor industry.

Portfolio with Résumé
Portfolios are often part of a creative résumé package. If your job objective is creative, use a one-page résumé and attach a laser color photocopy portfolio of your work for art job objectives; or send a nonreturnable videotape for desktop video and virtual reality jobs, or slides for technical illustration. For Web advertising or site design, briefly describe your site in your cover letter and let the employers visit it if they wish to. For writing jobs, attach photocopied, published clips or writing samples, and include a list of publications.

A creative résumé can be used for job objectives that emphasize imagination and analysis—especially for jobs with ad agencies or software design firms. In addition to art and writing, creative résumés can be used to show originality in programming or systems analysis, entertainment games design, software engineering, and the design of computer hardware architecture. (Hardware architecture design includes the engineering and design of hardware circuits, not the software.)

Artwork does not belong in the résumé itself. It should always be attached as a nonreturnable sample or shown in a portfolio. Use an 8½" by 11" sheet of good quality paper. Printed résumés are excellent as are quality photocopies on what some quick copy shops call résumé paper.

Cute résumés with teddy bears, scrolls, and résumés on computer disk and audiotape are all going to end up in the round file after the staff has a good laugh. If you use a creative résumé, keep it brief, serious, and business-like. Many employers now request faxed résumés in job advertisements. Therefore, it's acceptable, and may even be preferred, to fax your résumé. A mailed résumé can take from one to three days to get to an employer, whereas a faxed résumé takes only minutes to arrive.

Employers prefer computer artists to attach to the back of their résumés a nonreturnable portfolio of labeled artwork or slides accompanied by a table of contents. For interactive software and technical writers, employers ask to see a list of publications or published books and manuals and two writing samples or news clips of your published articles. Submit your best work, which should exemplify your creativity, imagination, and originality. In twenty seconds an employer will scan your résumé and samples for a quick first impression.

Persuasion
The creative résumé's purpose is to get you an interview. Creative résumés are fashioned after direct marketing letters. They are brief but powerful sales tools designed to convince companies to respond or to act. A creative résumé is like a marketing letter; it's written to be so interesting that a company buys the product—in this case, you. Direct marketing letters are often tracked to see whether they bring in sales. Track your résumé to see where it goes and who responds to it.

Training Shortages
You can design your creative résumé to address current training shortages in your field. Manufacturing employment in general is decreasing and downsizing in the United States. Yet ironically, training shortages

exist in the field of computerized manufacturing in many cities. When it comes to computerized manufacturing, minimal awareness of this field causes job seekers to overlook the burgeoning jobs in numeric control technology.

A creative résumé can emphasize how you will fit into the expanding and understaffed field of numeric control, or how you will create visibility for companies using numeric control technology, for example. On such a résumé you could show all the benefits of computerizing manufacturing and how you will fit in.

Create Your Own Job Description
Create your own job and job description. In this way, a creative résumé is used to create your own niche or job in a new technology you could introduce to a computer company. The firm may not know how to create a job for you that doesn't exist.

Your cover letter could use terms like the following to point out benefits of the new technology you are introducing: "increased accuracy, greater repeatability, and faster production." For example, there is an explosive growth of numeric control machines in the marketplace, but American companies have fallen short of attracting new workers into the changing manufacturing industry.

A creative cover letter could show how you would attract new workers. You want to convince management that if you are hired, you will show them how numeric control can make changes for the company's benefit, production increase, and profit. These facts explained in your cover letter would also be summarized or detailed briefly on your résumé.

Create Bridges by Finding Out a Company's Needs
If you are switching careers, a creative résumé could act as your bridge between the trades and the professions. Your résumé may appeal to a worldwide market. The creative résumé can accommodate computer-aided design and manufacturing, thus showing an employer the potential of a company's investment in you.

A creative résumé lets an employer know that you don't intend to be used in rudimentary ways and it can show a company how to stop using computerized equipment in rudimentary ways. Creative résumés, like all résumés, show that you've done your homework and that you've researched a company and its needs before applying for a job.

On-the-Job Training
Creative résumés often focus on training objectives and are also effective if you are applying for a training position yourself. If you are competing for a job as a trainer, a training manager, or a training materials designer, the winning résumé would explain that buying software and machinery isn't all you would do.

On-the-job training looks great on a résumé because it shows you have had the challenge of being pressured to produce while focusing on learning as well. Classroom training outside of the work environment doesn't show the same challenge because you don't have the demands of the workplace.

You can also change careers faster through on-the-job training. For example, if you are a machinist who wants to enter the computer industry, perhaps as a robotics technician, the creative résumé can help you change careers and get an employer to retrain you at company expense.

Respond to Changes, Competition
A correctly written creative résumé makes you more competitive. Computerized manufacturers are no longer competing with one another in a closed market. Your creative résumé can reveal how you can aptly handle working and communicating in a worldwide market.

A creative résumé responds to changes. The computerized medical products industry, artificial intelligence, robotics, and computerized manufacturing are receptive to creative résumés. A creative résumé is practical but also has a vision for the future that compels the employer to call you back.

Response Is All That Matters
Your creative résumé is an honest ad. A résumé, similar to a direct mail ad, is a type of writing where the quality of the words can be measured precisely, accurately, and scientifically. The measurement is based on how many interviews each résumé generated before you're eventually hired. Your résumé is measured by how much profit it made for you—or how much money it lost.

You can test your résumé against one written by another person with the same qualifications. The best résumé is the one that produced the most solid job offers.

In résumé writing, response is everything. Changes are occurring in the places least conspicuous. For example, while urban daily newspapers are merging and decreasing in number, the computer industry press is growing in terms of job openings for creative people.

There are many more computer industry newspapers hiring creative personnel like reporters and desktop publishing designers than there are urban daily newspapers absorbing journalism school graduates. The bad news is that smaller periodicals often pay less. Creative people in the computer industry frequently find higher-paying jobs with publishers of computer books and software user manuals.

See page 39 for a sample creative résumé format.

PRESENTING AND SUPPORTING YOUR OBJECTIVES

A résumé emphasizes your ability to do the job. Whichever format you choose, you'll highlight those qualifications that best support your objective. Most résumés today are hybrids. They are combinations of many components taken from chronological and abilities formats that most powerfully present your abilities.

The result of preparing an unforgettable, professional-looking résumé will be interviews. The résumé writing practice will prepare you for the interview, and the exercise in organizing your résumé will help you focus your knowledge, skills, and experience. Writing a résumé puts you in touch with where you are and where you want to go in your career.

If You Want to Get Hired, Help a Company Gain Recognition

Use your résumé when you join associations. Become an active member and get to know people with the authority to hire you. Sponsor awards or contests or scholarships to give others recognition and to help them grow in their jobs. This is the quickest way to gain recognition in the computer industry, even if you have no experience.

After you are hired, such activities will help your company gain recognition. As you further your image, you will be hired to continue similar activities to further your employer's image. However, as we will see later in this book, the first step in promoting your image is not always writing your résumé; it can also be writing a convincing cover letter.

Always Be First in an Employer's Mind

American businesses process 1.4 trillion sheets of paper annually. One sheet is your résumé. Many computer companies average 400 résumés for a job opening. Your résumé could be buried under towers of paper or software. In the computer industry, it's better to be a big fish in a microscopic pond. If you can't be first, reposition yourself. Enhance the image you have formulated by creating a niche.

In the next chapter, we'll explore how to create appealing and effective cover and follow-up letters. We'll also discuss six types of cover letters.

SAMPLE — CHRONOLOGICAL RESUME FORMAT

NAME
Street Address
City, State, Zip
Phone number with area code

JOB OBJECTIVE: Use exact job title or specific statement indicating the type of position you want and type of organization selected.

HIGHLIGHTS OF QUALIFICATIONS: Summarize your abilities, responsibilities, skills, qualifications, and achievements.

RELATED SKILLS: Begin each skill with an action verb. List skills and accomplishments. Relate and transfer skills to the position preferred. Draw from all volunteer and paid experience. Group skills under subheadings.

WORK HISTORY:
(DATES LISTED IN CHRONOLOGICAL ORDER) Begin with the most recent paid or unpaid work or activity, including computer related hobbies where you offer people training, how-to advice, or share information within computer user special interest groups. Include any freelance article or promotional writing (e.g., public relations, press releases for trade journals, associations, or businesses).

EDUCATION:
(LISTED IN CHRONOLOGICAL ORDER) List the most recent training first, name of school, degree earned, major area of study, or relevant coursework. Include workshops, GPA average of 3.5 or better. List any relevant seminars or work shops or continuing education in a computer-related field. List any licenses or teaching credentials.

MEMBERSHIPS IN ASSOCIATIONS: List any memberships in business, educational, professional, or computer-related associations, and offices/jobs you held, such as organization newsletter editor, convention and events planner, speaker, membership chair, or job referral director.

REFERENCES: Furnished upon request.

35

SAMPLE — ABILITIES RESUME FORMAT

Name
Street Address
City, State, Zip
Phone number with area code

OVERVIEW
(Job title) utilizing (specific name) software or hardware

HIGHLIGHTS OF QUALIFICATIONS

- Knowledgeable in various applications of _____.
- Hardworking, dedicated, and dependable; can be counted on to get the job done.
- Easily develop good relationships with coworkers, staff, and students.
- Adjust well to new learning environments.

EDUCATION AND SPECIALIZED TRAINING

A.S., Office Information Systems
Microcomputer Professional Certificate
San Diego City College, San Diego, CA

DBase IV+	WordPerfect	Database Management
Lotus 1-2-3	Ventura for Windows	Spreadsheets
PageMaker	Microcomputer Installation	Computer Presentations
AdPro	Disk Operating Systems	Adobe Illustrator
Graphics	CorelDraw!	

RELATED EXPERIENCE AND ABILITIES

- Organized _____
- Coordinated _____
- Revised _____
- Researched _____
- Determined _____
- Recorded _____
- Entered information from_____ into_____
- Processed _____
- Drafted _____
- Prepared _____
- Maintained _____
- Performed _____
- Tracked _____
- Inventoried _____
- Answered _____

REFERENCES FURNISHED UPON REQUEST

SAMPLE — EXPANDED RESUME FORMAT

NAME
Street Address
City, State, Zip
Phone number with area code

OBJECTIVE—To be responsible for _____ (use appropriate action verbs such as analyzing, solving problems, illustrating, designing, coordinating a specific department, writing/editing, researching, programming, troubleshooting, etc.).
To work with challenging projects with a leading provider of _____ (insert the specific type of industry such as "a leading provider of clinical laboratory services").
To have an outstanding growth opportunity with an organization providing _____ (e.g., data processing) services to _____ (e.g., the federal government).

SUMMARY: More than _____ years' experience in _____. Expertise in _____ (use action verb such as designed or coordinated). In one brief sentence state whether you have authored related articles, or books, illustrated any published computer art, or designed animation.

POSITIONS HELD: List names of employers, job titles, and dates (in reverse chronological order).

EDUCATION: Names of institutions attended, training programs, degrees, and certificates.

(The next section expands your experience into action-oriented accomplishments.)

SOFTWARE EXPERIENCE:
                   List all the software you know how to use and have had experience using. Indicate whether you install the software and design or modify it.

HARDWARE EXPERIENCE:
                   List the models of computers you use, the hardware equipment, whether you are knowledgeable in networking, whether the computers are PCs or mainframe, Cray supercomputers, or any other relevant hardware information. Indicate whether you troubleshoot and repair the hardware.

PROFESSIONAL EXPERIENCE:

Dates: Start with the most recent date and list your job title. Under the job
(Most   title list what you did recently using action verbs. Which division of
recent dates   what department or team did you work with within the corporation
first)   or institution? Use action verbs similar to the samples listed below

- Analyzed _____.
- Ran _____ programs.
- Solved _____ problems.
- Reduced costs by $ _____ in _____ (year).
- Increased gross sales by $ _____ annually for corp.

SAMPLE — EXPANDED RESUME FORMAT

NAME
page 2

- Made mathematical approximations.
- Interpreted _____.
- Established _____.
- Translated _____.
- Interfaced/interacted _____
- Produced documentation for_____.
- Met deadlines for _____.
- Published _____.
- Produced _____.
- Presented _____.
- Wrote _____.

TEACHING EXPERIENCE:
(Most recent dates first)

Date   NAME OF SCHOOL WHERE YOU TEACH OR HAVE TAUGHT
Job title (such as graduate assistant)
- Taught _____ to community college students.

Date   NAME OF SCHOOL
- Taught _____ to high school students as substitute and part-time hourly instructor.

Date   NAME OF SCHOOL
- Taught _____ to senior citizens at an intergenerational computer camp.

Date   •Lectured on _____ as a freelance public speaker.
(List places where you lectured or groups you spoke to.)

MILITARY SERVICE:
Dates   • BRANCH OF SERVICE, Job title.
(List job duties if related to your field now.)
State whether you were honorably discharged.

EDUCATION: Names of universities or technical schools.
Dates attended and degrees earned.

LANGUAGES: List any foreign languages you read and speak.

RECOGNITION IN PUBLICATIONS:
Set aside space on this second page to itemize a partial list of your published articles, books, or produced videos. If you have written many books or professional articles, attach a separate page entitled "List of Books and Articles Published."

REFERENCES AVAILABLE UPON REQUEST

SAMPLE — CREATIVE RESUME FORMAT

NAME
Street Address
City, State, Zip
Phone number with area code

OBJECTIVE

Information Packager

SUMMARY OF QUALIFICATIONS

- Gather information.
- Reshape information.
- Sell information in a variety of formats.
- Design information to meet different needs.
- Information is my most valuable resource.

EDUCATION/TRAINING

Degree, Major, Minor
College, University, or School
Certificates or Specialized Training

RELATED SKILLS

(Action verbs)	BENEFITS TO ORGANIZATION
• Created _____	• _____
• Produced _____	• _____
• Operated _____	• _____
• Selected _____	• _____
• Announced _____	• _____
• Illustrated _____	• _____
• Designed _____	• _____
• Wrote _____	• _____
• Edited _____	• _____
• Proofread _____	• _____
• Researched _____	• _____
• Analyzed _____	• _____
• Prepared _____	• _____
• Delivered _____	• _____
• Coordinated _____	• _____
• Managed _____	• _____
• Trained _____	• _____
• Volunteered _____	• _____

WORK HISTORY

Dates   • Most recent job first

REFERENCES ON REQUEST

Portfolio Samples Attached

3
COVER AND FOLLOW-UP LETTERS

This chapter gives you a format and tips for great cover letters. You will also learn how to use a cover letter to get your résumé noticed in a number of situations. Finally, follow-up letters that get you an interview are described.

THE COVER LETTER

The cover letter personalizes your résumé for each company. Before you sit down to organize your résumé, first write your cover letter. Your mind will be focused on the position as you begin to sort the many details that will form your résumé.

Your cover letter is really a sales pitch letter. Without it, an employer will have to wade through an entire résumé to find out how you will fit into the company. Your one-page cover letter introduces your résumé and communicates a specific message about your value to a company.

A great one-page cover letter begins by pitching (in the first sentence) exactly what position you want in a company. Define yourself as a specialist; today's job market belongs to the specialist rather than a generalist. A cover letter also serves as a powerful introduction to (or umbrella for) anything else included in the envelope and is a sample of your communication skills.

Hook Questions in Your Cover Letter

The first paragraph of your cover letter determines whether the reader will finish the letter. For your sales pitch, in the first brief sentence you need a positive hook. Introduce who you are, your skills, or services. Describe specifically how your skills will be used in the company. Hook the employer by stating how timely your services or skills are to the company. Or use a hook question such as, "What's the most powerful resource you have?"

Next, convince the employer to hire you. The simplest way is to give employers an observation they can verify themselves. The observation can be about their needs, or your skills. Computer companies are always searching for new ideas to plug holes or fill needs in the industry. Position your cover letter and résumé as a plug to fill a need.

Try using exclamatory hooks in the second paragraph of your cover letter. There are three types:

1. a fear hook—where you list a series of corporate or business fears and then tell how you'll solve the problems.
2. a story hook—where you briefly explain how you will provide benefits to the company, using professional expertise or media contacts.
3. an exclamatory hook or startling statistics—where you mention surprising numbers or statistics associated with your career that shock the employer in a positive way.

Finally, an imaginative cover letter closes by making you stand out from the crowd and get hired. (A résumé doesn't reflect the more action-oriented parts of your personality—it only states facts.) End the letter on a positive point. Show the employer how hiring you to apply your skills to the company's needs will bring positive results.

For further information on positioning yourself, read Al Ries and Jack Trout's book, *Positioning: The Battle for Your Mind,* Warner Books, NY, 1986. It provides advice about how to stand out from the crowd and win.

Cover Letter Tips

- Each time your résumé goes to an employer, it should be topped by a cover letter. The courtesy of a cover letter is held in such high esteem by employers that résumés coming in without them frequently are discarded.
- As your computer skills and experience expand, you will have to work hard to condense them in a one-page résumé or cover letter. Think of the entire computer industry as niches or areas of specialty. Your cover letter must be brief, but detailed enough to show your specialty or your unique qualities.
- Use your cover letter to personalize your communication and to establish a rapport with potential employers. Your goal is to build a relationship with someone who has the authority to hire you. A résumé without a cover letter is too impersonal.
- The cover letter should express your enthusiasm and energy. It's your unique style, strength, and personality type that should shine through and move an employer to think of ways in which you could benefit the company.

Junk Mail or an Attention Grabber?

In the computer industry, thousands of résumés a year may pile up on someone's desk. These résumés begin to overwhelm an employer, and some may begin to see them as junk mail. These piles are given derogatory names like "the slush pile" in electronic publishing, "the stable" in information processing and technical communications firms, and "portfolio puss" in the corporate animation industry. How can you stand out? Only an action-oriented cover letter saves a résumé from the heap.

Your cover letter can emphasize that you're an award-winning computer illustrator or have recently completed an internship in data analysis or programming. Maybe your volunteer work has won you recognition, or your sales record is outstanding.

If nothing outstanding has happened to you in your work or educational life, then join a professional or trade association and learn all about the newest products of several companies. Act as a volunteer contributor to a local computer industry publication, or volunteer to do research or help out on a professional association's special task force or speakers' panel in your area of interest at the next convention.

Most employers who place classified newspaper advertisements request cover letters to accompany résumés. The format of your letter is important. A cover letter format is on page 43 followed by a sample cover letter.

SIX KINDS OF COVER LETTERS

You send a résumé and cover letter when:

1. answering an advertisement.
2. writing to a specific employer—the informational cover letter.
3. asking a friend for job-related information.
4. consulting an employment or outplacement agency.
5. networking with members of a professional or trade organization.
6. attending a trade show, exhibit, convention, or conference.

Answering an Advertisement

Clip ads from trade journals, national employment newspapers, professional organizations' newsletters, computer magazines, and the publications of computer user special interest groups. Write down phone numbers from the tape recorded phone messages of job hotlines for members of trade and professional organizations. Clip ads from your daily newspaper's Sunday help wanted section.

The hidden (not advertised) job market appears mainly in trade journals, those magazines and newspapers directed to readers interested in a particular industry. Most jobs advertise qualifications for the ideal candidate. If the ideal job applicant doesn't respond, often the employer will take what's available.

Send your cover letters and resumes to the widest variety of ads possible, even if you only have some of the qualifications. One reason for this is that company paid training is sometimes available after employment. On-the-job training is offered when the technology is so new that little training is available outside the company. When new software is designed, technical trainers are trained on the job so they can go out to other corporations and train the new software users.

In a classified or display help wanted ad, job requirements are listed according to their rank of importance, with the most important skills listed first. If you don't have all of the requirements, list the capabilities you have and specify which requirements they meet.

COVER LETTER FORMAT

Your Name
Street Address
City, State, Zip
Phone number

Date of Letter

Name of person with the authority
to hire you in the department
in which you want to work
Title
Name of department
Company name
Street address
City, State, Zip

Dear Mr./Ms._____:

    Opening Paragraph—State the position you want. Tell why you want to work for that company. Make your sales pitch.

    Middle Paragraph(s)—Mention your two best qualifications (related to the job in question). Explain how your skills and/or experience would benefit the company. Point out any specialized training or skills that relate to company plans. Sell your abilities. Document your sales pitch with startling statistics or statements showing evidence of your talents. Don't repeat yourself by listing what's on the résumé.

    Closing Paragraph—Let the reader know that what's attached is your résumé or résumé and portfolio, list of publications, samples, or other itemized achievements. In the last sentence, let the employer know when you will call to follow up. (Don't wait for them to call you.) Your closing sentence should ask for a specific action from the company. Reread the letter to make sure nothing is vague. Make every word concrete and practical enough to be remembered. Anything vague is quickly forgotten. There may be hundreds of competing cover letters on someone's desk.

Sincerely,

(Your handwritten signature in black or blue ink, *never* another color.)

Your Name Typed

Enclosure

SAMPLE COVER LETTER

Jamesa Kintle
123 Mt. Penn Lane
San Justa, CA 92104-7177
(619) 555-1234

July 1, 1997

Ms. Rayanne Hart
Director of Employment
Video Game Corporation
100 Prince Road
San Justa, CA 92104-7199

Dear Ms. Hart:

   I want to serve Video Game Corporation. I create exciting, high profile Nintendo and Genesis games, working for the past year in the most fascinating industry possible. Your advertisement in the June 30 issue of the *San Diego Union-Tribune* for a video game artist matches perfectly my skills to your needs.
   I understand Video Game Corporation is a fast-expanding San Justa company offering the challenge, environment, and opportunity I'm seeking as an experienced artist specializing in computer graphics, video game design, and corporate animation. I have the ability to draw and paint cartoons and comic book-like characters or background using CorelDraw! on a PC.
   I also have illustration, desktop publishing, and desktop video production experience on PC and Macintosh computers. I'm experienced with PowerPoint, PageMaker, Microsoft Publisher, and Director.
   As detailed in my résumé, my experience centers on video game design and illustration. As an award-winning team member, I gained an appreciation of the cooperation it takes in a large computer video game company to coordinate the art function with all the other areas.
   My Special Studies A.S. degree in Computer Sciences and Fine Art from Grossmont College in El Cajon, California, included specific coursework in computer graphics design, presentation graphics, video production, animation, and fine art.
   Thank you for your consideration. Enclosed is my résumé and photocopied samples portfolio. You may keep the portfolio. My salary requirements are negotiable. I look forward to meeting with you. I'll call you next Friday at 9:30 a.m. Or if you prefer, you may reach me at (619) 555-1234 after 3 p.m. weekdays to schedule an interview.

Sincerely,

Jamesa Kintle

Enclosure

State how you will be an asset to the company. Take out all extra words; only list strengths in your cover letter. Let's look at an advertisement and analyze how to compose a cover letter.

> **SOFTWARE SYSTEMS SPECIALIST**
> *You will install user devices, diagnose hardware problems, load software maintenance releases, monitor system and subcontractor performance, maintain communications systems, assist customer end users, and perform other duties as assigned. Requirements include: a demonstrated knowledge of VAX/VMS or DSM operations, maintenance is a plus; a high school diploma/GED and five years directly related experience, or an AA in a related field and three years directly related experience. We offer a competitive compensation and benefits package. Please send your résumé and cover letter indicating department code for position of interest.*

The actual ad appeared as a display in the Sunday section of a major urban daily newspaper. The company name and address were listed.

Your first step would be to call the company and find out the name of the person to whom you would direct your letter. You can also ask about new company information, such as new products. In your cover letter, this information can allow you to tell the employer how you could help the company reach its goals.

Some interviewers hold résumés a long time before getting back to you. To offset this waiting period, send a mailgram cover letter. Be assertive and courteous. Call the staff manager first, before you are called, and ask to set up an appointment for an interview. The cover letter on page 53 is a sample of an answering-an-advertisement cover letter.

Blind Ads

How you respond to a blind newspaper ad is up to you. Some people never respond to blind ads (ads in which the hiring company is not identified). In a highly competitive industry, you may want to know in whose hands your résumé will fall, since it contains confidential information and your home address.

Thousands of companies use blind ads because they have economic reasons to remain anonymous. They may be placed by executive search firms on behalf of corporations. You must decide whether you want to discount potentially great opportunities by not responding to such ads.

WRITING TO A SPECIFIC EMPLOYER—THE INFORMATIONAL COVER LETTER

A different approach to your career search is to ask for information in your cover letter, rather than a job. Interview a department manager to make informed career decisions. This keeps you in touch with the company on a friendly, fact-seeking basis. Read the biographies of executives of major or fast-moving companies, which can usually be found in public libraries.

The department head for the area in which you want to work is the person who should receive your cover letter and with whom you should establish a rapport. Only the division specialist has the expertise in your area of interest, not the generalist in personnel. Address your fact-finding letters to the person who has the authority to hire you. Use a specific title such as Mr. Gene Wright, Manager of Information Systems, Day Computer Corporation, Inc.

Never send your letter to anyone without first calling and getting the correct spelling of the individual's name and title. Letters sent to the personnel or human resources department tend to get screened out. Often a personnel department's purpose is to weed out the unqualified.

You will have the best chance of getting hired if you send a mailgram cover letter and résumé with your business card. All job applicants should have business cards listing their three best skills and any degrees or technical school diplomas. Such a business card may look like this example.

TECHNICAL WRITER/SOFTWARE USER MANUALS
Dawn Whisper, M.A.
Public Relations, Training Materials,
Courseware Design
P.O. Box 123
San Diego, CA 92164
(619) 555-4321

Your database of employers may be gleaned from professional and computer journals, business publications, trade and professional associations, computer user groups, industrial directories, and the Yellow Pages. See Chapter 11 for additional resources.

Most of your research will be in finding out what type of software and hardware or applications systems are used in each company. Call the companies before you send them any letters or résumés and ask what systems they are currently using. Never waste your cover letters on unresearched companies.

You can also ask for a list of their suppliers and research those firms for possible job leads. For example, one salesperson didn't land a job at the company first applied to but found a great job with one of the company's material suppliers.

In addition to companies that supply computer corporations, there are other businesses that provide technical staff training with all of these companies. Networking expands the possibilities of finding jobs that match your skills. Employment agencies use this same kind of research to drum up job orders.

Keep in mind during your research that almost all corporations outside the computer industry use computers as tools. Most firms have information systems departments where data entry, word processing, and desktop publishing are accomplished. Also, corporate video production studios have computers connected to VCR machines and video cameras to create multimedia presentations, usually for training videos or product demonstrations called desktop video (DV) studios. Large corporations have management information systems (MIS) departments and computer operations divisions. Smaller companies have database management departments or data processing (DP) departments. Electronic publishing companies have desktop publishing departments and technical illustration or computer-aided design departments. Computer-aided manufacturing companies may use computer-controlled robots.

When you first telephone a company, ask for the director of computer operations or the manager of information systems. Either person can usually tell you which types of hardware and software are used by the firm. What you are seeking in your research are facts about a company's hardware and software, people, and job openings. Send out a dozen letters at a time to carefully targeted firms where you have already made verbal contact by phone or have interviewed directors of departments for company or product information.

Personalize all cover letters. Never send a form letter or a letter with a photocopied signature. End the letter with a question that makes it easy for the person to call you back with a product related or technical answer. By asking a technical question rather than asking for a job at first contact, you're seen as a potential customer. Emphasize how you can be of value to the business. This is a direct-mail campaign to show a company the specific advantages and benefits of your abilities.

See the sample cover letter to a specific employer on page 54.

ASKING A FRIEND FOR JOB-RELATED INFORMATION

This type of cover letter is used to gather job leads. Use it so that a copy of your résumé may be passed to people your friend meets at work or during meetings. You are not asking for a job in this letter. You only want information. Use the information to develop a profile of employers, companies, or job requirements.

Let your friend know you're looking for a certain type of job—maybe even with clients of your friend's company. Write an informal, friendly letter instead of a formal business cover letter, and have your friend pass the résumé only to personal friends and clients with authority to hire you. Sending three copies of your résumé with the letter is acceptable.

Ask for suggestions in the letter. Mention any plans for, or openness to, relocation. Let your friend know whether your correspondence is confidential. Leave out salary references. Human resources information is harder to obtain than product information. Some companies promote from within or pay a recruitment fee of several hundred dollars to any employee bringing in a qualified friend who fills a new job opening. Many new jobs aren't advertised to people outside the company until all employees are given a chance to apply. It pays to have a friend on the inside to pass around your résumé.

See page 55 for a sample personal cover letter asking a friend for job-related information.

CONSULTING AN EMPLOYMENT OR OUTPLACEMENT AGENCY

Target only those agencies that specialize in your field. For example, write to those agencies that specialize in placing military retirees, displaced homemakers, programmers, word processors and desktop publishers, database managers and systems analysts, accountants, software engineers, persons over age 55, recent college graduates, graphic designers, animators, drafters, technical writers or illustrators, temporary technical contract workers; or write to outplacement services for displaced computer personnel or other specialized jobs.

You can also write to executive search and recruiting firms and job consultants who work within placement agencies. Address your letter to the director. The purpose of a cover letter sent to an employment agency is to set up a personal interview. Ask to have your résumé kept in the active file. Include in your cover letter when you'll call to set up an interview.

Keep the cover letter to an employment agency brief. Most executive recruiters will rewrite your résumé according to their own formats. Ask to see your résumé before they send it out. If you don't, you'll lose control of how they present you on paper.

Find out whether your résumé will be downloaded onto a disk and sent electronically to companies across the nation or added to mailing lists.

A sample cover letter to an employment or outplacement agency is on page 52.

NETWORKING WITH MEMBERS OF A PROFESSIONAL OR TRADE ORGANIZATION

You can use a professional organization three ways:

1. Use their letterhead when you write your cover letter to an employer.
2. Send your cover letter and résumé to the director of a trade organization for job referral or use of the job bank.
3. A cover letter and résumé directed to the job-referral officer or job hotline coordinator of a professional organization can be helpful if you do some homework. Work on the job bank for the trade organization, where you can develop a portfolio or database of details about the companies you solicit for job openings to go in the organization's job referral databank.

Volunteer to work with a professional or trade association, a regional or national organization of people interested in a specific area of computing. A list of these organizations appears in the Appendix of this book. Select the area of your interest and explore. Once you are in a professional organization, seek increased responsibility to establish contacts and relationships with other members and to show your talents. Volunteer to speak on panels at conventions.

Most of these computer professional or computer user societies have task forces or committees, user groups, or networks of people employed in the same or related areas of computing. There are public relations task forces, newsletters, fundraising committees, membership drives, speaker special interest groups (SIGs), and job bank listings. If you are looking for a job, try the professional computer groups and trade organizations first and then the hobby user groups.

Target the job bank SIG. If you are part of this SIG, focus on calling employers to get job listings for the recorded telephone job hotline for your members. Your job bank task force might work alongside a committee that arranges internships for students, or recent graduates or retirees reentering the workforce (often the student membership committee).

After you have established telephone rapport with a recruiter or department manager at several of the corporations, you can call for the hotline jobs and then send your cover letter and résumé to recruiters with whom you've talked. Keep it brief, and mention your affiliation with the trade or professional organization.

You might ask your contacts to provide you with old job performance evaluations from former employees with jobs similar to yours. These evaluations will give you an idea of what people in the company thought of employees' skill levels. That way, you'll know what's expected of your performance on the job.

If your qualifications are appropriate for the job you want, include some of the job evaluation terminology in your cover letter to a prospective employer. At least knowing the details will help you fit in with the company on the same level of terminology.

Joining a professional or trade association demonstrates to employers two important facts about you:

1. What you can do as a volunteer and
2. How you handle responsibility.

Always include in your cover letter your volunteer association experience and the details of how you handle responsibility for your trade or professional association.

A sample cover letter used to network with members of a professional or trade association is shown on page 56.

ATTENDING A TRADE SHOW, EXHIBIT, CONVENTION, OR CONFERENCE

When you attend a convention or conference, visit the exhibit booths of each company. Ask the person at the booth the name of the department head, president, or person in charge of hiring for the department of your interest.

Write that person's name down on a sealed envelope containing your cover letter and résumé. Your cover letter would be addressed generically, for example, "Dear Exhibitor." Hand the envelope to the booth clerk.

If the person in charge of the booth or exhibit is the company president or employer, hand it over and start a conversation about the company's products, services, and personnel needs. Smile, chat, and leave a positive impression of yourself with whomever is representing the company at the exhibit booth.

If you know about a convention or trade show well in advance, volunteer to be on a panel or announce a workshop, even if you only introduce others or speak for five minutes. If you have experience, send your proposals to read a research paper, speak on a workshop panel, or give a seminar.

Many conventions have exhibitions of your state's task force in a specific field. Send your cover letter and résumé to your state advisory board on training and practice in your computer specialty. You might volunteer to join your state advisory committee board for drafting, or whatever your computer specialty is. For example, the Minnesota State Drafting Advisory Committee (MSDAC) is a task force located at the Department of Vocational and Technical Education of the University of Minnesota.

Consider handing out samples of your work with your cover letter and résumé at conventions and trade shows. If your job interest is in computer illustration or drafting, hand out nonreturnable samples in a miniportfolio to key representatives at trade shows. If you are a technical writer, include a list of publications and a published (or self-published) writing sample or news clipping with your cover letter and résumé.

A typical cover letter is on page 57, to be handed (with your résumé) to prominent speakers and company representatives at trade show exhibits, conferences, or conventions.

INTERVIEWS

Rarely will companies give first interviews at trade shows or conventions—unless the trade show is a job fair sponsored by several companies who are set up to recruit personnel at the gathering. Job fairs are usually sponsored by colleges or by professional and trade associations.

Some companies give only one interview. Others put you before several individuals from the personnel department. You then interview with the department manager. At a later date, you may be given a final group interview, before a board of subject experts who will decide whether to hire you. When each interview is over, send a different follow-up letter.

THE FOLLOW-UP LETTER FORMAT

A follow-up letter may be used at two different stages in the job hunt.

1. Right after every interview, send a follow-up letter of thanks to the interviewer.

2. You have sent your résumé with a cover letter. A few days later you made a follow-up phone call and still you were not called in for an interview. Now is the time to send a follow-up letter to seek the answer to the question "What stands between me and this job?"

The follow-up letter is more than a thank-you note or common courtesy. It's a reminder of your qualifications and continued interest in the company. The follow-up emphasizes to an employer that you want to work for the company, even if the job advertised isn't right for you this time around. If you didn't land the job for which you applied, another one will open.

Like the cover letter, the follow-up letter should be one page, usually three to six paragraphs. The format of a follow-up letter displayed on page 58 is followed by a sample letter.

SAMPLE COVER LETTER: EMPLOYMENT AGENCY

Fannie Meghan
659 Starview Terrace
Broadview, New York 02113
(212) 555-1234

September 1, 1997

Miss Tricia Knowleton Price
Careers For Women Over Fifty, Inc.
909 Crestline Avenue
New York, NY 09124

Dear Miss Price:

    Thank you for your exciting panel presentation on computer careers for workforce reentry women over 50 at the Displaced Homemakers' Center. As I mentioned in Monday's phone conversation, I feel my strengths are in computer sales and software retailing. A copy of my résumé is enclosed detailing my software sales experience.

    I have recently completed a course in sales given by the Broadview Chamber of Commerce. I am a full-time volunteer at the Broadview Computer Society and president of the Senior Computer Users' Special Interest Group.

    I've spent the last ten years involved in selling shareware and presenting exhibits of various software to computer user and hobbyist association members.

    I am particularly interested in working for database search companies, software libraries, and software location services, or selling software as a manufacturer's representative. I'm presently lecturing on Best Software for Screenwriters to the scriptwriting class of the Clarion Senior's Center. As a part-time software manufacturer's representative I often promote the software as a sideline when I volunteer as a public speaker, which is my avocation. For this reason I feel I could be very successful in a software sales and promotion job. I am a widow who is free to travel the country selling software wholesale or retail.

    As you review my background and areas of interest, you'll see benefits I can offer a manufacturer as a software representative. I am open to relocation anywhere.

    I'll call you next week to discuss an interview.

Sincerely,

Fannie Meghan

SAMPLE COVER LETTER: ADVERTISEMENT

Mary Ellen Kyle
1234 Grandview Terrace
Santa Rachel, CA 92104
(619) 555-5678

July 1, 1997

Mr. Leon August
Crest Computers
91011 Pacific Rim Gorge
Agua, CA 92105

Dear Mr. August:

    In response to your advertisement in the *San Francisco Chronicle* of July 1, 1997, for a desktop publisher and desktop video producer, I'm enclosing my résumé.

    I am deeply dedicated to both desktop publishing and desktop video. For the past two years I have been producing how-to computer videos as well as writing and publishing software user manuals for Windows software. I work at home as a freelance producer and writer using a PC with a variety of multimedia software for a variety of software designers.

    In the field of desktop publishing, I create software user manuals using WordPerfect and Microsoft Publisher. My self-published software manuals accompany my how-to videotape entitled "Everything You Want to Know About Windows." I also have an industrial broadcast quality video camera, Genlock equipment to interface my computer with my video camera, and a full range of videotape editing equipment. I am also able to produce minor special effects and animation in my desktop video productions. I'm experienced in using PowerPoint and Director software.

    I have the ability to handle all the requirements of your position in both desktop publishing and desktop video as well as multimedia presentations. I am an award-winning desktop publisher and video producer who can make technical subjects easy and entertaining to learn.

    My background includes a master's degree in English literature and an associate degree in desktop publishing and desktop video. I will call on July 14 at 10 a.m. to answer any questions and to set up an appointment at your leisure. Thank you for considering me for the position.

Sincerely,

Mary Ellen Kyle

Enclosure

SAMPLE COVER LETTER: SPECIFIC EMPLOYER

James Vincent
2911 Hyatt Drive
Greensboro, NC 21434
(555) 555-1009

June 4, 1997

Mr. Barron Bettingsen III
Cosgrove Computer Corporation
1253 Wellington Court
Greensboro, NC 21444

Dear Mr. Bettingsen:

    I know what to do with your clients who want a $1,000 project delivered on a $500 budget. I'm enclosing my résumé and portfolio samples to demonstrate how my award-winning computer designs serve all aspects of your current marketing program. The reason I'm applying for a position as a computer graphics designer at Cosgrove Computer Corporation is because I know you're looking for computer artists who can design on a tight budget. One of the most powerful marketing tools any company can wield is a cohesive design program.

    I'm a computer artist and graphic designer specializing in editorial illustration. My design strategies keep very low-cost designs looking great because I know exactly what to exclude from the design process. If I'm hired, I can promise memorable, award-winning, interactive 3-D designs.

    Your marketing department wants Cosgrove Computer Corporation to be noticed. I see an excellent fit between my computer art qualifications and your department's needs. I would appreciate the opportunity to discuss how I may contribute to your company's success. Please keep my portfolio samples on file to show your clients. I will call in two weeks to set up an appointment.

Sincerely,

James Vincent

(2) Enclosures

SAMPLE COVER LETTER: A FRIEND

Aniba Merimdeh
1756 West Byrd Street
Las Vegas, NV 80028
(702) 555-5777

December 11, 1997

Dear Brian,

    I met Karen Symmontree last summer while attending the Comdex convention in Las Vegas. She told me that you're using virtual reality technology at Laser Art Technologies to create special effects for the new television series, "The Time Hackers." She suggested that I contact you.
    I'll be finishing my desktop video internship in public relations at Blocks Cable Television in Las Vegas on December 23. (I wrote infomercial scripts and created press kits on a PC.) On January 2, I will relocate to Los Angeles and job hunt there for about four weeks.
    Since I saw you last, I've been writing freelance for *MIS* magazine and other computer trade journals and networking with friends in several computer industry professional associations as a volunteer newsletter editor.
    Would you know of a way to get into an emerging technology like virtual reality and still make use of my B.A. in English? I'd really appreciate any information or job leads you can pass on to me that could be helpful in my job hunting.
    I'd be happy to write a freelance article and publicize any aspect of your work or any aspects of Laser Art Technologies that would welcome visibility. I've enclosed three copies of my résumé. They can be circulated freely in the virtual reality industry or among virtual reality client and supplier businesses.
    I'm housesitting your mother's condo while she's in Europe. I'm looking forward to seeing you.

Sincerely,

Aniba Merimdeh

SAMPLE COVER LETTER: NETWORKING

Captain James Kendall, USAF (Ret.)
124 Coronado Court
Blakestown, MA 02154
(210) 555-1255

October 5, 1997

M. (Name of Current President)
Management of Data Special Interest Group (SIGMOD)
Association for Computing Machinery
P.O. Box 12114
Church Street Station
New York, NY 10257

Dear M. (Insert name of current president here):

    I'm retiring from the U.S. Air Force on October 30, 1997. (Insert name of member used as reference here), a member of your Management of Data Special Interest Group, recently informed me of an opening in your organization for a volunteer position as director of membership recruitment. I'd like to apply for that position as I enjoy networking with colleagues interested in data management. I have enclosed seven copies of my résumé. I am seeking information and job leads in order to make a transition in my career from military to civilian life. My goal is to find a new career in data management.

    For the past thirty years, my career in the Air Force as a recruiter centered on interviewing people and placing them in the right job. Now that I'm retiring from military service, I would like to devote the next twenty years or more of my work life to working with students interested in careers in data management. Last month I received my B.S. in Computer Information Systems (with an emphasis in data management) from National University, San Diego, and became a member of ACM.

    Please feel free to pass my résumé to any member or to download it to disk for any electronic job referral databank system that members might know of in the field of information processing. I look forward to hearing from you in person.

Sincerely,

James Kendall

SAMPLE COVER LETTER: TRADE SHOW/CONFERENCE/CONVENTION

Agape Theodakis
900 Bathgate Ave.
Forensic Park, IL 20208
(303) 555-9898

September 16, 1997

Exhibitors and Key Speakers
1997 Comdex Convention
Las Vegas Convention Center
Las Vegas, NV 80798

Dear Exhibitor or Key Speaker:

    I enjoyed networking with you at this year's Comdex Convention and electronic products trade show in Las Vegas. In January 1998, I will receive my B.S. degree in Computer Science (with a minor in accounting and finance) from the University of Illinois. I am interested in obtaining a programming position with a financial services corporation in February.

    I have recent experience programming in FoxPro for CPA Associates in Chicago. During my five years at the University of Illinois, I worked part time during school and full time during the summers at CPA Associates. My experience is in a personal computer environment utilizing Novell Netware. I have a knowledge of hardware and software (Lotus, WordPerfect, and Excel). I am willing to relocate to any area of major growth.

    My strongest areas are Novell Netware and Ethernet, 10 Base-T, and DBase. I have recent experience in network administration, PC installation, software installation, PC maintenance, network trouble shooting, and network performance analysis.

    I look forward to speaking with you and will call you next week.

Sincerely,

Agape Theodakis

SAMPLE FOLLOW-UP LETTER FORMAT

Your Name
Street Address
City, State, Zip
Phone Number

Date of Letter

Interviewer's Name
Title
Company Name
Street Address
City, State, Zip

Dear Mr./Ms._____:

    Opening Paragraph—Express sincere thanks for being given the opportunity of the interview. Mention the courtesies extended to you by anyone present. Indicate the job title, where and when the interview was given, and the date. Refresh the interviewer's mind with the most important part of the interview.

    Middle Paragraph—Restate your reasons for wanting to join the organization. Use your best one sentence sales pitch to close the sale. In one sentence state that you want the job because you will offer the following benefits and advantages to the company. If you left anything important out of the personal interview, include it now. Finish the middle paragraph with any sentence that enhances your abilities. State any specific qualifications that fulfill an important company need.

    Closing Paragraph—Offer to provide any information the company may want, such as reference letters, security clearance, or transcripts. Indicate when you're available for further interviewing at the company's convenience.

Sincerely,

(Your handwritten signature in black ink)

Your Name Typed

SAMPLE FOLLOW-UP LETTER

Jamesa Kintle
125 Mt. Penn Lane
San Justa, CA 92104-7177
(619) 555-1234

August 1, 1997

Ms. Rayanne Hart
Director of Employment
Dept. 300
Video Game Corporation
100 Prince Road
San Justa, CA 92104-7199

Dear Ms. Hart:

Thank you for the opportunity you provided. Interviewing for the position of computer video games artist was exciting. I look forward to joining Video Game Corporation and working with a dynamic manager like Anne Joan Levine.

As I mentioned during the special effects tour with Ms. Levine, I am familiar with all of the duties and responsibilities of the job. I spent the last year working in the special effects department of a video game design corporation and quickly learned the value of timely and original illustrations for the electronic game industry.

In addition to my experience in video game design, the knowledge I gained through courses in animation production and desktop video in my associate degree program will serve me well in fulfilling the requirements of the position. I can contribute significantly to your corporation with my award-winning illustrations and game designs.

Thank you again for the opportunity to interview with your company and for the fascinating tour. I enjoyed our informative discussion, and the new animation was breathtaking. May I publicize your forthcoming video game by writing an article about it for the local weekly computer newspaper, *The Byter?* I volunteer each month to send them a column reviewing and recommending new software and computer video games. I look forward to hearing from you at your convenience.

Sincerely,

Jamesa Kintle

ORGANIZING SKILLS ON PAPER

Looking at the variety of cover or follow-up letters and résumé styles in the previous chapters showed you some formats employers may prefer. Now it's time to focus on simplicity. This chapter will give you the framework to write your résumé concisely. It will help you organize your résumé by using a simple plan.

THE RESUME PLANNER

Interviewers use résumés to screen out applicants. Résumé reading is seen by them as a negative process. Often only a chosen few are referred to an employer for a decision. Many résumés never get past the interviewer to the employer because the résumé isn't simple to grasp at first glance.

To keep your résumé simple, devise a plan to organize work-related information. Employers will notice clear, concise résumés.

The Organized Plan

You know an effective résumé unlocks doors, but how do you filter all the information about yourself and present it simply? You need an organized plan to refer to while you are creating a first draft of your résumé. Organizing this plan means first asking yourself to itemize what's important. Organize your plan for writing a résumé by filling in your information in the following worksheets.

Only parts of the information on these worksheets may fit on your final résumé. However, sorting through all the details will help you market yourself more effectively and help you perform better in interviews.

Résumé Plan Worksheets

Identification Worksheet

Pencil in the following information on this plan.

Name _____

Address _____

City _____

State _____ Zip _____

Home Phone _____

Business or Message Phone _____

Fax _____

Confidential? Yes _____ No _____

Skills Worksheet
Listing your skills is required whether you're changing careers, reentering the civilian workforce after military retirement, or reentering the job market after being a full-time homemaker.

Employment Qualifications _____

_____
_____
_____
_____
_____
_____
_____
_____
_____
_____
_____
_____
_____

Are you changing careers? If yes, explain why briefly: _____

_____
_____
_____
_____
_____
_____
_____
_____

Best Abilities Worksheet

Training Worksheet
List your training, like your work experience, in reverse chronological order: your most advanced training or most recent course, workshop, seminar, internship, apprenticeship, or on-the-job training is listed first. Be specific and concrete about details. Include all dates, certificates earned, schools attended, or pertinent training information.

Job-related training: _____

Dates _____ Where trained _____

_____

On-the-job training _____

_____

Dates _____

Job-related continuing education _____

_____

Dates _____ Where trained _____

Apprenticeships _____

Dates _____ Where trained _____

Training internships _____

Dates _____ Address of internship _____

Computer training and coursework _____

_____

Hardware _____

_____

Software _____

_____

Repair _____

_____

Troubleshooting _____

_____

_____

_____

General Education Worksheet

List your formal education in reverse chronological order with your most advanced degree first. This section is for persons who have formal education beyond high school, rather than job training. If you didn't attend an accredited university, four-year college, or two-year community college, it's appropriate to list your post-high school continuing education and technical school courses under TRAINING.

Educational history includes all college degrees, dates, majors and minors studied, and any licenses or teaching credentials.

Advanced degree(s): _____

Date received _____

Name of university _____

Address of university _____

_____

Date received _____

Name of university _____

Address of university _____

_____

Undergraduate degree(s) _____

Date received _____

Majors _____

_____

Minors _____

_____

Name of university _____

Address of university _____

_____

Two-year college degree(s) _____

Date received _____

Emphasis _____

_____

Name of two-year or community college

_____

Address of college or school _____

_____

Diplomas, Licenses,   Date received _____

or Certificates_____   Name of school or training course _____

_____

Address of school _____

_____

Computer-related courses: _____

_____

_____

_____

_____

_____

_____

_____

_____

College-level internships served: _____

_____

_____

_____

_____

Job Objective Worksheet

If you choose to include an objective, list the job-related responsibilities you want. Simplicity rules here. Keep your objectives concise, remembering that employers will toss résumés with complex, wordy job objectives because they're too time consuming to ponder.

Use the job objective segment of your résumé plan as a terse, personal, and powerful ad. Dramatize your résumé's sales pitch. Your résumé needs flair. Pretend you are running it in the daily newspaper classifieds and have to state your job objective in less than 20 words. Try several different styles.

Hardware and Software Worksheet

Computer Models: _____
_____
_____

Software: _____
_____
_____
_____

Telecommunications Equipment: _____
_____

Local Area Networks: _____
_____

Operating Systems: _____
_____

Modems and Faxes: _____
_____

Computer Languages: _____
_____

Monitors and Access: _____
_____

Databases: _____
_____

Utility Packages: _____
_____

Peripherals: _____
_____

Telecommunications and Multimedia: _____
_____

Security Clearance: _____
_____
_____

Additional Information: _____
_____
_____

Subject Expertise Worksheet

EMPHASIS: _____
_____

Electrical Engineering Background _____
_____

Computer Science Background _____
_____

Mathematics Background _____
_____

Other Scientific Background _____
_____

Other Engineering Background _____
_____

Writing _____
_____

Public Relations/Marketing _____
_____

Sales _____
_____
_____

Art, animation, special effects _____
_____
_____

Data Processing _____
_____

Other: _____
_____
_____
_____
_____
_____
_____

The Day-in-the-Work-Life Worksheet
If you are currently employed, highlight each feature of the systems and programs you work with in your computer specialty. Write down your job roles in chronological steps. Include each job description—summarized concretely with details.

Write "a day-in-the-work life" page that details on an hour-by-hour basis what you do at work during a typical day. To get your specifics flowing, you might record your typical hour-by-hour activities on a tape recorder at work and transcribe them later.

A DAY IN THE WORK LIFE OF _____ (YOUR NAME)

SAMPLE WORKSHEET:

9 a.m.	Arrive at work and begin (action verb) _____
10 a.m	Program _____
11 a.m.	Analyze _____
12 noon–1 p.m.	lunch break
1 p.m.	Consult _____
2 p.m.	Sell _____
3 p.m.	Troubleshoot _____
4 p.m.	Demonstrate _____
5 p.m.	End of work day; or state whether you worked evenings, and describe your activities.
6–8 p.m.	Repaired systems on _____

Saturdays:

8 a.m.–1 p.m. Taught/trained/instructed _____

2 p.m.–4 p.m. Worked as a computer lab assistant at XYZ community college _____

Chronological Employment History Worksheet
Once you have filled in these worksheets, you are ready to itemize and detail your chronological employment history. Keep in mind that in the interview, you'll be asked to discuss the features of the systems and programs you worked on in each job in your field of experience. The questions will be taken right out of your chronological employment history if you use a chronological résumé.

Don't make the employer search for specific information and dates. Don't leave unaccounted for gaps in your history. Show how your chronological work history relates to your career plan. Employers hire people who specifically choose a company because it's part of their plan.

Your employment history also summarizes your qualifications. It tells the reader at a glance what you can do and how many years you've been doing it.

List the job title, company name and location, and years employed. Also list your responsibilities as accomplishments using action verbs. (Example: Implemented audience tracking system that saved company $50,000.)

Use an employment history worksheet to explain the nature of your career briefly and concretely. Start with your most recent job first. Include every job you've had since high school that is related to the new job or show transferable skills.

Leave no gaps unfilled. Instead of leaving gaps in those years you didn't work, fill them in with volunteer duties you handled, so that all time is accounted for by job-related responsibility. Use separate worksheet pages to detail all your jobs if you had several jobs within the same firm.

Never include salary information or reasons for leaving a job on a résumé. However, you can put them on your worksheet to help you define what you like to do most and what made you dissatisfied in a former job.

Remember: only part of the material on your worksheets will actually appear on the final draft of your résumé. Nevertheless, all the details you've sorted will ease you through an oral interview. Think about these details and practice answering questions about yourself in front of a mirror. List your work history in reverse chronological order.

Name of Company: _____

_____

Address of Company: _____

_____

_____

Job Title: _____

Dates from: _____ to: _____

Responsibilities:_____
_____
_____
_____
_____

Name of Company: _____
_____

Address of Company: _____
_____
_____

Job Title: _____
Dates from: _____ to: _____
Responsibilities:_____
_____
_____
_____
_____

Name of Company: _____
_____

Address of Company: _____
_____
_____

Job Title: _____
Dates from: _____ to: _____
Responsibilities: _____
_____
_____
_____
_____

Personal Requirements Worksheet

Willing to relocate: _____

Relocation areas desired: _____

Willing to travel: _____

Travel areas preferred: _____

Interests, hobbies, avocations: _____

Subjects or types of books read: _____

Types of magazines and newspapers preferred: _____
_____

Personality type, if determined through a personality test, such as the Myers-Briggs Type Indicator (MBTI): _____
_____

Prefer to work alone or with constant activity and people?
_____
_____

Introvert or extrovert? _____

Prefer usefulness/practical skills or imagination and learning for learning's sake? _____

Like flexible or rigid schedules? _____
_____

Highly organized person? _____

Prefer autonomy or supervision? _____
_____

Creative in your specialty? _____
_____

What conditions preferred at workspace? _____
_____
_____

Professional and trade association membership or volunteer work:
_____
_____
_____
_____

Publications, achievements, awards, productions, compositions, presentations, fellowships, scholarships, and kudos: _____
_____
_____
_____
_____

Foreign languages spoken or read, and ability: _____
_____
_____

Special skills: _____
_____
_____
_____
_____

Military service: _____
_____

From _____ to _____ Branch of service: _____
_____

Highest rank: _____
Service-related training or schools attended: _____
_____
_____
_____
_____
_____
_____
_____

References Worksheet

Never print the names, home phone numbers, and home addresses of your references directly on your résumé. It's common courtesy to protect their privacy. When you are asked for names and addresses of references, get your referent's permission first and then use only a current business address and business phone number.

Keep the names of your references and, if your reference letters were written long ago, contact them and ask for current letters of reference. Employers want to see references dated within the current year.

You should be aware, however, that former employers may be required by state law to report only the dates you worked for a particular firm, the job title, and a description of your job duties. Some states have privacy protection acts, information practices acts, and civil codes to protect confidentiality of information. Because state laws vary, check with your county law library to see which civil codes protect the privacy of employment, medical, and insurance records in your state. Your references may possibly no longer be allowed to comment on your job performance. For example, if an employer thinks Mary Jones did a wonderful job, but answers a request for references by merely confirming her job title, description of duties, and dates worked, it could be misinterpreted that something was wrong with her because the former employer held back comment on Ms. Jones's performance.

On an employment application, you will probably be asked to supply references from three people who know you professionally.

Name of reference: _____

_____

Job title: _____

_____

Organization: _____

_____

Business address: _____

_____

_____

Business phone number: _____ extension: _____

Name of reference: _____

_____

Job title: _____

_____

_____

Organization: _____

_____

Business address: _____

_____

_____

Business phone number: _____ extension: _____

Name of reference: _____

_____

Job title: _____

_____

Organization: _____

_____

Business address: _____

_____

_____

Business phone number: _____ extension: _____

Résumé Worksheet

Now that you have organized all your personal information on these worksheets, it's time to create a brief outline. From this outline, you will choose specific information to highlight and include in your final worksheet. This short outline is actually the first draft of your résumé.

Show exactly why you are qualified for the job in question. Choose only the job-relevant benefits, advantages, and practical information. Clarity is your goal. Now let's organize your outline further.

Pencil your information into the brief résumé worksheet that follows.

Name _____

Street address _____

_____

City, state, zip _____

Home phone _____ Business phone _____

OBJECTIVE (optional):

_____
_____
_____
_____
_____
_____

SUMMARY OF QUALIFICATIONS:

(Highlight your best skills and experience here.)

_____
_____
_____
_____
_____

EDUCATION AND TRAINING:

Institution

City _____ State _____

Degree/Certificate _____

or

Relevant computer coursework _____

Workshops/Seminars/Internships _____
_____
_____
Institution
City _____ State _____
Degree/Certificate _____
or
Relevant computer coursework _____
Workshops/Seminars/Internships _____
_____
_____

WORK EXPERIENCE:
Job title _____
Company name _____
City _____ State _____
Employed from _____ to _____
Major job responsibilities: _____
_____
_____
_____
_____
_____
_____
_____

Special awards, assignments, achievements in this job _____
_____
_____
_____
_____
_____
_____
_____
_____

Job title _____
Company name _____
City _____ State _____
Employed from _____ to _____
Major job responsibilities: _____

_____
_____
_____
_____
_____
_____
_____
_____

Special awards, assignments, achievements in this job _____

_____
_____
_____
_____
_____
_____
_____
_____

Job title _____
Company name _____
City _____ State _____
Employed from _____ to _____
Major job responsibilities: _____
Special awards, assignments, achievements in this job _____

_____
_____
_____
_____
_____

Job title _____
Company name _____
City _____ State _____
Employed from _____ to _____
Major job responsibilities: _____
_____
_____
_____
_____
_____
_____
_____

Special awards, assignments, achievements in this job _____
_____
_____
_____
_____
_____
_____
_____

Job title _____
Company name _____
City _____ State _____
Employed from _____ to _____
Major job responsibilities: _____
_____
_____
_____
_____
_____
_____

Special awards, assignments, achievements in this job _____

_____
_____
_____
_____
_____
_____

Special computer skills:
Include your knowledge of specific software and hardware. List any computer language you use for programming or design. List skills such as the following: word processing, desktop publishing, software operation and knowledge of electronic publishing software, database operation, spreadsheets, programming, systems analysis, local area networks, computerized accounting skills, scientific programming, computer-aided design and drafting, technical illustration, technical writing, courseware design, instructional technology, computer troubleshooting, repair, teaching or training on software or hardware equipment, graphic design, animation, Web site design or administration, or any related computer skills you can use on the job as well as teach. Include any office information systems equipment and software you use daily in any capacity—from data entry to management of information systems.

_____
_____
_____
_____
_____

Licenses and teaching credentials/certification: _____

_____
_____
_____
_____

Memberships in organizations:
List all associations in which you are involved that relate to the specific job you seek, such as computer associations, training organizations, creative organizations, or scholarly research groups.

_____
_____
_____

Awards, honors, scholarships, fellowships:
Include any special recognition you earned. _____
_____
_____
_____

Publications and productions:
Include any books you wrote, articles published, videos produced, artwork exhibited or published. _____
_____
_____
_____

Computer language knowledge: _____
_____
_____

Foreign language fluency: _____
_____
_____

REFERENCES: (Furnished upon request.)

Achievements Worksheet

Now that you've outlined the first draft of your résumé on this brief worksheet, you need to practice translating major job responsibilities into powerful phrases of achievement. Look at the list of action verbs at the end of this chapter. Instead of listing your accomplishments as duties, use these action verbs to make them as exciting, appealing, and forceful as a direct marketing advertisement designed to sell your qualifications.

The following examples demonstrate how powerful action verbs are used to describe a job applicant's achievements.

- Redesigned the entire computer room, changing the work flow of the office to meet ergonomic health standards, increasing output by 85 percent, and saving XYZ Corp. $200,000.
- Supervised the word-processing department's computers, valued at $1 million. Rerouted paperwork onto microfiche, saving the company $86,000 in 1993 and 2,000 cubic feet of storage space.
- Sold 1 million ABC software programs for XXY Corp., earning the company $20 million in gross sales in 1993. Won the best sales staffer of the year award. Trained 900 salespersons at 12 sites across the nation in software operation in 1993.
- Created three new system upgrades for_____software.

Now it's your turn to briefly describe your accomplishments using the action verbs provided. When you're finished, use your verbs to make a customized list of achievements. Create action-oriented phrases to sell your skills to an employer with an exact job in mind.

Organized _____

Planned _____

Established _____

Trained _____

Developed _____

Coordinated _____

Improved _____

Supervised _____

Created _____

Wrote _____

Presented _____

Illustrated _____

Designed _____

Analyzed _____

Managed _____

Initiated _____
Revised _____
Planned _____
Decided _____
Sold _____
Budgeted _____
Communicated _____
Evaluated _____

Action Verbs Resource Sheet

Accelerated	Augmented	Contributed
Accomplished	Authored	Controlled
Accepted	Authorize	Cooperated
Accounted	Automated	Coordinated
Accrued	Awarded	Corrected
Accumulated	Bought	Correlated
Achieved	Brought	Counseled
Acquired	Budgeted	Created
Acted	Built	Credited
Activated	Calculated	Critiqued
Actualized	Catalogued	Cut
Adapted	Chaired	Dealt
Adhered	Changed	Debriefed
Administered	Charted	Debugged
Advertised	Clarified	Decided
Advised	Coached	Deciphered
Affected	Coded	Decoded
Affirmed	Collaborated	Decreased
Afforded	Collected	Defined
Allocated	Commanded	Deflected
Analyzed	Communicated	Delegated
Animated	Compared	Deleted
Announced	Competed	Delivered
Anticipated	Compiled	Deregulated
Applied	Completed	Demonstrated
Appraised	Composed	Derived
Approved	Computed	Described
Arbitrated	Conceived	Designed
Arranged	Concentrated	Detailed
Ascertained	Conceptualized	Determined
Assembled	Conciliated	Developed
Assessed	Conducted	Devised
Assigned	Configured	Devoted
Assisted	Considered	Dialogued
Assumed	Constructed	Directed
Assured	Construed	Discovered
Attained	Consulted	Discussed
Audited	Contracted	Dispersed

Displayed	Grew	Managed
Distributed	Guaranteed	Manipulated
Documented	Guided	Marketed
Drafted	Handled	Mastered
Edited	Headed	Measured
Educated	Healed	Mediated
Effected	Helped	Merchandised
Elaborated	Hired	Merged
Eliminated	Identified	Met
Emphasized	Illustrated	Micrographed
Employed	Implemented	Ministered
Encouraged	Improved	Moderated
Energized	Included	Modified
Engaged	Increased	Molded
Engineered	Indexed	Monitored
Enhanced	Influenced	Motivated
Enlarged	Informed	Multiplied
Enlisted	Initialized	Narrated
Ensured	Initiated	Navigated
Entered	Inspected	Negotiated
Entertained	Inspired	Networked
Established	Installed	Neutralized
Estimated	Instituted	Normalized
Evaluated	Instructed	Normed
Examined	Insured	Notified
Excelled	Integrated	Notaried
Exchanged	Interested	Obtained
Executed	Interfaced	Officiated
Exercised	Internalized	Opened
Expanded	Interpreted	Operated
Expedited	Interviewed	Orchestrated
Explained	Introduced	Ordered
Explored	Investigated	Organized
Exported	Invented	Oversaw
Exposed	Inventoried	Participated
Extended	Inverted	Perceived
Extrapolated	Involved	Performed
Facilitated	Issued	Persuaded
Faxed	Joined	Photographed
Fixed	Judged	Piloted
Forecasted	Juried	Pinpointed
Formulated	Justified	Planned
Forwarded	Keyboarded	Played
Founded	Leased	Posted
Functioned	Lectured	Practiced
Furnished	Lessened	Predicted
Generated	Led	Preempted
Governed	Linked	Prepared
Graded	Loaded	Presented
Granted	Mailed	Presided
Graphed	Maintained	Pressed

Processed	Represented	Succeeded
Procured	Required	Summarized
Produced	Requisitioned	Supervised
Programmed	Researched	Supplied
Projected	Resequenced	Supported
Promoted	Reshaped	Surveyed
Proposed	Resolved	Syndicated
Proofread	Responded to	Synthesized
Protected	Restored	Systematized
Proved	Retained	Tabulated
Provided	Retired	Taught
Publicized	Retooled	Telecommuted
Published	Retrained	Televised
Purchased	Retrieved	Terminated
Qualified	Returned	Tested
Quantified	Revamped	Traced
Quickened	Reviewed	Tracked
Questioned	Revised	Trained
Raised	Rewired	Transacted
Ran	Robotized	Transferred
Reclaimed	Routed	Translated
Recognized	Scanned	Transmitted
Recommended	Scheduled	Treated
Recreated	Scored	Troubleshot
Reconciled	Screened	Typed
Reconstructed	Sculptured	Typeset
Recorded	Selected	Updated
Recouped	Sensed	Upgraded
Recovered	Served	Underscored
Recreated	Set objectives	Used
Recruited	Set up	Utilized
Rectified	Shaped	Validated
Recycled	Simplified	Verified
Redesigned	Sold	Videographed
Redecorated	Solicited	Videotaped
Reduced	Solved	Visualized
Reentered	Sorted	Vocalized
Registered	Specified	Voiced
Regulated	Spoke	Waited
Rehired	Sponsored	Waived
Reimbursed	Staffed	Weighted
Reinforced	Stabilized	Won
Related	Standardized	Word processed
Released	Starred	Wrote
Relocated	Stimulated	
Renewed	Streamlined	
Rented	Strengthened	
Repaired	Structured	
Replaced	Styled	
Replenished	Subcontracted	
Reported	Submitted	

EDIT THE RESUME

By now, you should have a good draft of your résumé. In this chapter, you will learn how to clarify the information in sample résumés and to use a checklist to edit your résumé. You will learn to see and solve problems in résumés and find what works and what doesn't. You will soon be able to apply these strategies to your résumé and enhance its job-getting appeal. Read the following résumés. Ask yourself if all time is accounted for, whether the information presented is appropriate to the position, and whether you'd hire these people.

FIRST DRAFT OF CHRONOLOGICAL RESUME

Anne Joan Levine

OVERVIEW: Telecommuting job desired, writing software user manuals from my computer or yours.

EXPERIENCE:

1975–Present Full-time freelance writer of business books and newspaper columns on computer businesses.

1990–1991 Adult Education Teacher of Literature and Creative Writing
San Diego Community College District Continuing Adult Education

Taught novel writing to senior citizens at senior centers and in adult education classrooms during summer and fall semester 1990–1991, one day per week (until class closed due to low enrollment after 15 weeks).

1980–1981 Typist/Word Processor
Various clerical temporary employment agencies. (Type 50 words per minute.)

Typed medical report records for the psychiatry department at University of California at San Diego in temporary assignments for a variety of temporary agencies for two-week assignments.

Typed medical records and reports for Sharp Hospital, San Diego, for short assignments.

1976–1979 Substitute English Teacher and aide,
San Diego Unified School District, San Diego

Taught English to high school, junior high, and elementary school students, kindergarten to 12th grade as a part-time hourly substitute for various one-day assignments until 1978.

EDUCATION: Master of Arts in English, SDSU, San Diego, 1979.
Winner of 1st Sigma Delta Chi Scholarship

Bachelor of Science in English Education,
New York University, 1973.

REFERENCES: Available on request.

SECOND DRAFT OF AN EXTENDED/CREATIVE RESUME

Anne Joan Levine

OVERVIEW: Writer of computer career books seeks a position as a courseware designer, instructional technologist, technical writer of software user manuals, training materials designer, or writer and editor of corporate or instructional video scripts.

EXPERIENCE:

1991–present: Scriptwriter, Instructional Videos, San Diego County Education Center, also wrote 500-page book for business services division at same site.

1987–1991: Independent Screenplay Author, Los Angeles, CA. Screenplays written for a variety of independent producers: Home video feature film scripts include: *Midnight Shift, Two Astronauts, Metalhead, Kiss Mommy, Playpen Hostages.* Animation: *The Amazon Hatchlings.* Stage play: *A Man's Woman.*

1985–1987: Instructional film/video scripts: "The Eric Computer System," 1976. "Elderly Abuse," 1987. "Self-Esteem," a video script, 1989. "International Child Abductions," 1990, budget feature film and television script. "How to Produce a Great Home Video," script. Plus two training film scripts written on distance education for independent educational film producers.

1980–1985: Typist/Word Processor:
Various clerical temporary employment agencies. (Type 50 words per minute.)

Typed medical report records part time for the psychiatry department at University of California, San Diego, in temporary assignments for a variety of temporary services.

Typed medical records and reports for Sharp Hospital, San Diego, for short assignments.

1976–1980: Grant Writer: San Diego Unified School District. Wrote grant proposal for Miramar Community School.

1975–1976: Chief Technical Writer/Editor: Creative Computer Sciences Corp., San Diego (rewrote Cobol manuals and scientific/technical reports.)

1973–1975: Speechwriter: Biomedical Media Planning, San Diego, CA. Wrote medical speeches for president of health planning organization contracted for public relations research.

SECOND DRAFT OF AN EXTENDED/CREATIVE RESUME

SOFTWARE:

Desktop publishing skills:
WordPerfect, Microsoft Publisher, and CorelDraw! software.

TEACHING EXPERIENCE:

1991–Present: Grossmont College, El Cajon, CA.
Taught Creative Writing 126 two nights per week as part of team teaching for five weeks of one semester with emphasis on scriptwriting and drama.

1990–1991: San Diego Community College District. Taught the following Saturday continuing adult education, semester-long workshops in creative writing:

San Diego Community College (part time). Creative Writing Workshop for Older Adults Midway Center: Taught course in composition, playwriting, autobiography writing. Taught "Home-based Businesses for Freelance Illustrators and Writers." Freelance business practices for animation script, comedy, writing feature films, writing for desktop video/home video, and corporate scriptwriting for instructional and industrial videos.

1981–1986: San Diego City College. Taught evening business communications course, Business Communications 119. Additional fiction workshops include: videobiography and writing.

1979–1981: Taught playwriting at North Shores Adult School, San Diego. Taught course titled, "Writing the Inner Personal Journal." Taught "personality type and writing style from both sides of the Brain." Taught "Writing the Historical Action Novel."

1976–1979: Substitute English teacher, secondary school, and kindergarten Teacher's Aide, San Diego Unified School District. Taught hourly and as an aide, helped teachers with secondary school English on a temporary, hourly basis taking attendance, lecturing, and doing clerical work for teachers as well as tutoring students in creative writing. Helped design learning materials for curriculum for teachers, worked with gifted students in creative writing workshops.

EDUCATION:

M.A. English, San Diego State University, San Diego, CA, 1979.
B.S. English Education/writing and psychology, New York University, NY, 1973.

REFERENCES AND WRITING SAMPLES ON REQUEST.

ANALYSIS OF ANNE JOAN LEVINE'S RESUMES

Why Employers Rejected the Résumés

Ms. Levine's résumés aren't focused on any specific skill in either draft. Visually, they don't make an impact. The information is scattered between gaps of time when she was a homemaker and part-time worker. Employers aren't going to spend time trying to make sense of the past 24 years of her life in this disorganized résumé. She has no obvious career goal.

The résumé must be reworked with emphasis on the transferability of her creative skills. To solve the problems in her résumé, her work history must first be simplified.

Practical Evaluation

Job Overview
Neither job overview is specific enough for the majority of employers to understand. Employers scan résumés for sequential facts and easy-to-follow format.

Experience
Work history in both drafts is unclear and not chronological. Too much emphasis is on issues not related to the job in question.

Education
The degrees are relevant to the job objective. There is no problem with the visual placement of the general education and degrees in the final draft. Rather than just list the majors, English and English education, in the first draft, Ms. Levine needs to specify the emphasis within her degrees: literature, linguistics, teaching, professional writing (nonfiction), or creative writing (fiction). An area of focus helps to fit the exact job title to the person's specialization or job responsibilities.

For example, suppose an employer is considering two applicants who majored in English for a job as an interactive fiction writer for a software game company manufacturing entertainment on CD-Interactive or CD-ROM. The person more likely to be hired would be the one whose English studies focused on creative fiction.

The writer more likely to be hired as a software user manual writer or software technical writer or editor would be a "professional writing" major (nonfiction), or a person who majored in English, technical writing, or technical journalism.

Overall
In the first draft, the sections aren't separated. Large gaps of unemployment exist. Also, superfluous experience is merged with important skills. In the second draft, her experience isn't sorted or organized into related segments that show how skills are transferred. Résumés need smooth transitions.

FINAL DRAFT

Anne Joan Levine

JOB TITLE: TECHNICAL WRITER OF SOFTWARE MANUALS

SOFTWARE EXPERIENCE:

- **Wrote book on applications software uses** for home-based business owners, published by Simon & Schuster, 1985.

- **Weekly national newspaper columnist** for *The Business News* (for small business owners). Write business strategies advice columns. Write software reviews.

- **Wrote video script** training teachers in the operation of the Eric computer system for educational research, San Diego County Education Department, Media Center.

TRAINING EXPERIENCE:

- **Professional Writing Instructor**, San Diego Community College District, 1990–1991. Specialist in nonfiction. Adult Education.

- **English Instructor**, San Diego Unified School District San Diego, 1976–1978 (substitute teacher on assignment).

RELATED COMPUTER SOFTWARE EXPERIENCE:

Writing: Author of 23 published 100-page pamphlets on computer art careers and careers in graphic design.

Word Processing and Desktop Publishing: Owner of a word processing, desktop publishing, and technical writing home-based business specializing in computer career information using WordPerfect, CorelDraw!, and Microsoft Publisher on a PC.

EDUCATION:

- Master of Arts in English (writing emphasis), San Diego State University, 1979.
- Bachelor of Science in English Education, New York University, 1973.

LIST OF PUBLISHED WORKS ATTACHED

REFERENCES ON REQUEST

ANALYSIS OF FINAL DRAFT OF ANNE JOAN LEVINE'S RESUME

Problems Solved

Ms. Levine's rewritten résumé is now focused on the targeted job title, that of a technical writer specializing in writing software user manuals. Although she has no experience in actually writing a software user manual, she has three related skills to emphasize, and she uses a bold visual appeal to display them:

1. Combined experience writing about software and the operation of home-based computer businesses.
2. Weekly newspaper business strategies column.
3. Prior teaching experience and education.

Related Jobs Using the Same Résumé

Ms. Levine could also apply for jobs writing, editing, or coordinating the publication of technical or literary training materials, developing curriculum materials, career books, and writing public relations literature for computer publishing companies or software manufacturing and design firms.

In the expanding field of electronic publishing, her knowledge of desktop publishing and word-processing software also qualifies her to write sales brochures and press kit materials for desktop publishing software firms. Desktop publishing skills are often used to obtain jobs as proofreaders, technical writers, or technical editors. One growth area is training materials courseware design for teachers of word processing or desktop publishing.

Practical Evaluation

Job Overview

The job overview has been eliminated. There is now the exact job title, "technical writer of software manuals." The employer can read under the experience cluster about Ms. Levine.

Emphasis on "telecommuting desired" was removed. In her interview, she can ask whether telecommuting is permitted, or whether the hours are flexible.

Experience

In the final draft, experience is focused and strengthened. Experience is now organized into three clusters that make smooth transitions without holes in time or other noticeable gaps in employment, and the information relates directly to the job title. Similar work is grouped together—writing with writing, teaching with teaching, and word processing with desktop publishing (listed under **Related Computer Software Experience**). With each **"Related Computer Software Experience"** specialty listed in a cluster, the job interest becomes more focused. To create visual appeal, she used bullets and put her specialties in bold.

Employers can refer back to **"Software Experience"** to see that she reviews software in her weekly column for a national business newspaper. These facts in sequential order build up her credibility and qualifications for the job objective.

The chronological work history dates were subdued. She omitted from her résumé the time periods when she was on the "mommy track" from 1973–1976 and from 1979–1990.

Nor did she list her occasional temporary typing jobs, which spanned the years from 1973 to 1981 or her typing speed. Her typing speed was a hint to employers that she would accept a lower-paid clerical job instead of a professional, higher-paid job as a technical writer or editor. List your typing speed only if you're applying for a word processing, medical transcription, secretarial, court reporting, or data entry job where people are hired for their keyboarding speed.

Related Software Experience
Ms. Levine wanted to emphasize the importance of her familiarity with computers and software, even though she had never taken a computer or software course. She's entirely self-trained in several kinds of desktop publishing software and owns her own computer.

To de-emphasize her lack of formal training, she highlighted running her own home-based desktop publishing and word-processing business. She lists the software as well as the specialty. The types of projects her business dealt with showed her knowledge of, or interest in writing materials about, computer careers, specifically computer art.

Education
Ms. Levine's fine educational accomplishment, a master's degree, remains listed. Since she is not looking for a teaching job, professional writing is emphasized, especially the writing of nonfiction, computer-oriented educational and training materials.

Her degrees in English add to her qualifications for a job as a writer, whether in the software field, instructional design, or in education. It's often easier to train a writer in programming than it is to train a programmer to be a writer specializing in making the complex simpler.

List of Publications Attached
Instead of the usual "references on request," it's more credible for a creative person to attach a one-page list of her books, pamphlets, articles, art, videos, or interactive fiction—with dates of publication/production.

The final version of Ms. Levine's résumé is unforgettable, impressive, powerful, and competitive with the hundreds of résumés that her targeted company will receive. The revised résumé has a far better chance of being taken seriously than the original résumés that she used for two years without receiving a single interview.

Now let's analyze another person's résumé.

FIRST DRAFT OF ABILITIES RESUME

Thor Tucker

OVERVIEW:	Applications Programmer, any field except finance.
EDUCATION:	
1990	A.S. Computer Science & Information Systems San Diego City College, San Diego 3.45 grade point average.
1987	Attended AT&T 4ESS Switching Machine School to learn how to repair 4ESS Switching Machine.
1972	B.A. Anthropology, American University, Washington, DC 3.0 grade point average
1973	18 graduate credits in Middle East Area Studies, American University, Washington, DC
HARDWARE:	4ESS, IBM, MAC
SOFTWARE:	Microsoft Word, WordPerfect, DeLuxe Paint DBase IV+, Paradox, Lotus 1-2-3. Local area networks with Novell.
COMPUTER LANGUAGES:	Assembler, Pascal, C, C++, Basic.
EXPERIENCE: June 1987 to Aug. 1997	AT&T Corp, San Diego, CA 92103 COMMUNICATIONS TECHNICIAN & SWITCHMAN Personally responsible for maintenance and repair of a 4ESS switching machine. Worked on machine translations and also fixed carrier systems that go to different cities. Analyzed schematic diagrams and analyzed Assembly language of maintenance programs.
1973– 1987	AT&T Corp., Los Angeles, CA 90028 COMMUNICATIONS TECHNICIAN AND SWITCHMAN Repaired microwave and carrier systems and private line circuits.

References on request.

ANALYSIS OF THOR TUCKER'S RESUME

Why Employers Rejected the Résumé

Experience is subdued in the bottom third of the résumé. He has written it too generally without itemizing what he actually did for the past 25 years on a daily basis that is fully transferable to a programmer's job. He doesn't link his 25 years as a telephone company switchman to new areas of telecommunications.

Mr. Tucker briefly lists three tasks he repeated daily for 25 years at the telephone company, but the details do little to convince an employer that he is a competitive programmer. Also, he asks to work in "any field except finance." Instead, he needs to focus on specific fields.

Practical Evaluation

Job Overview

Mr. Tucker wants to find an applications programmer's job in "any field except finance." But employers are looking for focus when they begin to scan a résumé. All we know is that he doesn't like the finance field.

He needs to replace his job objective with a more realistic job title, which would answer the question "In what field?" Several possibilities include:

- Applications programmer in telecommunications.
- Sales of applications software to telephone company spin-offs.
- Database management for telephone or telecommunications firms selling to corporations.
- Specialty items technology such as repair and installation of distance teaching telecommunications linkage equipment and related programming.
- Information systems technology or management.
- Local area networks (LAN) technology.
- Corporate telecommunications technology/repair, programming, or installation.

There's no emphasis on his 25-year outstanding performance as a telephone company communications technician/switchman.

Education

He has attended annual training at AT&T school to learn repair of the various telephone company machines but has left this off of his résumé, assuming that none of the skills are transferable to work outside the telephone company. Yet Mr. Tucker has had over 20 annual training sessions, lasting from two weeks to five months, at locations all over the nation.

His itemized liberal arts education in anthropology and Mideast area studies is irrelevant to his job goal as a programmer. It shouldn't have been given such prominence. He has overpowered his communications technician qualifications by emphasizing his early general education at the top of the résumé.

Experience

Mr. Tucker needs to show how his perceived narrow daily job experience, reading computer program errors in Assembler language code, transfers to wider fields outside the phone company. Emphasis on correcting errors in computer code serves as a bridge between the old communications technician job and a new job goal in applications programming.

Mr. Tucker needs to highlight his knowledge of programming in C Language, Pascal, Basic, and local area networks using Novell, learned in his community college courses paid for by his employer. These are professional quality skills that can be transferred to the new goal as a programmer. His whole career is not bound to telephone company switching machine maintenance and circuit repair.

Mr. Tucker needs to position the most programming-relevant skills at the top of his résumé and make bold the most important competency titles. Only practical skills and experience that can be easily transferred to other companies needs to be emphasized.

In the cover letter, Thor Tucker can refer to his excellent work evaluations and attendance award and use them later as references.

References

There's no need to take up a line on the résumé with "references on request" for a person who has only worked at one company for 25 years. The prospective employer will know to call the phone company to verify the employment or ask for the name of Mr. Tucker's immediate supervisor.

FINAL DRAFT

Thor Tucker

APPLICATIONS PROGRAMMER: TELECOMMUNICATIONS

OVERVIEW: Communications technician and computer software troubleshooter with 25 years of maintenance and repair service experience seeks programming position specializing in machine translations, analysis of Assembly language maintenance programs, and analysis of schematic diagrams.

PROFESSIONAL SKILLS

COMPUTER LANGUAGE ANALYSIS:
- Assembler language (4ESS)
- Machine language translations

PROGRAMMING LANGUAGES:
- Assembler, Pascal, C, C++, Basic, Cobol, local area networks with Novell

DOCUMENT PREPARATION:
- Prepare reports and schematic diagrams. Use of word-processing software, advanced use of database packages and spreadsheets.

EQUIPMENT REPAIR AND MAINTENANCE:
- 4ESS Switching Machines: Troubleshooting, maintenance, and repair of private line systems, microwave, fixed carrier systems, and telecommunications equipment that route to different cities.

EXPERIENCE

1973–1997   Communications Technician and Switchman
AT&T Corporation, San Diego, CA, and Los Angeles, CA, centers.

EDUCATION AND TRAINING

Associate in Science (A.S.)
Computer Sciences and Information Systems
San Diego City College, San Diego, CA, 1990

AT&T company school training for repair of 4ESS switching machine, 1987

B.A., Anthropology
American University, Washington, DC, 1972

ANALYSIS OF FINAL DRAFT OF THOR TUCKER'S RESUME

Problems Solved

Mr. Tucker's résumé is now focused on his skills in the specific area of telecommunications. This industry reflects the marriage of computers to a vast network of corporate telephone systems.

The revised résumé applies his 25 years of craft level experience working for one telephone company to new technology opportunities with a wide variety of telecommunications firms that link telephone systems with computer equipment and peripherals. His unique combination of company training and employer-paid computer training in college courses has been shown prominently, highlighting his programming skills and technician experience.

The new résumé will help Mr. Tucker transfer his skills to a wider variety of businesses within the expanding telecommunications industry. He needed to show how his former job competencies and continuous retraining in new programming languages could be used outside of the phone company.

Related Jobs Using the Same Résumé

He is now prepared to apply in the burgeoning field of wireless telecommunications for job descriptions so new that no one has yet had time to get experience in them. He can choose to target telecommunication companies involved with the maintenance and repair or distribution of satellite, fax, and modem equipment used for global teleconferencing.

Mr. Tucker can apply for positions as a programmer or technician with local area networks, or a combination of both. Corporations receptive to an applicant with such skills include those in wireless telecommunications, manufacturers of equipment used for distance teaching, global video-conferencing, electronic mail, and telecommunications firms involved in information retrieval from databases.

Practical Evaluation

Job Overview

Mr. Tucker has clearly targeted the telecommunications industry. The revised résumé lists the specific job title as applications programmer, a title that uses all of his competencies rather than only his mid-career training in programming.

He clarifies his telephone company technician skills, showing his ability to link computer equipment with telephone and wireless systems.

Focus is now on a concrete specialty. Mr. Tucker implies that after 25 years in maintenance and repair with the phone company, he would like to transfer skills learned through continuous retraining and computer programming courses to a new company in the expanding telecommunications industry.

Professional Skills

Since Mr. Tucker desires an applications programmer's position, he emphasizes his competencies in computer language analysis, programming languages, and document preparation using advanced database packages, spreadsheets, and word-processing software packages. He lists his equipment repair and maintenance skills last, in spite of the fact that he's used these daily for three decades. It's obvious he wants a break in the routine and prefers to program. Overall, the order in which the professional skills are now listed shows how important they are in seeking a new position as a programmer.

Experience

He's worked at one company since his graduation. There's no need to list companies in the order of importance or break experience into subdivisions, as would be done if he had worked at numerous firms.

Education

Mr. Tucker's degrees are listed at the end of the résumé. His computer-related education leading to the Associate in Science degree in Computer Sciences and Information Systems is now listed first. It shows he spent two years in evening community college learning six new computer languages and specific technical competencies.

His general education is singled out and not mixed with job training. The general education B.A. degree he received in anthropology was listed last, only to show he completed a well-rounded education before starting his technical career.

His 25-year career with the telephone company presupposes that the corporation sent him to company school to learn how to maintain and repair the 4ESS switching machine he worked on full time.

YOUR RESUME CHECKLIST

Every employer or human resource manager in the computer industry has individual pointers for what's organizationally correct on a résumé. Visual appeal is subjective, but all résumé readers prefer uncluttered résumés that spotlight job-related successes. Brevity and simplicity are important; redundancy will be noticed immediately.

Here are some commonly accepted do's and don'ts of résumé and cover letter writing. Use these tips as a checklist when editing your résumé and rewriting your cover and follow-up letters.

Do These Things!

1. Clarify skills valued by the employer in the job objective and overview section of your résumé.
2. Plan your résumé after you have learned everything you can about the job and the company.
3. Begin each sentence with action verbs that describe your competencies as you list concrete, specific, and job-transferable skills. Verbs should make statements positive yet not boastful.

4. Check and verify the facts on your résumé to make sure they're true before submitting it to an employer.
5. Be selective about your most important qualifications. Listing all your skills overwhelms the reader.
6. Simplify statements. Analyze your résumé for efficiency. Use sentences of ten words or less when possible.
7. Check for redundancies. Don't repeat the same idea in different ways on your résumé.
8. List your most important degree first. If you taught yourself about computers, then make it clear that you're a self starter.
9. Include your work permit type and your immigrant status if you're from another country.
10. Design your résumé like a story. All your experiences need to relate to your main plot. Stories can have subplots, but each must return to your main plot. Your résumé must stimulate a reaction in the reader.
11. Be specific and particular. State what you do best and what tasks you enjoy doing most in a job.
12. Track the responses to your résumé mailings until you are hired. Résumé tracking forms are located in Appendix A. Follow up the best prospects with letters each month for a year. Make monthly follow-up phone calls to see whether new jobs have opened and to check whether your résumé and follow-up letter are still active. Ask for referrals.
13. Put only required items on your résumé. List your licenses, teaching credentials, and security clearances only when requested.
14. Explain briefly how and why your education and/or your experience qualifies you to do the job.
15. Go with tradition. Appear conservative on your résumé when appropriate. Keep the tone or mood of the résumé professional. Give practical reasons why an employer should hire you.
16. Show how you will apply your creativity to the company's needs.
17. Highlight your problem-solving skills.
18. Include temporary, part-time, job-sharing, home-based business, telecommuting, entrepreneurial, freelance, contingency professional, or independent contract work only as related to the skills or experience required.
19. List sales and marketing profits if you previously worked as a sales and marketing representative or for yourself.
20. List your accomplishments in terms of the company's profit, not your personal profit (i.e., bonuses).
21. Show dedication to receiving a reply. In a follow-up letter, ask specifically what stands between you and the job.
22. Include dates for employment and education on all types of résumés as a reference point.
23. Provide your references' business phone numbers, not their home phone numbers.
24. Relate your military service to specific civilian job objectives.

If you're retiring from the military, include what you did in the service as a bridge toward a specific career.

25. List memberships in only those professional associations and trade or business organizations that relate to the occupation. Include relevant volunteer work for professional associations.
26. Write with enthusiasm for your work and for the employer or job.
27. Place bold headings and bullets on important titles in your résumé. Itemize your skills and responsibilities in order of their importance.
28. Create visual impact by using large amounts of white space.
29. Desktop publish your résumé, preferably using the most current desktop publishing software. A résumé has the best professional-looking appearance when laser printed.
30. Use the same fonts (type) for your résumé and cover letter.
31. Sell only what you can realistically offer an employer.
32. Proofread your résumé for errors three times on different days. Proofread after using a computer's spelling and grammar checker. Proofread your résumé again before having it duplicated for mailing.
33. Use 20-pound bond laser printer and duplicating paper, 100% cotton paper, or linen résumé paper to prevent smudging and tearing. The envelope and cover letter should be of the same color and weight.
34. Include experience that transfers general communication, organizational, or leadership skills to a variety of jobs. Track your growth with each new job.
35. Since most résumés that are faxed eventually are scanned onto a disc and put into a database or on a Web site, use sharp black fonts on white laser printer paper so the resume will be easy to scan, fax, or photocopy. Fancy font letterhead is hard to scan into a computer and photos don't reproduce well in a fax machine or black and white scanner. Color is hard to photocopy and usually reproduces with too little contrast to see. Stick to text-only résumés with large, easy-to-read type that will withstand computer digitizing.

Don't Do These Things!

1. Don't include personal information such as your religion, age, race, height, weight, marital status, child care provisions, ages of children, I.Q., GPA below 3.5, sexual preference, or any psychological testing results.
2. Don't include all former employers' names or staple old, handwritten reference letters to your résumé.
3. Don't list past salaries.
4. Don't send your photo.
5. Don't beg, plead, or manipulate an employer into hiring you out of pity because you're down on your luck.
6. Don't include odd-jobs experience that helped you pay your college tuition.

7. Don't complain—about anything.
8. Don't emphasize physical or emotional disabilities.
9. Don't exaggerate your achievements.
10. Don't describe yourself with a string of adjectives or passive verbs.
11. Don't say derogatory things about former employers or coworkers.
12. Don't let your overview overpower your entire résumé.
13. Don't proclaim ageism, sexism, racism, or any other discrimination, including jealousy or sexual harassment, as the reason you were fired from your last job.
14. Don't send unsolicited samples of your work and demand that your package be returned or held active in case a job opens.
15. Don't say that you'll gladly accept any job the company offers in any department—from sweeping the floor to the presidency.
16. Don't include your plan to someday open your own business after your employer has taught you the ropes and supplied you with a client list.
17. Don't emphasize how much more important your ideas are than production or profit.
18. Don't use the word *résumé* on your résumé.
19. Don't ask for tuition reimbursement for courses totally unrelated to the job.
20. Don't make it known that you have no time for lifelong learning and growth opportunities because you work so hard.
21. Don't advertise in your cover letter that you'll do anything illegal for a certain amount of money.
22. Don't give equal weight to each of your past jobs.
23. Don't ramble on about your military honors, travels, and experience unrelated to the job in question.
24. Don't tell your employer that you really don't need to work because your spouse pays the bills.
25. Don't label yourself with words that devalue you—such as "just a housewife for the past 20 years with a 1975 liberal arts degree seeking a creative job in the computer industry."
26. Don't demand to know where the company will be in five years and the role you'll play in it if you're hired.
27. Don't show how much you covet the power of the person with hiring authority or your prospective boss.
28. Don't include the fact that you can't drive and need to work near a bus line or telecommute.
29. Don't use your cover letter to ask employers to create nonexistent jobs in order to use your talents.
30. Don't crowd too much type onto one page.
31. Don't distract the reader with excessive use of italic, bold, and multiple fonts.
32. Don't send out unclear or flawed photocopies of your résumé.
33. Don't use dark or bright-colored paper that cannot be photocopied by the employer or is hard to read.

NONTRADITIONAL RESUMES

In this chapter and the next, you will learn how to support your strengths with concrete evidence. You will learn how to write a nontraditional résumé so clearly that you can't be misunderstood. You will also gain advice on how to take your nontraditional computing career and make it more attractive to employers, both in the private and public sectors.

When You Need a Nontraditional Résumé

You need a nontraditional résumé in these circumstances:

- Taking a long time out for study (more than a year)
- Running a business
- Rearing children, or caring full-time for aged or disabled relatives in the home for more than one year
- Retirement from military service
- Unemployment of more than one year's duration
- Switching careers after retirement
- Working flexible hours in part-time or temporary work
- Immigrating from another country
- Applying for an internship or a cooperative work-study arrangement
- Seeking a work/travel assignment
- Working part time for more than a year or switching from full-time work to part time work
- Job sharing for more than a year
- Public speaking full time
- Many years' work as a freelancer, consultant, independent contractor, entrepreneur, or intrapreneur
- Temporary work, or assignments for a temporary employment agency
- Many years spent unemployed because of illness, disability, or confinement
- Work outside the country for more than a year
- Creative artist, computer midi synthesizer musician or composer, or staff writer entering the fields of software design, interactive education/entertainment, or instructional technology for the first time
- Switching from one career to an entirely new industry

Why You Need a Nontraditional Résumé

If you are a person who diverges from typical corporate personnel habits, you need to be especially convincing about your talents. Your résumé must be so persuasive that the employer will find your unique skills profitable. Nontraditional résumés break patterns.

Nontraditional résumés itemize specific benefits, offered in the order of their importance to the employer. Collect data about yourself on index cards. Ask yourself, "Which of my ideas are interesting and exciting?" Now be specific. Back up a few selected ideas with facts and details that clearly show benefits to the company. You need to retrieve the facts that gave you profitable ideas in the first place.

Show Your Team Spirit

If your career has not followed a traditional path, an employer may be wary of hiring you. A prospective employee with a history of autonomy and independence, for example, may not work well or be productive as a part of a team-approach to business. Nontraditional résumés need special drafting to earn respect by their presentation. Strengths need to be emphasized in such a way that the nontraditional job applicant appears attractive and competent, and able to join a team.

Ask yourself what generalizations can be made about your skills that would fulfill the job-related needs of the employer. How can you tie all the relevant facts to a specific part of the computer industry? You need to give meaning to all those facts about yourself on your résumé that will answer an employer's concerns.

If you find you really are not comfortable working on a team, perhaps you can fit into a company niche or fulfill a specific need. Target those needs or niches. By tying together your facts and connecting them to a specific need in the company, you could represent yourself as a resource for other teams or departments in a company or government office. For information on résumés and government jobs, read Chapter 7, Retirees and Others.

Setting Your Résumé Apart from the Competition

Many jobs are never advertised because employers prefer to hire from within the organization or from similar jobs in other, related companies. This practice limits the résumés they must read and the interviews they must conduct. For example, an advertisement for a manager of information systems (MIS) usually draws a national group of applicants who are already employed as managers in similar settings.

Additionally, as many corporations downsize or hire temporary employees and independent contractors as computer consultants, many middle managers are displaced or laid-off. These managers are competing with a large group of computer professionals who have not yet worked as managers, but who are applying in hopes of being hired.

Job applicants applying for the MIS position can include military retirees entering the civilian workplace after 20 to 30 years of logistics administrative work in the services. Other job applicants may be displaced homemakers carving out their own niches after recent retraining. Some job applicants are recent MIS graduate degree recipients looking for management trainee positions.

Applicants include former entrepreneurs seeking to be "intrapreneurs." (Intrapreneurs work inside a company as independent contractors.) Some are computer consultants who want to work for one company on staff. There are many systems analysts, software engineers, local area network specialists, and programmers who intend to move into management.

The days when one ad for a manager of information systems brought in only groups of employed managers who wanted to move laterally are gone. Today, many individuals are trying to get a foot in the door at the top to avoid the crowd at the bottom.

To open that door for you—at any level—you need to approach employers with advantages and benefits that set you apart from the competition. Let's discuss strategies for students and those with an interrupted work history. In the next chapter, we will target retirees, temporary employees, and immigrants.

JOB DISCONTINUITY STRATEGIES

If your career or jobs have been interrupted by time or switches, the following tips are for you.

TIP 1: SHOW TRANSFERABLE (LATERAL) COMPETENCIES

Your first task is to explain in positive terms the breaks in your employment or the reason for your career switch to a new field. Instead of climbing the ranks from clerk to president in one firm, you may have moved laterally through many careers, collecting transferable experience and skills that can be used equally well in many careers.

Job continuity is no longer promised. Technology changes. You move forward only by training continuously, adapting to and learning to use new products. If you can show that your skills are useful to many types of firms, you can transfer from one career to the next.

TIP 2: LIST MARKETABLE STRENGTHS

What strengths can you sell? What strengths can you use to persuade, motivate, and inspire an employer to hire you? Show the employer by showing exactly and concretely how your strengths are going to be used by the company.

If you are a displaced homemaker with no outside paid experience, sell your ability to inspire, motivate, and promote other people or products in the computer industry. You may be able to sell your ability to oversee and nurture a product from its inception through all stages of its growth. In short, you could tranfer your parenting skills from person to product.

Market the usefulness of your skills to an employer. Whether you get the job or not depends on your ability to express to the employer what's in it for them.

TIP 3: USE A NONTRADITIONAL ABILITIES OR CREATIVE RESUME

Don't use the chronological work history résumé if there are large gaps in time or breaks in the continuity of your work between graduation and the present. Instead, emphasize all your transferable skills. Additional information on an abilities-type résumé is in Chapter 2.

TIP 4: BEAT AGEISM

The computer industry is marketing to mature people, including senior citizens' computer clubs that network nationally. If you are a retiree returning to the workplace, show how you can promote computer information or products to the rising tide of "over age 48" baby boomers—millions of computer users. Computer interest among people over age 50 is rapidly increasing. Who is going to serve this market's needs with computer products from investment software to creative innovations? More and more retirees are avid Internet users.

In contrast, if you are young and less experienced, use the same strategy to appeal to the youth market. Children begin using computers in preschool and will use software through college. A special segment of the Web was created just for kids. The computer industry is intergenerational.

TIP 5: SELL YOURSELF AS A CONSUMER

In the computer industry, feedback from consumers of computer products is coveted. Market yourself as a consumer of computer products or as a very knowledgeable navigator of the Web. To show how active and vocal you are as a consumer, write software reviews or columns on Internet/Web use and send them to newspapers, magazines, and computer user club newsletters.

Your common sense as a consumer of computers carries heavy weight in convincing a company to listen, improve products, and hire spokespersons or representatives. The computer world listens to consumers; that is why they use volunteer beta testers on new software.

TIP 6: ENROLL IN A COMPUTER-RELATED COURSE

Nobody networks better than working adult weekend/evening computer students with a course in common. Learn the latest technologies and software. Exchange business cards.

Find out about special fields and emerging trends, such as applied artificial intelligence used to forecast stock market trends. Learn the meaning of neural networks and fuzzy logic in the biotech industry. Take a course in local area networks and computer sharing, or in using the Internet. Join desktop computer animation enthusiasts, color desktop publishers, or graphic designers experimenting with new software at professional association seminars.

TIP 7: DO WHAT YOU ENJOY AND SHOW WHAT YOU CAN DO

Find out what feels comfortable in the world of work, what's easiest to do, and what skills come naturally. Take one of the personality questionnaires such as the Myers-Briggs Type Indicator (MBTI), the

Keirsey Temperament Sorter, or the personality quiz in this book to find your type and temperament. The results may help you match yourself to the job and company that are right for you.

TIP 8: WHY SHOULD THEY HIRE YOU?

Make a list of all the positive reasons why an employer should hire you—from the employer's point of view. List these points on your abilities résumé plan and first draft. Then select a chosen few to include on your final, polished résumé.

Research the company you want to hire you. Then research the job there. If you have no experience, use practical examples of how you use your abilities, skills, or talents. Your summary or overview, placed after the job objective/title and before your competencies, contains the action you take. If you think you have few skills, then emphasize how you motivate and inspire people through your actions. For example, if you are a volunteer fundraiser for your local charity, use an action verb to describe the skill—raise funds. Stress the title "fundraiser," not "volunteer."

TIP 9: LOOK FOR LINKS TO EMPLOYER

Find activities that link you and the employer—working on professional association panels or committees together, doing volunteer work, or taking the same courses with company staff. To be hired, your résumé must become a list that links or matches a company's needs to your skills.

Try placing a classified ad under the heading "employment (or situation) wanted" in a trade journal. When you advertise the best you can offer, and link up your interests, chances are you'll get more responses from employers than if you had sent your résumé in response to a "help wanted" classified ad appearing in a general daily newspaper.

STUDENT STRATEGIES

You are a full-time student with no paid job experience and you wonder how you can find a job when all the jobs require experience. Should you only look for help wanted ads that begin with the words *management trainee* or simply *trainee?* No. There is a wealth of ways to connect with companies before you graduate.

Use the following student strategies as bridges. Select what's most comfortable for you, and then list the involvement on your résumé. These tips will connect your school experience to the workforce.

TIP 1: USE PROFESSIONAL ASSOCIATIONS AS A BRIDGE TO EMPLOYMENT

Your first step is to connect with companies and begin relationships in capacities other than traditional employment. Look in the *Encyclopedia of Associations,* which you'll find in your public or school library. Choose several organizations or associations to join, at a reduced student membership cost, that are related to your field of interest.

In this book's Appendix is a list of computer associations that you can join at full-time student membership rates (lower than individual membership rates). Also look at the computer periodicals and publications listed and keep them in mind for making connections or networking.

Pick those associations that focus on your main interest in the computer field. For example, if you are interested in computer graphics, there are many different organizations dedicated to the use of computers for creating designs.

One example is SIGGRAPH, the computer graphics special interest group of the Association for Computing Machinery, or the American Institute of Graphic Art (AIGA) for commercial artists using computer illustration. If you are interested in technical writing, there is the Society for Technical Communication and the Association of Professional Writing Consultants. If you are looking forward to a career as a technical trainer or teacher of computer-related subjects, join national computer trainers' associations, like the Trainers Association of Southern California, or similar associations in your own state.

There is probably a national association to benefit almost any area of the computer industry. If there is no chapter or organization in your city, start one of your own. Ask your favorite employers to assist you in starting up a local chapter or to provide a meeting room at their company for after-hours seminars.

Ask several employers to volunteer as speakers for the local chapter meetings. Or plan an annual conference and invite those people you want to work for in the future.

Work on task forces, committees, and planning teams inside the special interest groups of national associations. If there is an annual convention, volunteer to be on the planning team. Offer to speak on a panel or to find experts to speak at conferences or meetings.

Publicize the professional association. Involve yourself in fundraising. Edit the newsletter for a year. Volunteer for take-charge activities that create visibility for you in the club. Leave the envelope stuffing and mailing chores to members who aren't looking for a job in a hurry.

Join Toastmasters and other public speaking groups that cater to a similar crowd of office workers, professionals, salespersons, business owners, and so on, or start your own chapter of Toastmasters or related public speaking groups for computer personnel.

If speaking on panels or public speaking in general isn't your way of creating visibility, try writing. Become a reporter or editor for the group's newsletter and use that as a bridge to writing company newsletters or manuals. Use computer magazines, newspapers, and national periodicals to report on your national organization's research.

Summer and part-time jobs can come out of working on task forces and committees of professional associations. That's how you make business connections to use as a bridge between school and employment outside of your academic department's office.

TIP 2: TUTOR YOUR COMPUTER SKILLS

If you are interested in education or corporate technical training, offer to tutor in computer science, office information systems, technical writing/editing, or computer-aided design/graphics at special schools. Volunteer or apply for a job as an instructional aide in a school that uses many computers. Offer to train corporate staff in new software and hardware equipment use within your specialty.

Use what you learned in computer school to instruct workers who are being trained on the job. If your background is in the humanities, train workers with basic literacy problems in written communications.

Computer training programs sponsored by the government and private industry councils are offered to low-income students. These programs are offered to people over age 55, displaced homemakers, the homeless, and persons in recovery or recently released from prison. Opportunities exist to become involved as trainers, aides, tutors, fundraisers, grant proposal writers, or volunteers to share your computer skills with others. The people you meet in the training business can form solid business relationships when you graduate—especially if you want to become a technical trainer.

TIP 3: TEACH COMPUTER SKILLS TO THE DISABLED WORKER

Many community colleges have special programs in computer instruction for the physically challenged. Volunteer to help these students learn computer skills. Volunteer as a student aide or tutor, or work on a team that trains them in their homes or in adapted classrooms.

Computer programs for students with disabilities emphasize such fields as computer-aided drafting and design, word processing, programming, desktop publishing, circuit design, robotics, and software specialist training. You can become involved with teaching computer skills to the disabled while you're still a full-time student.

TIP 4: SHOW HOW MUCH YOU'RE INTERESTED IN THE JOB

Apply for summer or part-time work that leads directly into your preferred career track. Ask for an internship. Express more interest in the company than in the position, without putting the position down. Don't mention advancement yet. Instead, emphasize how much you're interested in the job in your cover letter—and how much you're interested in where the company's heading. To find out the firm's direction and position, in comparison to its competition, research the company in the library or call the firm's public relations director and ask for a press kit with an annual report. Find out the same information for several companies you wish to target and compare them with regard to their growth as well as your goals.

See Tips 5–8 for advice on how to write your cover letter and résumé.

TIP 5: WHEN YOU DO APPLY—THE COVER LETTER

In your cover letter, include positive statements about the firm. Emphasize how much you want hands-on experience, in contrast to the theory you learned in college. Point out how many good facts you've heard about the company at college. Give a few examples; state how good the company's reputation is in the computer industry, how durable or beneficial the products are, and how much they fill a need in the computer community market.

Sum up with how anxious you are to learn from the company if you are hired—even if it's only for temporary work.

TIP 6: STATE WHY YOU'RE QUALIFIED TO PERFORM THE DUTIES

Your résumé can't qualify you through a work history, so let it qualify you with concrete evidence of your skills. Briefly point out how your skills qualify you for each of the duties required in the job description.

Highlight your motivation for the job. If it leads to your career goal or is on your career track, mention that. Be honest and direct. All you are stating is what the job duties are, why you are qualified to perform those duties, and what motivates you to want to work for the company.

Indicate on your résumé or cover letter the date you will graduate. If the job is seasonal or temporary, or if it is strictly part time, note that you're willing to stay on if any full-time position opens within a reasonable time.

TIP 7: EVALUATE THE JOB EXPERIENCE

The focus of your résumé will be clearer if you are certain of the reasons underlying your choice. Ask yourself what value you will get from working for a certain company. Will it pay off your student loan? Will you learn more about computers? Is there any on-the-job training you can't find at college? Or, after evaluating a position, you find you have experience in a field totally unrelated to your career goal? By carefully considering the position you may apply for, you avoid confusing a potential employer with résumé information unrelated or unimportant to the job.

TIP 8: SUMMARIZE YOUR INTENTIONS IN YOUR OVERVIEW

Your résumé packages your strengths for a job. In a one-paragraph Job Overview, listed under your Job Objective, summarize your intentions. The Job Overview is useful for students and others without prior paid job experience.

Three sentences should accomplish the summary that will market your overall abilities. For example, your overview might look like this paragraph:

Job Overview:
Second year Computer Information Systems student completing a B.S. in Information Systems, School of Business Administration, New York University, applying for the summer position as Software Engineer. Exceptional skills with Windows, Macintosh, OS/2, Unix, and DOS working in C++, C, Assembler, Basic, Cobol, and Novell Netware. Commercial PC software development, file systems, compression, networking, and localization courses qualify me for the software engineering position and support my goal of future permanent work with C. C. Corp.

TIP 9: USE TELECOMMUTING OPPORTUNITIES

Full-time students may also work at home using their computers in a freelance capacity. You can contribute articles, cartoons, or illustrations to computer publications, index computer books, create databases, design Web sites, or do record keeping at home if your computer is hooked up by modem or fax to a company branch or headquarters. This work-at-home employment is called telecommuting. It's different from work you do at home in your own business because you're employed by the company and considered part of its staff.

Ask whether you can connect your home computer by modem to a school or company to help process information or research databases. Doctors and lawyers sometimes hire information brokers to search professional library databases, the Internet, or other on-line services. These can be either freelance or staff employees.

The on-line field of information retrieval is called "the competitive intelligence industry." National clearinghouses of information and specialized as well as public libraries are linked to researchers through many private and government databases. Offer to use your computer to assist a firm with data analysis or other research in your field.

TIP 10: USE WORK-STUDY PLANS OR COOPERATIVE EDUCATION

Create your own cooperative work-study plan focusing on companies most likely to hire you after graduation. Many colleges arrange paid internships or part-time work and study arrangements in the computer industry. Use these opportunities to create a link between school and the world of work.

Use a work-study situation to obtain increased perspective on the computer industry, the company, or your special focus. In your cover letter, explain how you will adapt your skills to the work-study environment. Let the employer know in your cover letter how you will manage your time, juggling school requirements and work responsibilities.

7 RETIREES AND OTHERS

RETIREE STRATEGIES

Employers are looking for seasoned job applicants, especially in the computer industry. If they can wear more than one hat, that's a big plus. Computer industry employers would prefer to save recruiter's fees and hire mature, experienced workers who come to them first. Some employers don't have the budget to pay an agency to recruit young computer professionals, so they turn to older workers.

With recent college graduates facing tough competition, the older worker can fall victim to ageism in the workforce, however. If you're an older worker or military retiree, you need to have a selling point in your résumé and pitch a good closer at your interview that markets your experience and stability.

Therefore, to give yourself a competitive advantage and cut the time you may have to wait before finding your next job, begin your cover letter by showing your future employer how to reduce costs by hiring you.

In your résumé Job Overview (see Student Tip #8, Chapter 6), state that you're not retired; you're in transition. You're moving between levels of responsibility. Stress commitment and enthusiasm on your résumé. Show how you have used a combination of practical skills, people management ability, and task-oriented qualifications at each level of your career, regardless of the type of company.

Keep dates off your résumé if you're worried about covert age discrimination. It's unlawful under the Federal Age Discrimination in Employment Act to be turned down for a job because of age. The law applies to anyone over 40. However, the law is hard to prove if employers give competency, experience, or personality-related reasons for not choosing you.

Civil Service Positions

Retirees may wish to consider applying for civil service positions, although these positions are open to any candidate. Many military retirees apply for civil service jobs where they can earn veteran's preference points on civil service exams. Government applications require SF-171 for government or civil service work. Answer the questions directly on the form instead of sending a résumé. Request an SF-171 from your local State Employment Office.

The U.S. Office of Personnel Management, Los Angeles Service Center, has specific instructions on completing an SF-171 on its form FL-216 (8/92), titled "How to Complete an SF-171 Application for Federal Employment." You can also obtain instructions on how to fill out the SF-171 from the federal Office of Personnel Management or from most community college student job placement offices.

Here's what the U.S. Office of Personnel Management's form titled "How to Complete an SF-171" states

Some Important Things to Keep in Mind Before You Start:
The SF-171 is the standard application form used by most federal agencies. It is also a federal employer's first impression of you. As with any other application, a completed SF-171 is not only a reflection of the experience and knowledge you possess, it is also an indicator of the kind of employee you would be.

When reviewers evaluate your SF-171, they assess the extent to which your experience and education will allow you to successfully perform the duties of the position for which you are applying. Although you may have described your educational background and work experience clearly, spelling errors, grammatical errors, and/or a sloppy appearance could give an employer a negative impression of your abilities as an employee.

An SF-171 that is neat, clear, and error free is to your benefit. It is extremely important that all the information you provide is factual. The SF-171 is a legal document: falsifying any portion could prevent you from being hired, lead to your dismissal, or be grounds for criminal prosecution.

How to Complete the Form:
First, read the front page of the SF-171 carefully. It explains how to describe your experience, how to claim veteran preference, and how to reproduce the form for your future use. The SF-171 may be photocopied. In addition, you may describe your experience on separate sheets of paper. Be sure to include your name, social security number, and all other information requested at the top of the experience blocks. Every SF-171, or photocopy, must have an original signature and date in order to be accepted.

Guidance on how to complete the SF-171 follows:

Availability:
You will only be considered for positions for which you have indicated willingness to accept the pay

rate, working hours, and location. In most cases, the pay and job site are not negotiable. Please do not indicate that you are willing to work "anywhere." Indicate only those geographic locations where you are willing to work or are willing to relocate.

Military Service and Veteran Preference:
If you have never served in the U.S. military, answer "no" to question 17, and mark the "no preference" box in question 22. If you have served, be sure to read the "Veteran Preference in Hiring" section on the front of the SF-171 carefully. Item 21 is especially important to complete if you served in Operation Desert Storm and have earned a campaign badge or expeditionary medal.

Work Experience Blocks:
It is to your benefit to describe your work experience as clearly, concisely, and truthfully as possible. You will want to describe your experience in familiar, nontechnical language. The initial reviewer of your application may not have direct knowledge of the positions you have held. Be sure not to use excessive abbreviations or technical references that only apply to specific projects. You will want to describe the actual duties that you have performed and indicate the percentage of time you spent performing each duty.

Provide the actual month, day, and year you started and left each position, and the number of hours per week you worked in the position. Do not include excerpts from formal descriptions of your duties. Instead, describe the actual activities you performed and your professional accomplishments. If possible, briefly describe how your level of responsibility for accomplishing specific tasks increased with the time you spent in each position.

All this information is used by reviewers to quantify the extent of your experience and to determine its relatedness to the position for which you are applying. Please claim any experience you have gained through volunteer work or hobbies, if this information is applicable to the position for which you are applying.

Education:
Indicate your baccalaureate and/or associate degree major on the first line of item number 29, and your graduate major on the first line of item

30. The "Number of Credit Hours Completed" is the number of total units you have completed. Only completed courses will be credited. Also, remember to enclose a photocopy of your transcript (or OPM Form 1170/17, List of College Courses and Certificate of Scholastic Achievement) for verification.

Special Skills, Accomplishments, and Awards:
This section gives you the opportunity to claim credit for special skills you have acquired, achievements you have made, or honors you have earned that are not appropriate to mention in the course of describing your experience. This is the place to mention computer skills, public speaking skills, even personal developments that are pertinent to the position for which you are applying.

As with the experience blocks, attach additional sheets of paper if you need more space to describe your accomplishments. Items 33 through 35 ask you to claim your typing skills, licenses or certificates, and language proficiency.

References:
The references you list will be contacted. Include the full names, addresses, and phone numbers of individuals who can accurately attest to your character.

Background Information:
Answer questions 37 through 47 carefully and honestly. Be sure to review your responses in this section, and in all of the others. Reread your SF-171 while imagining that you are the reviewer. **Each application must have your signature in ink, not photocopied, and a date.**

Your Past Jobs Are Platforms

All the strategies for military retiree résumés can be applied successfully to the résumés of persons retiring from any type of work or for those switching careers later in life. The computer industry contains niches new enough to absorb those with little or no experience as long as training is current. Your best selling points are the practical skills that can be transferred from one job to the next. You have only one career but many different jobs. Look at each of your past jobs as platforms, levels, or foundations within one career. Retirees who have spent twenty or thirty years in an industry or the service have a lifetime of stages or levels of skills and responsibilities to transfer to new jobs.

CIVILIAN AND MILITARY RETIREES

Tips and Strategies

TIP 1: EMPHASIZE ENERGY AND ENTHUSIASM

A long service record sells your commitment to service and loyalty to duty. What is left to market is your enthusiasm and practical skills with computers and people.

The use of action verbs gives your résumé the feeling that you are blazing with energy. Show how efficient you are by listing measurable achievements on your résumé. List ten transferable skills you're going to offer an employer.

TIP 2: ADMINISTRATIVE WORK: A NATURAL TRANSITION

Many retiring officers prefer to transfer to administrative work. One example would be working as a law office administrator for a computer industry legal firm or department. Your main responsibility would be to free lawyers from managing the office and staff administrative tasks.

Law office administrative work is similar to what many officers did during their career with the military service. However, to get such a job, you would be competing with experienced legal secretaries who want to rise to a career in law office administration.

TIP 3: WHEN TO USE A CHRONOLOGICAL WORK HISTORY RESUME

A lengthy career in one industry or a military career fits easily into a chronological work history résumé. Neither the expanded nor creative résumés can usually accommodate 10 or 30 years of service. An abilities résumé wouldn't show the length of your service. Since you are selling dependability in terms of concrete skills, loyalty, and military achievements, the chronological résumé is often the best, most traditional vehicle for your kind of track record.

TIP 4: WHEN TO USE AN ABILITIES RESUME

Retirees who are making a drastic career change could successfully use the abilities résumé. Mature people who are switching careers may use the abilities résumé to reflect a transition of skills rather than traditional, long-term service under one employer.

TIP 5: SHORT-LENGTH MILITARY SERVICE

If your military service was relatively short, simply state your branch and the highest rank you achieved, dates of service, and provide the date that you were honorably discharged. Stating your military service, even if it's unrelated to your job objective, avoids unaccounted for time gaps in your employment record.

TIP 6: TIE YOUR QUALIFICATIONS TOGETHER

Include in your résumé a continuity section that summarizes and ties together your qualifications. This could be a brief Job Overview paragraph at the top of your résumé.

List any computer training you received in the military service. Include any technical training that could be transferred to a new job in the computer industry.

TIP 7: WHEN TO USE AN EXPANDED TWO-PAGE RESUME

You may wish to use a two-page expanded résumé to explain your responsibilities. Don't use it merely to elaborate on your executive status rank or to dwell on how much control or power you wielded. Responsibility should never be confused with rigid control, but rather as an accumulation of abilities and knowledge.

TIP 8: UPDATE YOUR SKILLS

Keep your skills sharp and up to date. If you trained long ago, it's time to take technical courses, attend conventions, and even organize your own workshops and seminars. You could then invite volunteer guest speakers to sell their products to your captive audience.

Join computer user groups and professional associations. Act as a liaison between your association, schools, and corporations. It will keep you actively seeking contacts. Learn how to use the most recent equipment and the latest software associations.

Keep volunteering in those associations while you call upon companies. The advice provided earlier in this book on creating visibility works equally well for retirees, students, and those with no previous job experience. The idea is to make yourself as unforgettable in person as your résumé is on paper.

TIP 9: SELL WHAT MAKES YOU UNIQUE—ACTION AND ACCOMPLISHMENT

Older workers in the computer field, as elsewhere, undervalue themselves. They don't realize or express the value of maturity and business experience.

Don't just chronicle past job titles; highlight solutions based on experience. For example show how you helped to solve problems for your past employers and brought profit to the company, or tell how you increased production. Reveal exactly how you see a task through to completion. Emphasize commitment. Highlight the value of your work ethic.

List qualifications that give you a unique advantage over the rest of the computer industry workers. If you are a retiree from the computer industry or a related technology and want to get back in, evaluate only the skills you wish to transfer to a new job.

TIP 10: FREQUENCY OF INTERVIEWS

Some personnel managers who look at résumés all day reject older workers based on false stereotypes that they are inflexible and cost more in terms of health care insurance and salaries. Other personnel managers hire older workers specifically because of low absenteeism and high work ethics; these managers realize the older worker's dependability and respect for authority (especially true of retiring military senior enlisted personnel).

Your résumé could land on the desk of either of those types of managers. The more managers who interview you, the better your chances are of finding a job quickly. Two interviews a day is a good target to aim for.

TIP 11: THE BEST JOBS ARE FILLED BY WORD OF MOUTH

Older workers are most frequently hired by word of mouth, not through newspaper ads. Use your wide circle of business contacts, neighbors, and friends to recommend you.

Some older workers or retirees who travel find employment by building friendships during vacations that draw older people.

TIP 12: TEMPORARY OPTIONS

Consider working on a temporary or contingency basis. This is often a desirable route for retirees. Additional information on this job strategy is outlined in the next section.

TEMPORARY EMPLOYEES AND INDEPENDENT CONTRACTORS

Temporary Service Employment

A temporary worker may be a "contingency professional," a temporary technical worker, day laborer, or temporary clerical employee.

According to one temporary employment service owner, when referring to temporary work, the term agency is never used in conjunction with temporary employment. It's called a temporary service. Agency refers to an employment agency that places job seekers in permanent positions for a fee. Not all temporary services have employment agency divisions.

Computer personnel are often contingency professionals working on temporary jobs for long or short-term assignments, such as technical writers, desktop publishers, database managers, programmers, computer operators, and paraprofessionals. Contingency professional employment often means hiring persons on a continuing but temporary basis. A larger number of temporary workers are office staff replacements doing word processing, desktop publishing, retail store demonstrating, convention registering, or related clerical work. A smaller but rising number are technical professionals, computer programmers, software manual writers, or day laborers. College students often apply for temporary work during the summers to gain more experience.

According to workers, some temporary services charge the employer one fee per hour for a temporary clerical worker; for example, $15 per hour for a word-processing operator, and $30 per hour for a technical writer. The temporary service may pay the actual worker another fee, such as $10 per hour for word-processing specialists and $15 to $20 an hour or more for the technical writer working on contingency. The employee is never charged a placement fee for referral to a temporary job, regardless of the length of the assignment.

Temporary workers can cost the employer less than hiring full-time permanent employees. Insurance costs for the temporary employee, such as health benefits or pension plans, often are paid for by the temporary service. In contrast, independent contractors working solely on their own as freelancers must pay for their own health insurance and retirement plans.

Sometimes retirees return to contingency work within a year after retirement, asking for flexible or part-time hours. They may choose to work two or three full days per week or just during a season, in different parts of the country, or as a traveling temporary worker.

Temporary employees may work for many temporary employment services or only one. The temporary worker is sent to one or many businesses for each assignment of varying length, from one day to several months.

Temporary Work Is Increasing
Unlike contingency professionals, temporary clerical employees and certain paraprofessionals don't have the continuity of working for one service that leases out the worker to a company for many years. Temporary clerical workers and some technical paraprofessionals, such as desktop publishers and word-processing specialists get the feel of doing temporary work on short assignments to fill in for vacationing or sick staff employees.

Who's an Independent Contractor?
The independent contractor can be anyone who sells a service or product on an as-needed basis by contract with a client. The independent contractor may work alone as a freelancer or work with assistants or partners.

The client or customer can be an individual or a company. Independent contractors also may work as intrapreneurs, entrepreneurs, contingency professionals, temporary or part-time workers, and as permanent staff employees (moonlighting after work) at various times.

Examples of some independent contractors in the computer industry include the following occupational titles:

- animators
- beta testers
- human resource recruiters
- computer press: journalists
- programmers
- systems analysts
- technical and software user manual writers
- local area network (LAN) specialists
- graphic designers
- drafters
- technical illustrators
- architects
- engineering graphics specialists
- desktop publishers

- desktop video producers
- computer graphics presentation specialists
- computer trade show planners
- sales and marketing
- word-processing specialists
- computer technicians
- desktop videographers
- video game artists/designers
- special effects specialists
- multimedia specialists
- technical trainers
- managers of information systems
- documentation analysts
- computer-aided designers
- computer presentations graphics designers
- robotics and numerical control technicians
- designers
- software engineers/designers
- manufacturing technicians
- cable television/producers
- software reviewers
- software talent agents
- Web site designers
- Web trackers
- Webzine writers/editors

Advantages to the Company

An employer doesn't have to pay any health insurance or benefits to an independent contractor. Independents don't receive worker's compensation from an employer. You may have to pay your own health insurance expenses as an intrapreneur, although some firms give perks that include insurance.

Financial responsibility to find clients, collect payments, and follow up leads rests with the independent contractor, not with the client or company hiring you. However, you take orders from the company that contracts with you to perform a service or supply a product.

Most clients won't contract with you based solely on your résumé or cover letter. In addition to a creative or abilities résumé and a business card, you'll probably need a brochure or flyer that details your expertise and services.

Written communication may get you into corporate or institutional offices for interviews. There, you bid to supply your service or product against competing businesses. Evaluate honestly what you will offer.

Independent contractors may be in bidding competition with foreign businesses that import and export computer peripherals, software, and services. There's a burgeoning foreign market for computer industry independent contractors and consultants (for example, foreign computer animators).

Tips and Strategies for the As-Needed Worker

TIP 1: TEMPORARY EMPLOYEES—WHICH RESUME?

If you are seeking temporary employment, use a chronological work history résumé. Skills are most important. The skills could be word processing, programming, accounting, desktop publishing, or software manual writing. List the computer languages and software you work with, and detail all hardware and software used. List speed of data entry if applicable, such as. "Word processing on a PC with MS Word at 80 words per minute." List past employers and exact job duties as they apply to the skill you're selling.

If necessary, use an abilities résumé, an expanded résumé, or a creative résumé to focus on your abilities and responsibilities; special work history résumés are needed for approaching contingency professional employment services. Your résumé will highlight different areas of your unique skills and training background. Flexibility is emphasized. Many contingency professionals prefer flextime or flexible hours. If you customize your work or résumé to suit many individual employers (as an independent consultant would do), contingency employment could be for you. Often, contingency workers get two- or three-year leases to work for one employer. The employee may receive health benefits and possibly other perks but temporary work does not usually offer as many benefits to the short-term workers, and perks differ with each agency.

TIP 2: FLEXTIMERS MUST GROUP SKILLS

Group your skills and abilities. Can you name each job-related task you can perform? Every part-time or shared job consists of a series of competencies and practical skills used on an as-needed basis. If flextime is your goal, sell your qualifications to make that clear.

TIP 3: JOB SHARE

You can create and customize a job according to your individual preferences and share it with another person. Use an abilities or creative résumé to do this.

Pick someone in a situation similar to yours, maybe a person close to retirement or a double-income-with-small-children employee who wishes to work fewer hours. Job sharers, like flextimers, are looking for a chance to work flexible hours or to work on preferred days. Perhaps you prefer to work at home, part time; or you're retired and want to come back into the work force a few days a week. Perhaps you are going to school; or you want temporary work for a few years, not a few days.

Advertise in a business magazine or professional association newsletter for someone to job share. You are looking for an associate with a full-time job who wishes to cut back to two or three days a week or half-days. Offer to work the other half the week. Ensure that your skills and goals are compatible.

TIP 4: INDEPENDENT CONTRACTORS

Use a creative résumé as a brochure or flyer to offer your clients a healthy bottom line. Independent contractors prefer the creative or abilities résumé that is formatted to look like a business brochure to secure clients or customers. At the back of the résumé, attach a one-page list of clients, and services provided. If you are an artist or writer, include a miniportfolio or list of publications with your résumé.

RESUMES FOR NEWCOMERS IN A CULTURALLY DIVERSE WORKPLACE

Immigrants come to North America from all parts of the world seeking jobs, clients, or customers in the computer technology industry. What does a newcomer to the United States or Canada who seeks work put on a résumé?

Cultural diversity is prevalent in today's global computer industry. You will find software in most major languages sold in the United States, and computer products catering to the needs of people from around the world available in major U.S. cities.

Many computers continue to be built in the United States. The wide variety of software available is designed and manufactured primarily in the United States. Import and export of computer parts is a huge industry here. For example, most computer hard disks sold here are assembled in Asia.

Cultural diversity in the workplace includes the entertainment industry's use of computers for special effects. Most computer animation for the television and film industry is currently created by computer special effects in Europe and Asia. Corporate desktop animation and special effects for ad agencies are created mainly here through multimedia desktop video.

Despite the reality of growing cultural diversity, employers still look for work patterns and values familiar to U.S. corporations. Employers want information they can understand quickly when reading your résumé. What are the most important points an immigrant can emphasize in a résumé or cover letter?

TIP 1: MAKE YOUR GENDER OBVIOUS ON THE RESUME OR COVER LETTER

If you are foreign to the United States, as a courtesy you may want to state your gender in the Job Overview section on your résumé. The person reading your résumé may not know your gender by the spelling or sound of your name. Consider putting Ms. or Mr. with your name on your cover letter.

TIP 2: TRANSLATE YOUR SKILLS INTO COMPANY VALUES

Picking from among your many abilities is difficult, so list only those skills that are highly valued by the company. Research the company's labor needs at a library, or ask an employee what skills the company seeks. Look at the job description and briefly explain how your skills apply. Identify what you do best in terms of what the employer values most. Focus on an employer's greatest need. For example, explain how an employer will save time and money by hiring you. Qualify and quantify your reasons. Include company-valued details about your abilities and work performance on those past jobs of special interest to the new company.

TIP 3: LOOK FOR NICHES WHERE YOUR SKILLS CAN BEST BE USED

Sort your experience into categories. Sort your educational courses or technical training into categories that are comparable to levels of education in your new country. Show similarities to the U.S. corporate workplace. Clarify and explain your education where needed.

Call a few employers or human resource managers and ask them what job descriptions and job responsibilities in your computer specialty sound most familiar to U.S. (or Canadian) employers.

If your English is not good, see a résumé writer or a teacher for advice, or take a course in résumé writing at a community college.

TIP 4: KNOW WHERE YOU WANT TO WORK

Travel to areas where you would like to live and work and where there is enough computer industry growth in your field. Send your résumés to appropriate companies in that area. It's best to attend a few professional conventions in your chosen geographic area to network with people in your specialty. By making business contacts you may find some good tips about working in that area.

TIP 5: MAKE YOUR RESUME CONVINCING

Convince the employer that your international skills translate into experience familiar and useful to U.S. corporations or institutions. Use statistics to verify how good your skills are. Quantify the skills in your résumé as in the following examples:

"Word-processing speed is 90 words per minute with zero errors. Specialize in statistical keyboarding and data entry on XYZ computer using ABC software."

"Two years' experience operating NMB computers in the biotech industry."

"One year's experience in database management using Paradox software on a PC."

TIP 6: LIST YOUR IMMIGRATION STATUS

Let the employer know on your résumé whether your visa is that of a student or a resident alien, or whether you're waiting to become a citizen. It's important for them to know whether you are legally in the country and have a work permit or "green card," and how long you intend to remain here, if you're not a permanent resident.

List your status simply and briefly at the end of your résumé, without drawing undue attention to it. You can elaborate on it in the interview.

TIP 7: LIST YOUR ENGLISH PROFICIENCY AND ANY COURSES TAKEN IN THE UNITED STATES

State your English language proficiency level. The employer wants to know that you understand and speak English well enough to handle the job. If you have a heavy accent, take some speech coaching to improve your English diction. List any English training or courses taken in the

United States. Explain that at your former jobs here or elsewhere, fluency in spoken and written English was required, if this is true.

TIP 8: EXPECT TO WAIT LONGER TO FIND WORK

It may take a new immigrant longer to find a job than someone who has lived, studied, and worked in the United States for many years. You may be offered less pay if you're not yet a U.S. citizen. You may be rejected for a job because you don't have the right level of security clearance; you may seek redress in this area for some situations. However, your age, not your ethnicity, will often determine how many weeks you may spend trying to find employment.

Now that you have learned how to customize résumés and job search strategies, let's move on to customizing your career. In the next two chapters you will learn how to choose a computer career according to your special preferences and personality type. You will be able to use this information to focus your résumé and target the job that is right for you.

WHICH JOB IS THE RIGHT JOB?

This chapter is designed to increase your self-awareness and help you to find the job that is the right match for you.

If your résumés frequently elicit form letters that state, "Your credentials are impressive, but they don't fit our requirements at this time," perhaps you have not been applying to businesses that need what you do best. Maybe you are not writing your résumé according to your personality preferences.

Would you like more power to choose the job that works for you? The personality questionnaire, or preference classifier, which you are about to take in this chapter applies specifically to career choices within the computer industry.

The questions ask what types of work you feel most comfortable doing in the computer industry. Use the completed answer sheets to self-score the sixteen preference types and find your personality type. Then look under your personality type. There you will see a list of the job titles recommended for each.

The personality questionnaire is a tool for understanding normal differences in the way people organize skills. It may also help you understand and appreciate the differences between all types of people working in the computer industry.

What Interests and Skills Come Naturally?

Ask yourself what skills are most easy to learn and to practice. What comes naturally? What's harder to do—so hard that you become depressed, irritable, or stressed out and exhausted from doing it all day?

Which tasks would you rather be doing at work? Computer industry personnel differ in their work preferences as they do in their job tasks. Some like to analyze. Others are artistic. There are those who like to sell and talk. Some like to train or teach.

Do you like to work alone using the computer as a tool to express or reflect inner thinking or feeling? Would you prefer to use the computer as a tool to do other jobs—such as architectural drafting or industrial design?

Whether you are sending your résumé to a corporation or you already work in a paid job, employers are going to ask, "Do you mind doing things our way?" When you do mind, it's because your preferences are different from your employer's.

How Can You Use Your Personal Strengths to Improve Teamwork?

The preference classifier will reveal your personal strengths. You will learn how to apply these strengths to improve teamwork on your job.

You will come to appreciate the personality type difference of others in a variety of jobs. And you will learn how to apply your understanding of personality type, in a specific way—to selected computer industry job requirements.

What Are Your Real Preferences?

Your type, as determined by this preference classifier, reflects how you felt when you answered the questions.

Preferences can change under stress. Or you could be hiding your real type in order to pursue a career you want because of the security, status, or better pay. Your real preferences are those you feel when you aren't under pressure or aren't out to prove anything.

Understanding Others' Types

You need to apply your knowledge of personality type when your usual behavior no longer works on the job. Once you recognize your type, use it ethically. Don't let it prejudice you against coworkers with different types and different needs.

Use your knowledge of personality type to help your coworkers fit into their most comfortable niches at work and use their natural preferences. You will find people at work who get great pleasure out of filling in the details and grounding you in practicality. Other types may feel that their dreams for the future are being wasted by attention to details in the present.

Detail-oriented people are clear and precise; they look for common sense. You may wonder why employers so often give the creative, imaginative, and visionary work to people impatient with details, common sense, and usefulness. Detail-oriented people can be just as imaginative in practical ways.

People with a preference for sensing (using their five senses before using their imagination) might prefer to complete tasks step-by-step in sequence. They prefer practical, detail-oriented skills that rely on common sense.

In contrast, people with a preference for intuition (using their imagination before using their five senses) might feel more comfortable completing tasks by first using creative skills that express ideas or visions about the big picture. They are interested in the future and possibilities. They enjoy forecasting trends and predicting everything from the weather to jobs of the future.

Intuitive people may not want to write down step-by-step sequential plans for how they will implement the big picture at first conception. It's easier to examine ideas and visions about the finished plan before drawing up the details.

Thinkers in the Computer Industry
Analytical or technical thinkers like to design models and matrixes, or put ideas in categories and label them. They troubleshoot and repair computers or sell technical equipment to other businesses, or they invent, build, or research aspects of the computer industry. Such thinkers are found in great numbers in the computer industry. Their favorite niches include management, administration, design, engineering, systems analysis, robotics, and computer repair technology.

Artists who are thinking types may enjoy computer-aided drafting specializing in circuit design, architectural illustration, computer video game design, and engineering graphics. Thinkers frequently major or minor in courses using computer equipment to analyze and solve problems in science, technology, or design.

Feelers in the Computer Industry
Feelers in the computer industry are interested in creating software that is easy to use by people with more diverse interests and in various applications. Feelers may wish to use computers as tools to communicate with people and to package or disseminate information. They write computer books and software manuals, publicize and market ideas, people, and products.

Feelers run the electronic bulletin boards and databases that communicate or broadcast information to researchers (the information brokers). Frequently feelers work as trainers where they can share information. They are also found in educational sales, instructional technology, and courseware design. Feelers are eager to communicate how to use computer technology to make life easier. The term user-friendly may have been coined by a group of feelers who empathized with those wanting easy-to-learn software.

Feelers are frequently hired to make the language of complex operations clearer and simpler for beginners to understand. For them, making software easy to learn is as important as the software's function. A sizable number of feelers are English majors hired to simplify and clarify complex language in instructional brochures or manuals.

Feelers may major in nontechnical fields, taking several computer courses as electives to gain entry-level job skills or to switch careers. They often go into personnel work in the computer industry. Some focus on recruiting people for computer jobs. Many become human resource managers. They may also work with outplacement agencies or as career consultants for computer industry workers in transition.

Some feelers concentrate on imaginative, artistic expression. They enjoy creating illustrations and corporate animation using computer graphics. Others focus on crafts, such as computerized toy design and manufacturing, or desktop video and multimedia production (presentation graphics).

Feelers and Thinkers Decide Differently
Feelers tend to make decisions by asking questions that focus on emotion or inner values, such as: "Is this job worth my being so stressed out?" and "Why do I care so much?" Thinkers weigh the pros against the cons more scientifically or impersonally before making decisions.

Other Personality Tests
The personality test you are about to take is a tool to enhance your self-awareness, appreciate your coworkers' talents, and improve teamwork on computer-related jobs.

This preference classifier is not the classic Myers Briggs Type Indicator (MBTI®), one of the world's most popular personality tests. This classifier resembles other common questionnaires, inventories, sorters, and indicators of personality preferences that give you a four letter type. This type is based on the principles of the MBTI®, which is based on the theories of psychoanalyst C. G. Jung and is validated with statistical research.

If you want to take the MBTI® to find out your four-letter personality type without vocational preference questions about computer careers, or to take other popular vocational preference inventories, such as the Strong (formerly Strong-Campbell) Interest Inventory, write to Consulting Psychologists Press, Inc., 3803 E. Bayshore Road, Palo Alto, CA 94303, or call 1(800) 624-1765. Ask for their catalogue.

Most colleges and adult education counseling offices offer the MBTI® or other indicators and vocational inventories to the public at low cost, or sometimes at no cost to students. Counselors and consultants offer interpretation of the results and career counseling. You can also interpret these questionnaires on your own.

If you'd like to read more books and pamphlets on personality types, or temperament and the MBTI®, also write to Type Resources, Inc., 101 Chestnut Street, #135, Gaithersburg, MD 20877, or call (301) 963-1283 or 1(800) 456-6284. Other related books include *Introduction to Type and Careers,* and *New Directions in Career Planning and the Workplace.*

You may want to read the book *Do What You Are,* by Paul D. Tieger and Barbara Barron-Tieger (Little, Brown & Co., Boston, 1992). The book includes a professional personality test.

To understand your temperament, see *Please Understand Me* by Dr. David Keirsey and Marilyn Bates (Prometheus Nemesis Book Company, Del Mar, CA), a book that includes information about job choice based on temperament. It contains the Keirsey Temperament Sorter, an inventory of preferences, and it details four temperaments and sixteen types.

Where Do *You* Fit in the Computer Industry?
The preference classifier you are about to take is designed exclusively for computer personnel. Think about what kind of work environment you prefer. What tasks are easier to do? Before you look for a job in the computer industry, find out where you fit.

After you finish this questionnaire and score your preference type on the answer sheets provided, keep a record of your preferences or computer-related personality type (in the broadest sense). Then look at the list of jobs under each preference type to see what would feel most comfortable. The recommended job list follows the answer sheets.

All computer-related jobs have in common the use of different technical, clerical, analytical, artistic, or imaginative skills to solve problems. Like most jobs, all computer-related jobs also have in common the need to get along with people. The jobs suggested in this book are only a few of the many that exist in the computer industry. Any type can and does work in any job. How comfortable or satisfied individuals are with their jobs is another issue.

Increase Your Workplace Comfort Level
There are no right or wrong answers. Use the following Computer Career Preference Classifier to increase your workplace comfort level, which could be different on paper (theory) than in reality. Never hire or work with people on the basis of their type.

Do you often dwell on what you would like to be rather than what you are deep down? Were you ever afraid of revealing a core personality in your job that was too different from the job description—too free-spirited and entrepreneurial, or too practical and security-seeking?

Have you ever avoided revealing your real preferences on your résumé or on personality inventories? Were you told that the skills you prefer to use weren't practical, useful, or realistic for a particular job? Are you afraid that "the real you" won't fit in with a group at a particular company—or even in some segments of the computer industry in general?

There are economic reasons why people won't admit, even to themselves, the job they would really love to do if they knew they could get hired. They may never match their résumés to those companies that are looking for what they do best. Without exposing preferences (which are motivating and lead to further skill-building), there is no way to find companies that apply what you do best to technology, business, or training.

The Computer Career Preference Classifier clarifies which work situations are more comfortable for you. Now let's take the preference classifier.

COMPUTER CAREER PREFERENCE CLASSIFIER

Directions

The classifier contains 74 questions. Answer on the separate answer sheets that follow the questions. An extra blank answer sheet is provided in case you want to answer this questionnaire with a friend or take the classifier twice.

1. Read each of the work-related situations. Mark A or B next to the corresponding question number on the answer sheets provided at the end of the classifier. Note that the question numbers are not in exact sequence on the answer sheets but are divided between page 1 and page 2.
2. To score your answers, total columns A and B. Add the totals under each column in the boxes marked with a letter. Then circle the highest score in the lower boxes closest to the bottom of the page marked E or I, S or N, T or F, J or P. Finally, enter the four letters of your highest scores on the line marked "Your Type." (Your type on this classifier means your classified preferences based on your personality and level of comfort with your choices.) A sample self-scored answer sheet is provided after the two blank answer sheets so you can see what the completed, scored answer sheet looks like.
3. When you have found your four-letter type, look at the explanation and suggested job titles that follow in the next chapter.

1. You received a B.S. in Computer Science and Information Systems last month. This month you began an entry-level sales and marketing job with a major designer of computer video games and educational software. You would rather

   A. actively sell the CD-Interactive software to a wide variety of consumers by giving live presentations and demonstrations.
   B. work alone in a private office with the door closed to market the software by direct mail without face-to-face or phone contact with people.

2. Computers are your hobby. At work you have time to practice your hobby during your two-hour lunch break in your flex-time job. You choose to:

   A. play computer virtual reality martial arts video games purely for entertainment.
   B. design programs for forecasting the weather daily for 100 years into the future.

3. You would enjoy a job that requires you to

   A. select from many details in corporate computer animation special effects and point out which details need improvement in shape or color, and keep accurate records of facts.

      B.   examine how artificial intelligence, neural networks, or fuzzy logic affect people's attitudes about the computer industry.

4. A large corporation has two openings. Which job would you take?
    - A. Financial database manager: where you will analyze stocks and stock market trends and apply artificial intelligence strategies to forecast upturn or downturn. You will also analyze computer systems.
    - B. Director of human resource development: where you will use your understanding of people to head the personnel department or research training and human relations in the corporation. Your main duty is to place the right people in the right jobs.

5. You are told to fire an employee for taking too long to come back after maternity/paternity leave. You
    - A. terminate the person as ordered, telling the employee that the company cannot afford the loss of productivity and profit directly attributed to the individual's absence.
    - B. refuse to terminate the person as ordered. You advise the employee to sue the company for family leave discrimination and side with the person because of circumstances.

6. When asked to take a day off to purchase a new computer for your firm, you
    - A. visit many different stores all day looking for exactly the right machine at the best price and quality.
    - B. impulsively buy the first computer you see that fills the boss's requirements for the make and model so you can take the rest of the afternoon off.

7. You paid $200 last month to reserve a nonrefundable ticket to attend a computer graphics convention five months from the present in Las Vegas. Today you found out there's a virtual reality convention on the same day in Egypt, which you find more exciting. You are
    - A. comfortable sticking to your original plans to attend the Las Vegas computer graphics convention because it doesn't require change.
    - B. feel deprived of a fascinating experience and wish you could afford to lose the $200 and take off for Egypt at a moment's notice instead.

8. To give yourself more visibility among colleagues you would
    - A. take a paid weekend job hosting a two-hour radio talk show, answering questions on the air about computers or software in your specialty.
    - B. take a two-hour weekend job writing a column for a computer industry newspaper about your own interests, reading, reflections, or research.

9. You would take an assignment in the computer industry in order to have
    - A. job security and a high salary to spend any way you please.
    - B. the chance to have your work made into a film and plenty of worldwide recognition at conventions, and receive only $1,500 for your work.

10. You'd rather take a job that uses your
    - A. realistic attitude and practical skills in logistics.
    - B. your imagination to create software that sells escape.

11. You wish you had majored in a subject at college that
    - A. would have allowed you to think logically and objectively so that now you could analyze strategies, map out models, or keep records to solve problems about production and profit at work.
    - B. would have helped you to understand what people value most about their careers.

12. On which three specialties would you focus within a college major in computer science and information systems and a minor in liberal arts, business, or education?
    - A. Systems analysis, programming, and math
    - B. Computer graphics illustration, professional writing, and technical human resource management

13. Your supervisor gives you an assignment to write an article for the company in-house employee newsletter on ten home-based businesses you can operate with your personal computer. You would prefer to
    - A. create a plan and outline first; follow it exactly to organize the article; then write the article.
    - B. write the article first, from whatever springs into your head at the moment and then weed out what doesn't belong when it's finished.

14. You're researching an international electronic database for a long list of articles and books on UFO abductions in Russia for an Ivy League university professor of psychiatry. You get a call from a Nobel-prize-winning astrophysicist asking you to stop your work immediately and tape record what he has to say before he leaves the country. You prefer to
    - A. finish your research for the psychiatrist and tell the astrophysicist you'll write to him later. It's annoying to have to stop in the middle of a project and switch to a new task.
    - B. drop what you're doing and look forward to the surprise, change in routine, and excitement of taping the astrophysicist's startling statistics on a different subject.

15. You meet many strangers of both genders at work who ask you whether you're married, what you majored in, what's your hobby, what you do for fun, and how old are you because they want to know you

better. All of you will be working as a team in your new job. You tell the strangers

    A. everything you can think of about yourself. You reveal all that interests you. You ask all the strangers to lunch.
    B. you are a private person and don't want to reveal personal information, but you'll gladly ask and answer questions about anything related to the job.

16. You want a high-paying, prestigious job in the computer industry that uses all you have to offer and that you'll be able to keep until

    A. you retire in 40 years with major benefits such as health insurance, a paid-off home mortgage, and an adequate pension.
    B. a better job offers you an opportunity to use your imagination for adventure, change, intellectual achievement and/or creative expression.

17. On Thursdays, your employer lets all employees out at four to attend personal enrichment classes. You have a choice of two workshops. Which one would you attend?

    A. How to repair your personal computer.
    B. How to write novels about the future of computers.

18. You are asked to evaluate an employee. You would first consider
    A. the employee's productivity and profit to the firm.
    B. the employee's warmth and personal service to customers.

19. You have a choice of working for two supervisors. You would prefer

    A. the boss who talks to you straight about how to analyze a database system but uses harsh words and sarcasm to make you improve while keeping your relationship from getting too personal.
    B. the gentle boss who tells polite lies to protect you from knowing why your work was rejected, then asks your immediate supervisor to reprimand you for errors.

20. Your job finishes at 5 p.m., but your department manager says you can leave early if you want or hang around and start tomorrow's work. You won't be paid extra or less either way. No one's left in the office to see you working. You

    A. start tomorrow's work and leave exactly at five, according to your usual daily schedule. You'll know exactly which place to start again in the morning with no confusion.
    B. drop everything in midstream, take off, and head for that new movie you're eager to see. Leave tomorrow's work for tomorrow, and have fun when you can.

21. Your computer work is always

    A. completed and well organized long before the deadline.
    B. finished exactly at deadline or just after. You enjoyed the exhilaration of rushing to complete it on time.

22. You are asked to train a group of visiting computer science students in systems analysis and advanced programming in machine language. You're more comfortable

    A. giving an oral presentation and live hands-on demonstration to a large group in the company conference auditorium. You love talking face-to-face with large groups of people who share your interests in computers or related products.
    B. distributing the latest software manual you wrote to the students. You wish they could learn independently on their own machines in school, at their own place of employment, or at home. You find giving an oral presentation to a group positively exhausting. You would rather train students by letting them read what you write (books, manuals, articles, or newsletters) as part of a correspondence course.

23. In the computer industry, you would be happier as a

    A. business-focused logistics executive grounded in the present time and the real world who deals with troubleshooting and repair of computers or in the sorting and selection of details in accounting, database management, or financial programming.
    B. future-looking professor who uses neural networks technology from the biotech industry to create new possibilities in programming, computer hardware, and robotics to mimic human life.

24. You bought a computer at the best price you could find. Three years later you

    A. still use your computer as is. If it ain't broke, you don't need to fix it.
    B. upgraded your computer to keep up with technology. Everything has room for improvement and change.

25. When asked what you think of the concept of time, you're most likely to say

    A. the concept of time as a theory is impersonal.
    B. you feel guilty if you don't use it to help people. Time is concrete.

26. There are two job openings. You have all the qualifications for both. You choose to

    A. design software to track government legal cases and to merge databases with a secretly modified "back door" to allow intelligence agencies to access foreign computer systems for their own espionage purposes.
    B. be a journalist who achieves visibility while investigating the software tracking program as well as banking and intelligence agencies' scandals.

27. You find it easier to

    A. follow directions exactly as planned or told to you by others at work. You would rather do the company's thing.

    B. break regulations and do the work your own way. You find it harder to follow someone else's plans to the letter because you can't get into the other guy's head to know what he wants, and there's no way you can please him.

28. You're better at

    A. time management.

    B. adapting to unexpected changes in schedule.

29. You are an unemployed and homeless typist down on your luck with a nickel in your jeans. An employment agency with a government grant pays for your training in word processing and sends you on two jobs. Both employers want to hire you with equal pay for similar firms near the same location. Which job would be least stressful?

    A. receptionist guiding heavy traffic all day in and out of the office, answering constantly ringing phones while typing reports and running errands.

    B. back office word-processing specialist in a quiet, one-person office where the boss is usually out and no one comes in or calls. You can have total solitude as you type one long software manual after the other.

30. You would prefer a job where most of the projects you deal with have these characteristics

    A. common sense, practical, useful, direct, realistic, actual, down-to-earth, factual, specific, and traditional.

    B. futuristic, conceptual, inspirational, motivational, random, possible, intellectual, imaginative, fantastic, theoretical, ingenius, generalized, nontraditional, and creative.

31. The computer firm where you are employed is adding a corporate animation department. You are offered a choice of two jobs. You decide to take the job as a

    A. marketing and sales manager of computerized toys and video production of corporate animation.

    B. designer and researcher of animated robot cartoon characters, and scriptwriter of cartoon commercials.

32. People who work around you usually say you would prefer to do what's

    A. fair and truthful than do what will make people happy.

    B. needed and valued to make people like you or to accommodate colleagues.

33. It's more important to you

    A. to be right than liked.

    B. to be liked than right.

34. You want a computer industry job where you can

    A. thrive on order and know what your work day will be like.

B. explore the unknown without being pinned down. You want to keep all work options open.

35. You prefer a job in the computer industry where you can
    A. complete projects and get them out of the way by the end of each day.
    B. turn your job into play. You believe if your work can't be fun, you won't work in that particular job.

36. A large software firm offers you a choice of two jobs handling their customer base of Fortune 500 accounts at the same pay and benefits. You ask to be placed
    A. in the sales department to use your telephone skills.
    B. as a computer operator working alone monitoring runs.

37. If you were promised the same salary and job security, you'd prefer to spend the next four decades as
    A. a communications technician with the phone company reading assembly language code on the 4ESS switching machine, which makes use of your common sense to handle phone company breakdowns from inside the various computers. You prefer to deal with details instead of your imagination to fix what's broken on the job.
    B. an investigative journalist and suspense novelist who writes about the connections between competing computer corporations. You prefer using imagination to absorb global impressions or create new ideas instead of checking, locating, or troubleshooting details for accuracy at work.

38. You would rather be a multimedia presentations specialist who
    A. makes judgments based on past experience.
    B. makes decisions based on gut-level guessing.

39. The type of people you wish you could be more like are
    A. able to stay calm and objective when others panic.
    B. able to walk ten miles in another's shoes.

40. If you could pick your mentor at work, that person would
    A. welcome challenge, rebuttal, and confrontation, sacrificing harmony for clarity.
    B. prefer harmony, even at the sake of sacrificing clarity to avoid conflict.

41. You prefer to associate with employees who
    A. always want everything in its place.
    B. don't plan to have a place for everything, because they'd rather wait and see what the job demands at different times.

42. You are hired to interview job applicants for the personnel department of an educational software manufacturer. You have plenty of time to spare. You would prefer that each job applicant

A. come only at the scheduled time of the interview.
B. walk in off the street when they felt like it and surprise you with their impressive credentials.

43. A major food processor has hired you to direct the internal management information systems department. You would prefer to manage

A. public relations and marketing to vendors, suppliers, internal users, and regulatory agencies, including managing the electronic data interchange program.
B. computer operations, telecommunications, and systems and applications programming where you'd get more of a chance to work alone without interruptions.

44. You find the future

A. best put off until it comes because it's too scary.
B. full of exciting possibilities.

45. In your computer classes you most enjoyed the courses that emphasized

A. hands-on practical skills leading to a comfortable job in the real world as quickly as possible.
B. theory about the futuristic possibilities computers might be capable of once microchips are enmeshed with human DNA molecules to form neural networks.

46. All the computers at work break down at the same time. Your first impulse would be to

A. keep things in perspective and push for precision and clarity when directing others to fix what's broken.
B. try to understand how human error impacts the people affected by the computer meltdown.

47. In a computer career, you would rather

A. solve analytical problems and increase efficiency.
B. express your creativity by improving communications or helping consumers.

48. You are asked to write a software user manual. You would rather

A. keep the original outline goal-oriented and reach a closure as soon as possible.
B. stay open-ended without goals because new information may come in by deadline.

49. As a documentation analyst, you are asked to manage the technical writing department. You would like to

A. hurry permanent decisions, turn solutions into action, and implement communications right into the word-processing department.
B. keep the staff from going with the first decision, keep offering better solutions, and hold communications until you've cleared it with the technical illustration department—before turning the current iteration over to the word-processing department.

50. You just graduated from college. Two employers are eager to hire you. Each offer equal benefits. You would rather
    A. train many people, employees and students, in how to operate VAX hardware and use VMS (DCL) software and the VMS backup utility. Do lots of demonstrations for people.
    B. be a VAX computer operator for a healthcare management firm monitoring production runs and performing backups of corporate data, working alone.

51. You prefer to work in a niche of the computer industry that deals mainly with
    A. using practical, real, tangible, specific, common sense, hands-on troubleshooting skills based on practice, usefulness, and experience.
    B. using your imagination to forecast trends that show others how to find hidden escape routes, back doors, advantages, alternatives, theories, and new ways of doing things.

52. If you were a salesperson in the computer industry, you'd rather sell
    A. tangible products, like computers, modems, and peripherals, financial database software to accounting firms, or medical records technology and transcription software to hospitals.
    B. ideas, advertising, public relations, public speaking, logos, desktop video productions, technical writing, event planning, neural networks and fuzzy logic, artificial intelligence solutions, trend forecasting, interactive fiction, presentation graphics productions, virtual reality games, and Internet services.

53. You're a person who has worked your way up through the ranks in the computer industry. Colleagues are most likely to call you
    A. a tough-skinned, hard-headed employee who clawed your way to the top by your achievements, intelligence, persistence, and education.
    B. an empathic, persuasive, self-made employee who always put the customer's needs first.

54. You're asked to give a presentation to fellow employees at a computer industry convention. You'd prefer to
    A. convince the audience by logical analysis to clarify definitions, facts, or trends.
    B. persuade the people by communicating to their values, sentiment, and identity with a stirring videotape or film.

55. When searching for a career, you
    A. grab the first job you find so fast that you're disappointed later.
    B. switch careers as frequently as you switched majors in college or tech school.

56. You want a good job in the computer industry that is
    A. reliable, stable, serious, secure, unchanging, controllable, orderly, routine, familiar, scheduled, methodical, organized, and dependable.
    B. flexible, adaptable, leisurely, playful, fun, spontaneous, changeable, open-ended, and creative.

57. Deep down, lots of people contact at work makes you feel
    A. energized and eager to talk and share your life experiences. Your office door is kept open for the sounds of people networking.
    B. sick, drained, exhausted, anxious, and bored by a continuous, crushing crowd on whom you wish you could close your office door.

58. A software company asks you to review their new database software or state-of-the-art paint and draw programs. As a gift for reviewing their software for a computer magazine, the company says you can keep the expensive software. You use the software to
    A. produce a new product that will appreciate in value over the years, even when the software becomes outdated. You patent the new product and save the profits in your retirement plan.
    B. have some fun teaching kids how to use it and then donate the software to an imagination-stretching computer camp high in the mountains of Aspen, Colorado. Afterwards, you enjoy a ski vacation as a guest of the computer camp.

59. You have a choice of two conferences to attend during the holiday season. You'd rather attend
    A. a conference on improving your practical skills, which will allow you to pass a qualifying exam for a more secure job at a higher salary.
    B. a conference on UFO abductions, advertising evidence presented by a distinguished military general, a Nobel prize-winning physicist, an Ivy League university professor of psychiatry, and three security guards who witnessed autopsies on space aliens at a secret military testing site's underground base.

60. When you read a software user manual, you are more apt to see
    A. the errors of clarity and organization and how it can be improved or made more efficient. You want to critique and analyze it, or see how and where it went wrong. You welcome challenge and rebuttal. You want a software manual that remains objective and impersonal.
    B. the way it motivates, inspires, and persuades you to understand the subject by its smooth-talking style. You praise it for simplicity and harmony.

61. You're hired to train advanced information systems students in programming the latest versions of C++ computer language. You let the students know that

    A. you're more interested in the computer language capabilities than in the student's personal problems, learning needs, or motivation.

    B. you're more interested in the student's personal needs and motivation, inspiration, and growth than you are in the programming language.

62. You'd rather take a job as a

    A. tape librarian or computer operator where every minute of your workday is planned and scheduled, and you use a day planner (book or software). You wouldn't mind if your keystrokes were counted as you enter data into a computer. You don't mind following someone else's rules to the letter. You prefer to make lists.

    B. multimedia presentation graphics producer where you have many hours of free time to see what spontaneous activities can be molded into video productions and computer graphics presentations without others requiring you to be an exacting, methodical perfectionist in detailed work, scheduling, and organizing. You would mind very much if your keystrokes were counted or you had close supervision. You hate to be evaluated on how closely you follow another person's plans.

63. On weekends you

    A. make a list of every chore that needs to be done and every item you have to buy. You visit computer stores only when you need to buy a specific product on your list.

    B. let whatever happens spontaneously take over the day, depending on your energy level, who calls, or what movie is playing. You enjoy spending an afternoon browsing in computer stores, even if you don't need to buy anything.

64. On your résumé you would be certain to emphasize

    A. your interest in giving presentations, speeches, or talks on your area of interest or experience.

    B. your preference for communicating via the written word in memos to coworkers and doing as little face-to-face talking as possible.

65. You would rather take those thick software manuals and

    A. review them for a practical, how-to personal computer magazine.

    B. turn them into spectacular 60-minute multimedia instructional videos for beginners.

66. You would rather repair

    A. people's computers.

    B. people's attitudes.

67. You want to duck out the door and take a break when
    A. coworkers cry openly.
    B. you say something negative that you really don't mean, but you believe it must be said because it is logical and fair.

68. You wish your résumé and cover letter could
    A. analyze, challenge, and confront ageism with the truth.
    B. deny that ageism exists in your specialty and convey optimism, energy, and enthusiasm for the job.

69. To start and finish a job, what you need most is
    A. an agenda with handouts and flow charts.
    B. room to move in all directions by self-pacing—a chance to change the agenda and diverge from the original plan.

70. You'd rather
    A. do the best quality work you can on each project so you can be proud of yourself, even though no one else ever notices. (You may secretly keep records in a log book.)
    B. have self-determination.

71. You are always willing to
    A. share personal experiences at work by talking and expressing your opinions; volunteering to work on committees and attend meetings, functions, office parties or after-work cultural or sports events; and speaking on panels at conferences.
    B. write a personal journal that involves research, reflection, meditation, and challenge—especially when a coworker interrupts you in mid-paragraph.

72. On your résumé, you would prefer to
    A. list only those realistic, practical, useful, routine, hands-on skills or experiences that specifically fulfill the requirements of the job description.
    B. express yourself by abilities or examples of creativity and persuade the employer to consider job possibilities that don't yet exist but that accommodate your ideas.

73. Your employer is giving you an "Employee of the Month" award. You'd prefer the prize to be
    A. an award for successfully beating rival firms.
    B. a psychology book on why women see competition as loss of self.

74. You spend too much time
    A. feeling rigidly impatient with exploring your career.
    B. gathering information.

COMPUTER CAREER PREFERENCE CLASSIFIER

Sample Self-Scored Answer Sheet
Answer Sheet: Page One

(Note: Question numbers go in order from left to right across the seven columns on these two pages.)

	A	B
1	X	
8	X	
15	X	
22		X
29		X
36		X
43		X
50		X
57		X
64	X	
71		X

TOTAL

4	7

4	7
E	I

	A	B		A	B
2		X	3	X	
9		X	10	X	
16		X	17	X	
23	X		24	X	
30	X		31		X
37	X		38		X
44		X	45		X
51		X	52		X
58		X	59		X
65		X	66		X
	3	7	72		X

TOTAL → | 3 | 7 |
          | 4 | 7 |

7	14
S	N

COMPUTER CAREER PREFERENCE CLASSIFIER

Sample Self-Scored Answer Sheet
Answer Sheet: Page Two

	A	B		A	B
4		X	5		X
11		X	12	X	
18		X	19		X
25		X	26	X	
32		X	33		X
39		X	40		X
46	X		47		X
53	X		54		X
60	X		61	X	
67	X		68	X	
	4	6	73		X
				4	6
TOTAL				4	7

	A	B		A	B
6	X		7		X
13	X		14		X
20	X		21		X
27	X		28		X
34		X	35		X
41		X	42		X
48		X	49		X
55		X	56		X
62		X	63		X
69		X	70		X
	4	6	74	X	
				4	6
TOTAL				1	10

8	13
T	F

5	16
J	P

YOUR PREFERENCES REVEAL YOUR TYPE   I N F P

COMPUTER CAREER PREFERENCE CLASSIFIER

Answer Sheet: Page One

(Note: Question numbers go in order from left to right across the seven columns on these two pages.)

	A	B
1	X	
8		X
15		X
22	X	
29	X	
36	X	
43	X	
50	X	
57	X	
64	X	
71	X	

TOTAL

9	2

9	2
E	I

	A	B		A	B
2		X	3		X
9	X		10		X
16		X	17		X
23		X	24		X
30		X	31	X	
37		X	38		X
44		X	45	X	
51	X	X	52	X	X
58	X		59	X	
65		X	66		X
			72		X

TOTAL → | 3 | 8 |
        | 4 | 8 |

7	16
S	N

145

COMPUTER CAREER PREFERENCE CLASSIFIER

Answer Sheet: Page Two

	A	B		A	B
4		X	5	X	
11		X	12		X
18	X		19	X	
25		X	26	X	
32	X		33		X
39	X		40	X	
46	X		47		X
53		X	54		X
60		X	61		X
67		X	68	X	
			73	X	
			→	4	6
		TOTAL		6	5

	A	B		A	B
6	X		7		X
13	X		14		X
20	X		21	X	
27	X		28		X
34		X	35	X	
41		X	42		
48	X		49		X
55	X		56		X
62		X	63		X
69		X	70	X	
			74		X
			→	6	4
		TOTAL		4	7

10	11
T	F

10	11
J	P

YOUR PREFERENCES REVEAL YOUR TYPE E N F P

COMPUTER CAREER PREFERENCE CLASSIFIER

Answer Sheet: Page One

(Note: Question numbers go in order from left to right across the seven columns on these two pages.)

	A	B
1		
8		
15		
22		
29		
36		
43		
50		
57		
64		
71		

TOTAL

	A	B		A	B
2			3		
9			10		
16			17		
23			24		
30			31		
37			38		
44			45		
51			52		
58			59		
65			66		
			72		

TOTAL →

E I

S N

COMPUTER CAREER PREFERENCE CLASSIFIER

Answer Sheet: Page Two

	A	B		A	B
4			5		
11			12		
18			19		
25			26		
32			33		
39			40		
46			47		
53			54		
60			61		
67			68		
			73		
TOTAL					

T F

	A	B		A	B
6			7		
13			14		
20			21		
27			28		
34			35		
41			42		
48			49		
55			56		
62			63		
69			70		
			74		
TOTAL					

J P

YOUR PREFERENCES REVEAL YOUR TYPE ___ ___ ___ ___

YOUR PREFERENCES AND TYPE

Now that you have your four-letter type, what do you do with it? Use it as a guide to achieve job satisfaction. A résumé balances your need for job satisfaction with a company's drive to control its production and profit.

To move the balance in your favor, your résumé must contain something measurable on it to make an impact and to position you first in the employer's mind. Your four-letter type can give you clues about what to put on your résumé that's measurable. How you have applied your personality preferences to skills, and skills to production and profit, is only part of the picture.

To understand how your preferences relate to job satisfaction, you need to know the characteristics of the four letters of your type. A list of suggested jobs follows the discussion of each letter. Let's discuss the differences between extroverts and introverts. Your first letter was either *E* or *I*.

ARE YOU PEOPLE ORIENTED?

E Is for Extrovert
Extroverts get their energy from being around people and doing people-oriented activities. Extroverts get power from being with others and thinking in broad, horizontal terms. Introverts energize by being alone with their ideas, reading, and through deep concentration. Introverts tend to be specialists and extroverts tend to be generalists.

If your first letter was *E*, you see yourself at this time as an extrovert. (It's also possible to be a closet extrovert, and list yourself as an introvert; or to be an introvert at your core and list yourself as an extrovert because that's what you would rather be to fit in.)

In résumé writing, you act as an extrovert when you talk about each part of your résumé with people you meet at professional associations and job fairs, with computer industry employees in your field, and people on job search committees. You are comfortable working around a steady flow of people and lots of people-processing activity.

Look for jobs that require you to be outgoing, sociable, interactive, and enterprising. Look for breadth of skills or job activities rather than depth of expertise and concentration.

You find it hard to maintain concentration on a solo activity if there is any interruption or distraction by people. Extroverts make excellent receptionists, customer relations persons, vendors, and teachers or trainers. About 49 percent of computer programmers are extroverts and nearly 52 percent are introverts.[1]

You need extensive contact with clients because people contact energizes you and being alone drains you. Attend events such as conventions, conferences, and meetings.

Involve yourself in planning events for the computer industry such as trade shows and exhibits. You are energized by talking, so volunteer to do public speaking on panels at conventions and meetings of professional associations. An ideal job in the computer industry would be where you can manage people, technology, or events.

If you are an extrovert, look for a job in the computer industry that allows you to do the following tasks:

- Run national associations of computer professionals.
- Do public speaking and presentation graphics work.
- Sell and market computer tangibles (products) or intangibles (ideas).
- Produce software videos.
- Train employees how to use software or hardware, or teach in a school.
- Open a computer matching service for business partners.
- Organize computer camps.
- Do many things at once.
- Work in an environment where distractions are routine.
- Work in the computer press arena as a journalist.
- Sell wireless telecommunications equipment and car phones.
- Do demonstrations for stores.
- Plan campus computer fairs.
- Direct marketing research and consumer tracking.
- Manage a large staff.
- Attend meetings and volunteer on committees.
- Put your opinion in the company newsletter; be a columnist so you can interview supervisors and employees.
- Work in the public relations and marketing communications department of a computer firm.
- Create visibility for all your ideas, working with a partner who can help you make your ideas realities.
- Produce audio or videotapes.
- Practice listening skills.
- Get daily feedback from coworkers and employers on how you're doing. Don't wait until job evaluation time.

---

[1] These statistics are from *Manual, a Guide to the Development and use of the Myers-Briggs Type Indicator* by Isabel Briggs Myers and Mary H. M. Caulley, Consulting Psychologists Press, Palo Alto, 1989, p. 245, "Ranking of Occupations by Preference for Extroversion/Introversion." (This percentage does not reflect a worldwide study, only the sample from the more than 250,000 MBTI® records at the Center for Applications of Psychological Type, Inc. in Gainesville, Florida.) Scoring in the *Manual* was done between 1971 and 1989.

I Is for Introvert

Approximately 30 percent of the U.S. population are introverts. Introverts are energized by introspection, concentration, and working alone. They prefer depth to breadth in job duties.

If your first letter was *I*, precision, vision, understanding, insight, analysis, objectivity, and reflection are your best skills. The more quiet time you have, the more creative you become. Market your precision in written communication.

Introverts need more time to think and reflect on questions before they speak. Many jobs in the computer industry fit the needs of introverts desiring solitary activities where they can think, analyze, or express their creativity for long hours at a time.

If you are an introvert, you are territorial. The job you can thrive in must allow you to concentrate on one long project at a time with the office door closed for privacy. Your skills focus in depth on one or two subjects. If the focus is too wide, you feel scattered. Target a niche. Become expert in what gives you energy. Your worse mistake would be to become a generalist or jack-of-all-trades. A second skill can be used as a backup when the first subject becomes obsolete or is no longer needed by employers.

You are drained by people. Find a job that will conserve your energy levels by allowing you enough time to work alone. Your work is going to be guided by your internal reactions and reflections on your subject of expertise. Working alone or with one or two other people on long projects requiring deep concentration, such as writing computer books, might satisfy you.

Introverts are complex people who usually don't show everything they are feeling without thinking about it first. In a live interview, introverts may keep their best points to themselves, preferring instead to put them in their résumé or cover letter.

Interviewers may not allow for different response times from candidates, and could confuse introversion with a lack of enthusiasm for the job. Résumés and cover letters of introverts can use direct mail marketing techniques to illustrate enthusiasm and circumvent this problem. If you have an "I," highlight the skills in your résumé, brochure, or cover letter by showing samples of your work and a list of your achievements.

If you are an introvert, look for a job in the computer industry that allows you to do the following tasks:

- Work alone as much as you need for recharging.
- Write or illustrate.
- Choose long projects, like books, to concentrate on with the office door closed for privacy.
- Deal with people through mail order or computer bulletin boards.
- Limit your public speaking commitments.
- Choose distance teaching and correspondence courses if you are a teacher.

- Conserve your energy.
- Travel less than an extrovert if you are in sales.
- Stop working when you are exhausted and take a break.
- Write what you have to say and reflect on it.
- Concentrate on creative or analytical work.
- Interview people one at a time with as few interruptions as possible.
- Work outdoors where you spend more time alone than directing people face to face.
- Telecommute or work in a home-based consulting business.
- Review software and books or tapes.
- Sell your listening skills.
- Hire a publicist to promote your ideas, talents.
- Do radio and TV interviews by telephone hook-up to your home.
- Develop your artistic talents with software.
- Restrict your telephone time.
- Communicate in writing.
- Design courseware and instructional technology.
- Perform computer technology and robotics repair. (Customer interaction is minimal.)
- Work alone at night.

HOW WE TAKE IN INFORMATION

Your second letter was either *N* or *S*. There are two ways we take in information, by intuition or sensing. Intuitives (N types) like to gather information holistically, under a theoretical umbrella. Sensors (S types) like to gather information factually, chronologically, sequentially, and specifically.

Misunderstanding or lack of communication at work or in the home often is due to the differences between those giving out information as sensors and those taking in the information as intuitives. Let's look at the differences between sensors and intuitives.

N Is for Intuitive

Intuitives are in the minority. Only about 30 percent of the world's population take in information using intuition. Therefore, it's going to be hard to do things your supervisor's way, unless you happen to match your type with the organization's character.

If you are an intuitive, your résumé needs to show how much you inspire and motivate people with your theories about the future. You deal in randomness and possibilities, rather than concrete logistics. Intuitives thrive on theory. Whether you are an introverted or extoverted intuitive, if your second letter is N your best skill is your ingenuity.

Intuitives Need Change and Diversity

You wouldn't be happy for long handling routine daily details, such as keeping records of accounts payable and accounts receivable or typing title insurance policy forms in the word-processing department. You need diversity and change on a job—many projects, ideas, and possibilities.

You would be happy working as a computer newspaper or magazine reporter writing a different article each week on a variety of subjects rather than teaching word processing each semester using an upgraded version of the same software.

Look for a job where your main skills would be to persuade, motivate, and inspire alternatives. Introverted intuitives are happy writing, programming, analyzing, illustrating or designing courseware, or creating on-line services. Introverted intuitives would feel more comfortable selling by direct mail order catalogues or electronically, where constant face-to-face contact wouldn't occur. Extroverted intuitives are energized by being training managers, speaking in front of audiences, managing people at all levels, and creating marketing ideas. Extroverted intuitives could sell intangibles such as ideas to advertising agencies. They are also excellent at motivating and inspiring others to enter the computer industry.

Intuitives are catalysts who bring people together from different walks of life, and they make great event planners for computer conventions. As an intuitive, you would enjoy designing or writing a corporate video or managing a nonprofit organization that recycles used computers for use in schools.

Programming appeals to intuitives. Many combine diverse backgrounds, for example in health care or environmental sciences, with computer programming for research, design, or training.

Intuitives Need to Use Their Imaginations
Intuitives prefer to use fantasy and escape rather than facts to sell products or ideas. If you are intuitive, you may want to develop a skill for making all your good ideas reality and then selling them. Any personality type can be creative or imaginative, but intuitive types are more frequently creative in general and future-oriented ways. Sensor types are often imaginative in specific, present-oriented ways.

If you are an analytical intuitive, the best computer-related jobs lie in designing computer video games, selling your interactive fiction, teaching and training others in your specialty, and working in theoretical disciplines.

If you are not an analytical-type intuitive, try corporate animation, desktop video, desktop publishing, technical writing, on-line journalism, computer graphics, designing Web sites, and the more creative aspects of computing. Many intuitives prefer to work at home as telecommuters with their computers hooked up to employers and others via modems, VCRs, and fax machines.

Intuitives Look for Alternatives
Use your intuition to study the possibilities in your résumé. Besides your ingenuity, your ability to look at alternatives and consider what else can be done is valuable.

Looking for alternatives energizes you. You could be an ideal resource person. You can find a thousand ways to market a product or service, or a hundred businesses that utilize one skill.

If you are an intuitive, look for a job in the computer industry that allows you to do the following tasks:

- Think of many things while working on one project.
- Work out alternate routes or new possibilities.
- Leave the details to sensors (sensing types).
- Work flexible hours—as late as you want.
- Analyze how computers work.
- Work with words and creative writing.
- Explore hidden meanings; create "back doors" in software.
- Find out how different things are connected.
- Question authority.
- Give general answers to specific questions without arousing anger in others.
- Work without always following others' directions.
- Sell escape fiction, such as games and stories of fantasy.
- Explore your creativity. (Desktop publishing/design and interactive, multimedia, desktop video are good fields for you.)
- Keep out of the accounting department, unless you're managing an accounting firm's public relations or personnel department.
- Perform analysis of complicated problems for research departments and think tanks.
- Do computer engineering, where the emphasis is on computer language analysis rather than on continuous sorting of sequential details.
- Look into new uses of computers, and virtual reality used in new ways. Look to international markets and the Internet for new possibilities.
- Forecast trends.
- Use foreign language abilities to design translation software.
- Evaluate and analyze inventions or work with inventors and patent attorneys.
- Improve or develop new products that use old things in new ways.
- Use computer technology in psychotherapy or rehabilitation.

S Is for Sensing

Sensors like to gather information literally. The résumés of sensors reflect the perspiration more than the inspiration that drives their work. About 70 percent of the world's population are sensors.

The job most likely to be a comfortable fit for you will be direct, realistic, down-to-earth, steady, specific, and geared to the present. You would prefer to sell tangible products rather than ideas. You like to sell what you can touch, smell, hear, or see through your five senses.

Sensors want to see ideas applied to real solutions. To sensors, intuition means playing hunches, and hunches aren't backed up by concrete facts.

Sensors Are Literal
You are literal about data. You enjoy the tactile experiences of textures, videos, sounds, sights, and smells. Virtual reality is your stage. You want a job that uses your hands-on skills or troubleshooting ability. You are a master of facts or tools.

Your ideal job needs a here-and-now aspect to it, such as in analyzing or programming financial databases. You would prefer to leave the theorizing to physical scientists and mathematicians. You like computer courses in which the content is applied to real world problems. Sensors are comfortable in the business world.

If you are a sensor, look for a job in the computer industry that allows you to do the following tasks:

- Deal with details and specifics.
- Find solutions using common sense rather than theory.
- Explore computer security and computer law professions.
- Work with applied sciences. (Theory puts you to sleep.)
- Enjoy lots of physical activity at work. Move around. Walk.
- Troubleshoot and repair technology.
- Learn computer-aided drafting or engineering graphics.
- Deal with accounting or applied mathematics.
- Apply your financial knowledge to artificial intelligence.
- Create technical illustrations, typography, or applied art.
- Work with robotics technology and computer-aided manufacturing, which require your hands-on skills.
- Concentrate on one project at a time.
- Take jobs that offer immediate, tangible results. (You want to see where your efforts lead).
- Work at jobs that deal with the present. (Thinking too much of the future wastes your time.)
- Work with figures or facts. Routine is important.
- Choose programming specialties in financial database management or health care fields.
- Work sequentially and chronologically.
- Learn step by step and teach computer subjects the same way.
- Simplify the complex using facts and details.
- Supply exactness and not sweeping generalities.
- Give clear instructions and ask for the details immediately.
- Question authority before taking anything literally.
- Look for the trees, not the forest.
- Keep daily logs, dated memos, and records of your work environment and activities, or anything unusual that occurs.
- Instead of trying to fix what's not broken, ask an intuitive to show you all the ways something can be improved.
- Shop comparatively.
- Use software for fashion design.

HOW YOU MAKE DECISIONS

Your third letter was either *T* or *F*. There are both thinkers (T types) and feelers (F types) in the computer industry. Let's look first at thinkers, who are found in large numbers in programming, software engineering, scientific research, and systems analysis positions. Fifty percent of the world's population are thinkers. However, two thirds of the thinkers are male and one third of the thinkers are female.

T Is for Thinking

Thinking deals with how you make decisions. Here is where you focus your need to come to closure when you make a decision, be it what to put on your résumé or where to work. Thinking means you reach conclusions through logical analysis. You often step back from becoming emotionally involved in a decision.

According to Otto Kroeger, management consultant and author of *Type Talk at Work, (How the 16 Personality Types Determine Your Success on the Job)* (Bantam, Doubleday, Dell, 1992), 96 percent of top corporate executives are thinking judgers (TJ types). Only four percent of corporate executives who have risen to the top CEO level are not thinking judgers.

For example, suppose you are a thinking, judging person. According to Kroeger, "As long as our system is profits and productivity driven, TJs will rise to the top." Profit is a key factor in determining how those who run the computer industry make their decisions. On a résumé, how much money you made for a company last year influences how desirable you are to employers.

So if you are a T or TJ, connect with organizations that have a similar character. (The same advice applies to the other preferences: connect what you are to where you work.)

Hard Heads and Firm Words

As a thinker, you will try to be logical, calm, and unemotional. Sometimes your clear-headedness will be perceived as hard-headedness. You will talk truthfully to others rather than make up polite lies to avoid hurt feelings. You believe there is always room for improvement in people's work, and you will evaluate and critique the work of others. You are best at analyzing the work of others and making it clearer and sharper.

Being natural skeptics, it's comfortable for a thinker to critique. They will question authority if the authority's conclusions aren't backed up by factual, scientific evidence. They may insist that the boss is wrong until the boss proves he or she is right. It's more important for a thinker to be right; if you are a thinker, you couldn't care less who likes you. You don't need harmony at work.

A thinker likes to organize either facts (if he or she is also a sensor) or ideas (if he or she is also an intuitive) into logical order. Thinkers hate redundancy. In the computer industry, many thinkers are business-like, brief, and curt in conversation. Thinkers are impressed with logic.

Thinkers enjoy solving the problems of machines, software, business, or technology more than solving the problems of people—unless they can administer or manage people without getting involved in emotional issues.

If you're a thinker, look for a job in the computer industry that allows you to do the following tasks:

- Settle disputes objectively.
- Analyze securities, facts, or computer systems.
- Troubleshoot and repair computers or peripherals.
- Sell technical instruments.
- Write technical software or hardware user manuals.
- Design software or hardware.
- Design and program computer games.
- Handle accounting problems.
- Manage financial databases.
- Invent more efficient computers.
- Sell cable television to telephone companies.
- Investigate computer security problems or crime.
- Practice computer, tax, or computer-related entertainment law.
- Design computers for military robotics.
- Write technical textbooks.
- Open an electronic university to teach computer sciences.
- Teach critical thinking to employees or college students.
- Make decisions.
- Become a computer consultant, solving problems.
- Work as a systems analyst.
- Be an expert witness.
- Use computers for scientific, economic, or financial research.

Feeling Types
F stands for feeling types. About two thirds of all females and about one third of males in the United States are feeling types. Feelers seek rapport with coworkers, either through correspondence or in person. Feeling types avoid conflict and need harmony in the workplace and in their work tasks. Feelers like to give feedback, and consider the emotions of everyone around them before making a decision.

Although thinking types can be found in music, art, and literature, their verbal language and technical illustration tends to be complex and analytical. They seek to evaluate or critique. Feeling types, however, seek to praise rather than critique, evaluate, or analyze. They seek inner values leading to serenity in the project or work environment.

If you are a feeling type, a computer job or task may be both technical and creative. However, if the work can't be directly applied to helping people or enhancing people's lives, environment, imagination, or healing, you aren't too interested in it. You ask, "Is it worth working for?"

The Journey, not the Destination
You are process-oriented rather than task-oriented. Your overview and career goal is always centered on self-growth, service with a smile, or ensuring that there is value to your work.

Feelers can be found in everything from artificial intelligence and neural networks to nanotechnology and biotechnology. They are frequently found working as trainers, editors, public relations directors of software companies, writers, illustrators, and event planners.

You have a great need for affiliation and rapport with those around you at work, even if it's only through correspondence. You are loyal to your boss as long as the workplace needs for harmony and rapport aren't overlooked.

When you are under stress, rather than list the pros and cons to make a decision objectively, you'll ask yourself whether the outcome is worth it. What does the work mean to your growth and the growth of those around you who use the product, service, information, or idea? You trust your feelings.

The Feeler's Niche Is Communication
In the computer world, software is viewed as a tool for business and education, for learning through entertainment, or as creative arts therapy. Sell software that you feel upholds your values about work and life. Emphasize software as a tool to make communication easier and better. Your niche is probably in a communication field like one of the following: CD-Interactive courseware design, CD-ROM, virtual reality, animation, desktop video, desktop publishing, the computer press and journalism, public relations, human resource management, people-oriented research and personnel trend studies, electronic publishing, video production, psychology, multimedia, special effects, telecommunications, local and wide area networks, wireless communications, the Internet, music and graphics design or illustration.

Feeling Types Frequently Design Software
Educational technology, designing or selling software as entertainment or education are areas where you do well. You would feel comfortable designing preschool software and games, helping people see value in computers, on-line services and the Web, or expressing yourself using computers as tools for an aesthetic, communicational, personal, or visual experience.

If you are a feeling type, look for a job in the computer industry that allows you to do the following tasks:

- Write articles or books about careers in the computer field.
- Design computer software to teach through entertainment, idealism, or service.
- Capitalize on your communication and interpersonal skills.
- Sell software to hospitals.
- Speak to sales groups.
- Direct public relations.
- Work as a journalist in the computer press.
- Design instructional courseware.
- Use computers to enhance the environment.
- Use computers in psychology and therapy.
- Animate corporate training films.
- Use computers and video in multimedia productions.
- Record information on CD-ROM.
- Use desktop publishing or desktop video to create books or ads.

- Write software user manuals to help people learn a skill.
- Manage the marketing communications department.
- Plan events, trade shows, and conventions.
- Publish a newsletter on ergonomics.
- Work as a computer illustrator or graphic designer.
- Teach computer skills to the physically challenged.
- Place employees in jobs.
- Work in outplacement for retiring personnel.
- Open a software talent management agency.
- Design computer games for the learning disabled.
- Teach creative writing using word-processing software.
- Teach computer-aided design and illustration.
- Use computer equipment to create music, work with sound and lights, or edit films.
- Create national clearinghouses for new databases.
- Start a business or professional association.
- Introduce computers and software training to a preschool or senior center.
- Bring together international businesses or groups for a common interest.
- Use computers for therapy in special education.
- Work as a documentation analyst.
- Train corporate managers.
- Telecommute so your time can be as flexible as possible.
- Combine sculpture and animation for 3-D technology and software.
- Operate an environmental information camp.

HOW DO YOU STRUCTURE YOUR LIFE?

Your fourth letter was either *J* or *P*. There are both judging types (J) and perceiving types (P) working in the computer industry.

Many times it's the judging or perceiving preference that is the reason some employees are terminated for "not fitting into the group." They are competent but are matched with people of the opposite preference in a particular work situation.

In fact, the J or P preference may cause all types of conflict, tension, hostility, and arguments at work—from tardiness to disorder, from rigidity to delays.

Why does judging or perceiving cause so much conflict? The J or P preference deals with the way you structure your environment. The judger wants order. The perceiver wants flexibility. The need for structure opposes the need for spontaneity.

If you are a P type, your résumé reflects someone who needs a flexible working environment with flexible hours. You can adapt to many types of work situations on demand. As a spontaneous, creative person, you can meet unexpected needs as they arise.

When you send your P type résumé to a J type employer, it may get tossed in the round file. The J type employer is looking for an applicant who is productive and comfortable in a routine. The person in the employer's mind must be decisive, orderly, deliberate, and work well under pressure during certain hours. If you diverge from the J character of the employer, you will feel there's a wrong fit.

As a P type, you want to keep your mind open for new information. The J type wants quick closure that makes sense. Judgers will want advance notice of changes instead of adapting themselves to the constantly changing information. When a judger is staying on a predetermined course in the face of change, and a perceiver is adapting to change instead, there is conflict. The perceiver may feel exploited and reactive.

J Is for Judging

About 55 percent of the world's population, and 90 percent of top level executives, are judgers. Judgers seek structure in everything—"the planned life," as Isabel Briggs Myers writes in her book, *Gifts Differing*. Everything has a place in your system of order.

If you are a J, you are a natural leader, a person who likes routine, stability, security; you may work for the same company many years. You are a saver rather than a spender; relaxation does not come easily.

In your career, you seek closure. You want everything at work decided on as quickly as possible, and you want to make the decisions. You are traditional in many ways and need to belong to a group. This structure-seeking behavior shows on your résumé.

You are methodical, scheduled, and organized. There is a definiteness about the way you organize your résumé. It's usually chronological, organized, and exact. You use a plan for everything, from writing your cover letter to the last follow-up call, entered in your computer.

You make use of day planners and clocks and are a master of time and records. You like to count, measure, and control. You hate constantly changing information. The biggest problem with writing your résumé is revising it. J types have a harder time relaxing than P types.

In a job, you need to seek balance and moderation. Instead of becoming angry at P types for taking too long, look to them to provide alternative routes to the same goal. Look to the spontaneity of the P to teach you how to enjoy work more.

P types see you as an authoritarian figure to be feared. Perceivers see you as the girdle into which they are squeezed whenever their self-determination grows. You see yourself as the parent scolding a P type child, instead of equals at work.

If you are a judger (J type), look for a job in the computer industry that allows you to work in the following areas:

- Records management
- Executive level or junior executive trainee work in computers
- Programming
- Accounting
- Systems analysis

- Financial database management
- Applied artificial intelligence
- Software engineering
- Clerical supervision or clerical work
- Word processing
- Desktop publishing
- Computer security
- Drafting
- Robotics technology, computer-aided manufacturing
- Numerical control
- Electronic mail processing
- Manage multiple projects, objectives, and deadlines

P Is for Perceiving

About 45 percent of the world's population are perceivers. Tight schedules cramp your style if you are a P type. You like to wait and see what happens. Surprises are welcome.

You wish to create your own deadlines and work whenever you feel the inspiration or motivation to do your thing. You won't work to meet anyone else's deadline unless the recognition of your creativity or your entire financial security depends on it. You are "laid back." However, you often do your work too near ther deadline, cramming everything into the short time you allowed yourself. You may thrive on the adrenaline. As a stress avoider, you also may avoid work if it makes you tense—or get it out of the way early so you can have fun.

Your work must be fun or you won't do it. If you adapt yourself to a J type's rigid schedule or plan, your health could be affected. Your spontaneity would make you a good police officer on a foot patrol—or the equivalent in the computer security field. Your résumé will change its slant many times as you work at temporary jobs in different fields.

P types are free-spirited intrapreneurs, entrepreneurs, independent contractors, and freelancers who often work for someone else if there's autonomy and flexibility on the job. Above all, a job must offer you a chance to move freely. Express your creativity and need for movement and change on your résumé, and explore the more innovative areas of the computer industry. Stay away from records management jobs where you have to organize and file facts all day.

If you are a perceiver (P type), look for a job in the computer industry that allows you to do the following tasks:

- Explore new uses of computer technology.
- Allow spontaneity to dominate your work life.
- Learn all you can about your employer or your job.
- Choose a job where you'll know what others are doing.
- Start up many different new businesses.
- Work with alternatives and possibilities for change.
- Sell software.
- Research, working with think tanks where you can design your own models—especially if you're also a thinker/intuitive.
- Design video games.

- Seek variety in your work assignments.
- Explore the relationship between computers and robots and the needs of the physically challenged.
- Keep technical writing options open.
- Design robots.
- Write interactive fiction for CD-Interactive and CD-ROM laser discs.
- Plan computer industry conventions and trade shows.
- Learn skills that are transferable from one career to the next.
- Use computer rather than paper files.
- Expand your job search internationally.
- Depend on last-minute spurts of energy.
- Think on your feet.

Now that you have some understanding of the personality preferences, you can see how they may combine to form 16 personality types. These are based on the principles of the Myers-Briggs Type Indicator (MBTI®). The 16 types are as follows:

ISTJ	ISFJ	INFJ	INTJ
ISTP	ISFP	INFP	INTP
ESTP	ESFP	ENFP	ENTP
ESTJ	ESFJ	ENFJ	ENTJ

WHAT THE LETTERS STAND FOR: THE 16 PERSONALITY TYPES

ISTJ	introverted, sensing, thinking, judging
ISTP	introverted, sensing, thinking, perceiving
ESTP	extroverted, sensing, thinking, perceiving
ESTJ	extroverted, sensing, thinking, judging
ISFJ	introverted, sensing, feeling, judging
ISFP	introverted, sensing, feeling, perceiving
ESFP	extroverted, sensing, feeling, perceiving
ESFJ	extroverted, sensing, feeling, judging
INFJ	introverted, intuitive, feeling, judging
INFP	introverted, intuitive, feeling, perceiving
ENFP	extroverted, intuitive, feeling, perceiving
ENFJ	extroverted, intuitive, feeling, judging
INTJ	introverted, intuitive, thinking, judging
INTP	introverted, intuitive, thinking, perceiving
ENTP	extroverted, intuitive, thinking, perceiving
ENTJ	extroverted, intuitive, thinking, judging

These 16 personality types are found among all people in the world, according to the principles of the MBTI®. Recommended computer industry jobs for each type follows.

RECOMMENDED COMPUTER JOBS FOR EACH TYPE

The job recommendations below represent only a fraction of the jobs that exist in the computer industry. New jobs are created each year whose titles never before existed.

ISTJ
Accountant, data manager, computer security investigator, auditor, software engineer, attorney, economist, career military and civil service computer administrator, business information technologist, numerical control specialist, comptroller of financial databases, law office administrator, paralegal, medical software transcriptionist, medical records technician, software manufacturer's representative, applied mathematician, financial operations manager.

ISTP
Computer-aided drafter, computer-aided manufacturing specialist, robotics technician, computer repair technician, business computing programmer, applied systems analyst, systems engineer, astronaut, virtual reality specialist, defense and weapons computer simulations instructor, traveling computer security specialist, information systems consultant, defense weapons vendor or designer.

ESTP
Real estate software sales, computer program radio talk show host, computer marketing personnel, peripheral retailer, wholesaler, importer of computer products, design automation publicist, auditor, traveling software distributor, cable TV multimedia producer, wireless telecommunications manufacturer's representative, promotor of new hardware and software products.

ESTJ
Law office administrator, paralegal, computer security specialist, computer lawyer, investigator, manager, business information technologist, data communications engineer, programmer, information retrieval specialist, database manager, records manager, numerical control manager, robotics engineer or technician, accountant, financial programmer, marketing manager, banking programmer or systems analyst, insurance database specialist, wholesaler, international database manager, executive recruiter, broadcasting multimedia executive, hospital and health services administrator, computer science and information systems instructor, production and operations manager, public administrator, logistics specialist, insurance investigation, systems engineer.

ISFJ
Local area network (LAN) specialist, telecommunications equipment technician, organizer, word processor, desktop publisher, teacher, librarian, medical software technology designer, telephone company craftsperson, communications technicians, switching machine operator, computer operator, data-entry clerk, secretary, paralegal, applied computing programmer, applied computing specialist, records manager, court reporter, wireless telecommunications equipment technician,

nurse practitioner, health care software transcriptionist, medical records administrator, data communications specialist, telecommunications technologist, computer science education specialist.

ISFP
Medical transcriptionists and health care computing operator, word processor, secretary, bookkeeper, computer illustrator, crafts person, computer software fashion designer, computer repairer, computer peripheral retail sales clerk or manager, medical records technologist, medical records, software manufacturer's sales representative, desktop publisher, mail-order customer service manager, preschool computer specialists (games for teaching preschool), computer midi synthesizer music composer or vendor, exhibit designer.

ESFP
Software talent agent, computer laser light show performer, sports computing specialist, manufacturer's software representative, retail computer store sales clerk, virtual reality entertainment retailer, computerized theatrical production specialist, software video producer, computer animation advertising agency representative, public relations account executive, traveling computer sales, computer music (midi synthesizer and special effects) performer, physical therapy and rehabilitation computer trainer or sales representative, software fashion designer, merchandiser, nurse practitioner and trainer, vendor, computer camp counselor, travel agent.

ESFJ
Database manager, medical secretary or transcriptionist, medical records software technician, programmer, computer store retail manager, sales and customer representative, communications technician with phone company, telecommunications sales representative, computer animation advertising account executive, publicist, professional associations convention planner, computer professional association national organizer, special events planner, Peace Corps organizer, trainer, nurse trainer, business education teacher, office information systems manager.

INFJ
Computer illustrator and designer, animator, technical writer, software user manual writer, teacher, courseware designer, instructional technologist, on-line librarian, tape librarian, ergonomics designer and researcher, biomedical computing specialist, interactive fiction writer for CD-Interactive/CD-ROM, electronic publishing consultant and color desktop publishing specialist, mediator, human resource manager, outplacement director, personnel consultant, recruiter, exhibit designer, Webmaster.

INFP
Freelance writer, freelance editorial illustrator, computer press columnist/journalist, grant proposal writer, software user manual writer, computer career book author, cartoonist, desktop animator, desktop video script writer, courseware designer, newsletter designer, writing teacher, consultant, computer camp counselor, organizational development specialist, electronic publisher, Webmaster.

ENFP
Counselor, computer camp resort recruiter, "technostress" psychologist, computer personnel researcher, computers for the physically handicapped trainer, vendor, ergonomics vendor, professional speaker, career book writer, computer press journalist/columnist, temporary agency recruiter, organizational development specialist, outplacement interviewer, convention and event planner, publicist, trade show and exhibit manager, cruise ship computer room director, courseware designer, personnel agency manager, small business opportunities, publisher, corporate training video producer, animator.

ENFJ
Public speaker, trainer, teacher, computerized job bank counselor, retail salesperson, manufacturer's representative, interactive multimedia producer, audience tracker, organizational development consultant, office manager, recruiter, human resource development manager, event planner, computers and society researcher, computers and human interaction researcher, traveling seminar specialist, public relations account executive, video producer, computer graphics presentations designer, Webmaster, total quality management trainer, traveling salesperson and manufacturer's representative, computer personnel researcher, computer uses in education trainer.

INTJ
Allied health fields researcher, automata and computability theorist, biomedical computing programmer and systems analyst, computer architect, design automation specialist, documentation analyst, symbolic computing and mathematics researcher, software engineer, biotech computer specialist, biomedical engineer, information broker, competitive intelligence specialist, computer security investigator, software manufacturer and designer, object-oriented programmer, financial analyst, applied artificial intelligence financial forecaster, trend forecaster, economist, computer science educator, neural networks and fuzzy logic programmer/designer, electronic publishing vendor, molecular biology software developer.

INTP
Computer architect, numerical mathematician, robotics engineer, measurement and evaluation computing specialist, simulation specialist, software engineer, computational linguistics researcher, educational researcher, securities analyst, systems analyst, programmer, scientific programmer, operating systems specialist, programming languages designer, microprogramming researcher, software designer, computer game programmer, biomedical computing programmer, automata and computability theory researcher, trend forecaster, atmospheric and environmental forecaster, satellite technician or tracker, mathematician, educational researcher, biostatistician, numerical control robotics researcher, inventor, electronic engineer, technical writer/science writer, graphics designer.

ENTP
Instructional technologist, marketing research manager, labor trends forecaster, economist, inventor, software engineer, designer, multimedia

and presentation graphics designer/producer, electronic publisher, wireless communications developer, telecommunications network engineer, technical public speaker, organizational development specialist, outplacement consultant, entrepreneur, intrapreneur, manufacturer's representative, traveling salesperson, computer camp owner, computerized photographer, special effects designer, corporate animator, public relations account executive, advertising agency account executive, promotion director, data communications vendor, documentary/training films filmmaker, programming languages designer, hardware, peripherals, and robotics designer, virtual reality designer, computer and video games programmer/designer, Web site designer, systems analyst, physician's training video producer, independent contractor, computer marketing consultant.

ENTJ
Data manager, organizational development researcher, general manager, entrepreneur, operating systems director, career military officer, lawyer, computer security director, design automation researcher, programmer, systems analyst, entrepreneur, intrapreneur, organizer, planning director, time management trainer, software developer, hardware importer/exporter, computerized genetics researcher, environmental investigator, electronic engineer, software engineer, venture capital broker/banker, executive recruiter, analog/digital circuit engineer, fundraiser, marketing analyst, wireless electronic security wholesaler, weapons systems specialist, public speaker, hardware design engineer, network switching software engineer.

The following chart describes the computer industry niches that fit the various types most comfortably:

Computer Software/Hardware Research, Design, Invention, Analysis	INTJ, ENTJ, INTP, ENTP
Software, Hardware, Courseware Development	ENFJ, ENTJ, ENTP, ENFP
Technical Services, Programming, Administration	ESTJ, ISTJ, ESTP, ISTP
Troubleshooting, Computer Repair and Debugging	ESTP, ISTP
Database Management, Manager of Information Systems, Production	ESTJ, ESFJ, ISTJ, ISFJ
Telecommunications Technician	ISFJ, ISTJ
Sales of Computer Products	ESFJ, ESFP
Sales of Ideas, Advertising, Public Relations, Abstract Concepts	ENFJ, ENFP
Public Speakers, Sales Trainers	ENFJ, ESFJ, ENFP, ESTJ, ENTJ
Secretarial, Guy Friday	ISFJ
Medical Transcription or Medical Records Technology, Software Manufacturer's Representative	ISTJ, ISFJ, ESFJ
Clerical and Customer Service With Direct People Contact	ESFJ, ISFJ
Clerical with Machines Transcribing Equipment	ISTJ, ESTJ
Administration, Organization	ESTJ, ENTJ
Inventions (Hardware) and Robotics	ENTP, INTP, ISTP
Software Design	INTP, INTJ
Art, Educational, Design Writing Software	INFP, INFJ

Accounting	ISTJ, ISFJ
Personnel, Interviewing, Human Resource Management	INFP, INFJ
Art, Illustration, Computer Animation/Design, (Including Preschool Software Design)	INFP, ISFP, ENFP
Interactive Fiction/Learning With CD-I and CD-ROM Scripts, Training Films, Software for Education Design, Product Publicity, Technical Advertising Copywriting	INFP, INFJ, ENFP
Systems Analysis	INTJ, INTP, ISTP, ISTJ
User Friendly Software/Hardware Design	ENTP, ENFP, INFP
Video Producers, Multimedia, News Cable Producers	ENTJ, ENTP, ENFJ, ENFP
The Computer Press	INTJ, INFJ, INFP, ENFP, ENTP
Midi Music Synthesizer Composition, Special Effects	INTP, INFP, ISFP, ESFP, ENTP, INFJ
Corporate Animators, Special Effects Designers	INTP, INFP, INFJ, ISFP, ENFP, ESFP

By this point, you have probably learned how to match your personality type with the character of the organization for whom you choose to work. Select those action verbs and preferences that emphasize your best qualifications. Finally, use words in your résumé or cover letter that describe your personality type strengths to direct attention to the job you want.

Writing résumés is all about packaging yourself as information. People seek work for a variety of reasons, but if you are insightful, introspective, or reflective, you know intuitively that it takes as strong an ego to turn down a promotion so you can be happy in your career as it does to climb the ladder. It's hard to resist a promotion or the offer of a prestigious job, even when you know you would be happier doing what excites you. Status is valued by society, but you may place more value on freedom in your job.

10
SAMPLE RESUMES

In this chapter, there are 58 résumés to guide you as your write your **résumé.** They are classified by each category found in the computer industry to help you observe details that target different niches. Compare them to your résumé details.

Some of the job applicants' names, addresses, and company names in the résumés are fictitious; some are real. However, all the job descriptions, titles, duties, and responsibilities are real employment requirements in the computer industry. It's important to study the job duties in the résumés.

The golden strategy of résumé writing is "do unto employers as they would have you do unto them." Value their company's needs. Observe how qualifications listed on the sample résumés match the needs of the position. When you send your résumé out, keep in mind the character of the company. Does it match your preferences?

At the end of this chapter, you will find record-keeping pages to help you track your résumés so you can follow up as new openings occur in any company. The 58 sample résumés in this chapter apply to the following areas of the computer industry.

- artificial intelligence
- biotech computing
- biotech medical writer
- communications analyst
- computer-aided design
- computer convention/events
- computer graphics
- computer journalism
- computer law
- computer operations
- computer security
- computer technology/repair
- database management
- data entry operations
- desktop/electronic publishing
- desktop video/animation/special effects
- digital special effects/image manipulation
- document production manager
- drafting/medical
- drafting/engineering
- fashion design/software

- information services/systems analysis
- interactive design
- interactive fiction writing
- interactive résumé writing
- Internet/intranet
- marketing communications
- marketing management
- medical records technology
- medical transcription
- multimedia
- network systems engineering
- neural networks
- numerical control
- personnel management
- programming
- quality/regulatory assurance
- robotics technology
- sales and marketing
- scientific programming
- software engineering
- software talent agenting
- software test manager
- software writing
- systems analysis
- systems engineering
- tape librarian
- technical illustration
- technical writing
- technical training
- video computer games design
- videoconferencing
- virtual reality
- Web site design and administration
- wireless communications
- word processing

ARTIFICIAL INTELLIGENCE/NEURAL NETWORKS

MICHAEL B. CHIFTELESEN

89 Setton Lane
Manchester, IL 60603
(303) 555-1999
mchift@myisp.com

JOB OVERVIEW
Permanent employment as an applied artificial intelligence financial database manager specifically in stock market trend forecasting. Seek to become part of a growing software development company.

SOFTWARE/HARDWARE
C++, C, Pascal, Basic, Novell, Unix kernel, GUI, SCSI interface development in C, on IBM AS 400 hardware, and IBM PC.

EDUCATION
B.A. in Economics with applied mathematics minor, University of Chicago, December 1992. Second minor in computer science and information systems.

SOFTWARE EXPERIENCE
December 1992 - Present
MEREET INVESTMENT SOFTWARE DESIGN, INC., Chicago, IL
Database Manager, Software Designer, and Programmer
Identified a particular stock market situation and environment as one that resembled a known period in history. Applied artificial intelligence tools to stock market forecasting. Designed forecasting software. Produced videos and gave seminars.

RESPONSIBILITIES
- Automated investment advisory service.
- Developed software within a closed network.
- Created an end product of presentation software.
- Designed and developed data management software.
- Coordinated with national database services to obtain current quotes.
- Developed an array of artificial intelligence technology including the following:
    - Statistical processes.
    - Extrapolation and trend analysis.
    - Pattern matching to historical development of indicators.
    - Neural networks expertise system and heuristics.
    - Measured breaks in stock market prices for changes in direction.

References on Request.

Amyra C. Cohen
49 Rowbrook Blvd.
Sinclair, CA 92000
(714) 555-1212

JOB OVERVIEW

Clinical documentation specialist. Responsible for document control and archives to meet government requirements for clinical studies within a biopharmaceutical company developing innovative products in medicine.

SOFTWARE/HARDWARE

Lotus 1-2-3, dBase, Paradox, Excel, WordPerfect, PowerPoint.
IBM-compatible PC.

DOCUMENT CONTROL EXPERIENCE

October 1979–1993   LOMBOCHE PHARMACEUTICALS, INC., Pendleton, CA

<u>**Clinical Documentation Specialist**</u>
- Responsible for document control for clinical studies.
- Maintained department archives to meet FDA requirements.
- Tracked and reported study status.
- Maintained all pharmaceutical documentation in databases using a variety of dBase and spreadsheet software.
- Prepared pharmaceutical documentation for FDA audits.
- Utilized medical terminology extensively.
- Administrative support activities included heavy use of word-processing software and spreadsheets.

June 1974–October 1979   ST. MICHAEL'S HOSPITAL, Oceanside, CA

<u>**Medical Records Technician and Transcriptionist**</u>
- Coded medical records and transcribed medical terminology in medical records department of an acute care hospital.
- Operated IBM 129 computer.

EDUCATION

<u>**B.S. in Business Administration**</u>
with minor in health sciences, San Diego State University, June 1979.
<u>**A.S. Medical Records Technology**</u>
Mesa College, San Diego, 1973.
<u>**Certificate in Medical Transcription and Medical Office Administration**</u>
Mesa College, San Diego, June 1972.

References available upon request.

BIOTECH MEDICAL WRITER

Anne Jeanne Smith
4455 Texas Street
Wilmington, DE 20304
(302) 555-7895

OBJECTIVE

A permanent staff position as an advertising medical writer with a health care company, medical advertising agency, or computer corporation specializing in medical software, video, and multimedia presentation technologies.

SUMMARY OF QUALIFICATIONS

- Gather information.
- Reshape information.
- Sell information in a variety of formats.
- Design information to meet different needs.

RELATED SKILLS

- Interpreted complex clinical research and development data into easy-to-understand marketing support materials.
- Interpreted, wrote, and edited: monographs, presentations, video scripts, sales aid layouts, and clinical/marketing research claims support materials.
- Managed projects from inception to completion.
- Authored three self-help and nutrition books published by major New York publishers.
- Wrote many multimedia computer presentation graphics scripts.
- Wrote medical advertising copy for a variety of advertising agencies for Fortune 500 international health care firms.

EXPERIENCE

1964–Present: Independent contract medical writer,
A.J. Smith Medical Writing Productions,
(self-employed), Wilmington, DE.

EDUCATION/TRAINING

B.S., English Education
New York University, NY, 1980
Continuing Education in Medical Writing
American Medical Writer's Association
Continuing Education Seminars, 1992

REFERENCES
Upon Request

COMMUNICATIONS ANALYST

Wanda Barston
1756 Eastwell Drive, Borne, MN 30324
(217) 555-1678 • Fax (217) 555-1679
wbars@myisp.com

GOAL A permanent position as a communications analyst in a large-scale LAN/WAN information systems and services department managing and troubleshooting network projects.

OVERVIEW
- Six years of LAN/WAN experience with an in-depth knowledge of interconnect technologies.
- Technical and working knowledge of synchronous/asynchronous protocols, TCP/IP and SNA network methodologies.
- Three years of hands-on experience with bridges, routers, 10base T cabling systems, modems, MUXes, and telephone company services (T1, 56k).
- Six years of experience with network test equipment (LanAlyzer, Firebird).

SOFTWARE Knowledge of Microsoft, LAN Manager, Novell, Unix, DOS, and e-mail.

EXPERIENCE
January 1987–Present: **Communication Analyst, Able Data, Inc.,** Bloomington, MN.
Managed the Information Systems and Services Department of a large-scale LAN/WAN corporation. Troubleshooter on network projects.

EDUCATION B.S., Information Systems; Certificate in Telecommunications
Borne Computer College, Bloomington, MN, 1986
A.S., Computer Science and Information Systems
Bloomington Community College, 1983

REFERENCES On request.

COMPUTER-AIDED DESIGN

Robert Vine

2394 Crestview Ridge, Brooklyn, NY 11230
(212) 555-9007 ▪ Fax (212) 555-9000
rvine@myisp.com

OVERVIEW

Eight years of experience, with increasing responsibilities, as a technical illustrator, with in-depth exposure to AUTOCAD engineering graphics, design, and drafting. Focus on blueprint reading, dimensioning, tolerancing, assembly drawing, and airbrush illustration. Four years' experience designing special effects. Seek a position as a computer-aided designer in industrial design.

ABILITIES

- Detailed drawing of complex concepts in engineering graphics.
- Assembly drawing and cutaways.
- Airbrushing.
- Presentation graphics design on Macintosh, focusing on multimedia and video.
- Computer applications on Cadds 4x computers.
- Technical illustrations in Freehand and Illustrator software.
- Computer tracing from originals.
- Macintosh production and traffic management.
- Desktop publishing with PageMaker and QuarkXPress, specializing in color separations.
- Strong design using AUTOCAD software.
- Computer illustration with CorelDraw! on PC's. Finished designs using line or airbrush.
- Corporate computer animation, special effects, and desktop video using Morph and VideoDirector on the Macintosh.

ACHIEVEMENTS

- Developed detailed, cutaway drawings of computer hardware.
- Designed drafting blueprints of hardware using AUTOCAD software.
- Illustrated parts brochures with Adobe software on the Macintosh.
- Created three award-winning corporate animation videos using the Amiga computer and Video Toaster, focusing on special effects.

EMPLOYMENT

June 1985–Present: Technical Graphics Artist and Computer-Aided Designer/Drafter, Creative Media Technical Advertising Agency, Brooklyn, NY.

EDUCATION

Associate in Applied Science
Technical Illustration and Desktop Video
Brooklyn Community College, 1985

References available upon request.

COMPUTER CONVENTION/EVENTS PLANNER

FRANCINE SHOEMAKER
9 Mae Lee Drive
Hagerstown, MD 30389
(217) 555-7855 • Fax (217) 555-7800
fshoe@myisp.com

OBJECTIVE

Experienced computer and electronics events planner seeks affiliation with convention, trade show, and exhibit planning agency or national association of computer professionals.

ABILITIES

– Computer trade show, exhibit, and convention planner with Mann Computer College Annual Job Fair.
– Knowledge of exhibit design and booth sales.
– Public relations, tours, and press conference planning.
– Site selection and budgeting.
– Coordination and organization from inception to completion of computer and electronic trade shows, exhibits, conventions, conferences, meetings, seminars, workshops, and job fairs with institutional and hotel sales and catering managers.
– Sold 250 booths at annual Computer Equipment Dealer's convention.
– Personnel interviewing, screening, and hiring of exhibit designer's crew and carpenters.

EXPERIENCE

June 1992–September 1993: Sales Manager, convention and conference space, Mann Computer College, Hagerstown, MD.
June 1987–May 1992: Exhibits Designer and Events Planner, Glentackie Technical Events Planning Agency, Chevy Chase, MD.

VOLUME

Average annual exhibit booth sales of $600,000, 1992–1993.
Average annual exhibit booth sales of $350,000, 1987–1992.

EDUCATION

Certificate in Events Planning
Certificate in Desktop Publishing
Baltimore Community College,
Adult Continuing Education Division
Baltimore, MD, 1987

References on request.

THERA SANDOR

4494 Rest Ridge
San Diego, CA 92104
(619) 555-1387 • Fax (619) 555-1388
tsand@myisp.com

EDUCATION

Associate in Applied Science
Commercial Art
San Diego City College, 1980

OVERVIEW

Thirteen years of experience, with increasing responsibilities, as an ad agency staff graphic designer. Focus on heavy advertising, agency brochure, print, greeting card, calendar, and electronic design. Seek a position as a staff illustrator in the advertising department of a large corporation, or as a staff illustrator/graphic designer/desktop publisher or desktop video producer with a major advertising agency.

ABILITIES

- Detailed drawing of complex concepts in advertising design.
- Illustration of children's books, and editorial design.
- Airbrush illustration.
- In-depth experience with CorelDraw!, Ventura Publisher, and Ventura AdPro in graphic design on PC's.
- Design multimedia presentation graphics on Macintosh using QuarkXPress, Adobe Illustrator, PhotoShop, and Freehand.
- Computer tracing from original art.
- Ad agency traffic management, routing, and media buying.
- Desktop publishing with PageMaker software on both the Mac and PC.
- Specialist in computerized color separations.
- Corporate computer animation, special effects, and desktop video using Director and MS PowerPoint on a PC and Adobe Premiere on a Mac.

ACHIEVEMENTS

- Designed 4-color editorial illustrations for newspaper ads, for ad agency.
- Illustrated ads for brochures with Adobe software on the Macintosh and CorelDraw! on PC's.
- Created an award-winning animated corporate training video on health tips for truckers, using the Amiga computer and Video Toaster. Included special effects.

EMPLOYMENT

June 1980–Present:
Graphic Designer (Staff Artist/Illustrator),
Barnett Public Relations and Advertising, San Diego, CA.

References and portfolio on request.

Amida Browne
54 Orange Terrace
Kansas City, MO 64106
(816) 555-4542 • Fax (816) 555-4540 • abrow@myisp.com

JOB OBJECTIVE:
Journalist covering the computer industry seeks a senior editorial position on a trade publication. Experienced in QuarkXPress on the Macintosh.

EDITING EMPLOYMENT:
1988–Present: Managing Editor of *Technical Education,* a national computer trade journal for trainers.
1983–1988: Senior Acquisitions Editor, *Computer Investor,* a monthly national trade magazine.
1981–1983: Associate Editor of *Telecommunications and Computers,* a national weekly business newspaper for the computer industry.

INVESTIGATIVE REPORTING:
1981–Present: Developed computer industry sources. Published investigative reports in periodicals for owners of desktop publishing businesses. Wrote a weekly investigative reporting column on electronic publishing.

CITY REPORTING:
1980–1981: Reporter, *The Daily Kansas News.* Covered local business news for an urban daily newspaper with a circulation of 300,000 in a city of 750,000.

FREELANCE WRITING:
1970–1980: Full-time freelance reporter: national magazines. Wrote more than 300 business articles.

PROFESSIONAL ASSOCIATIONS:
° Computer Press Association.
° Society for Professional Journalists.

EDUCATION:
Bachelor of Arts in Journalism
New York University, NY, 1970

REFERENCES AND CLIPS ON REQUEST.

Phillip Treston

5699 Grand Terrace
Vista View, OR 95984
(402) 555-3444

JOB TITLE:
PARALEGAL/LEGAL RESEARCHER: COMPUTER OR PATENT LAW

CASEWORK:
- Interview and discovery interrogation and background research work for computer law cases pending before the courts.
- Researched state and federal computer and patent laws, judicial decisions. Wrote briefs for attorneys.
- Prepared preliminary arguments and pleadings in computer law.
- Obtained affidavits.

COMPUTER LAW DOCUMENT DRAFTING:
- Drafted contracts under supervision of attorney.
- Prepared separation agreements, tax returns, incorporations, computer security statements, patent filings, and trust agreements.
- Prepare reports and schematic diagrams.

LEGAL SUPPORT:
- Assisted computer law specialists in preparing hardware and software patents, contracts, applications, shareholder agreements, benefits plans, loan documents, software development documents, packaging agreements, and annual financial reports of computer-industry corporations.
- Use of word-processing software, advanced use of database packages and spreadsheets.

EXPERIENCE:
June 1988–May 1993:
Computer and Patent Law Paralegal
Bryan, Steen & Bates, Attorneys-at-Law, Vista View, OR.

EDUCATION:
Certificate in Paralegal Studies
Specializing in Computer and Patent Law
Vista View State College, Division of Extended Studies
Vista View, OR, 1988

References on request.

COMPUTER OPERATIONS

Tom Lewein

79 Brook Road
Orange, CA 92000
(714) 555-1212

GOAL
A position in the insurance field as an AS/400 computer operator using personal computer support systems, using my experience in a Novell Network environment.

SOFTWARE
Lotus 1-2-3, dBase, PowerPoint, WordPerfect, Paradox, Excel, Ventura Publisher, and PageMaker.

HARDWARE
- #100M, #101EM, AS/400, VM/MVS operator.
- PC and Novell technical environment.

DOCUMENT CONTROL EXPERIENCE

October 1993–1197
LORE INSURANCE INC., Orange, CA
Computer Operator
- Operated AS/400 computers for four hours daily for three years in an insurance environment.
- Operated #100M, #101EM, VM/MVS (and IBM-compatible computers for PC support) in an insurance environment four hours daily for four years. Heavy use of Novell Network technology.
- Maintained department archives.
- Tracked and reported policy title status.
- Maintained all documentation in databases using a variety of dBase, word-processing, data entry, and spreadsheet software.
- Performed first level problem recovery/resolution for client base. Strong customer service orientation.

June 1988–May 1993
PRIME TITLE INSURANCE CO., Orange, CA
Word-Processing Specialist
- Administrative support included extensive use of WordPerfect.

EDUCATION
A.S., Records Management and Office Information Systems
Orange Community College, June 1994

References available on request.

COMPUTER SECURITY

Commander Tim Warden, U.S. Navy (Ret.)
90 Muncie Street
San Francisco, CA 91509
(415) 555-9008

OVERVIEW

Experienced computer security investigator and researcher with more than 25 years' military intelligence security background seeks affiliation with computer security investigation or research team of major corporation or national computer security investigation firm.

COMPETENCIES

INSTITUTIONAL
* Military police officer in the U.S. Navy.
* Naval intelligence officer, computer security services.
* Knowledge of computer security law and law enforcement.
* Experienced computer systems analyst and scientific programmer.
* Systems troubleshooting and repair technology for U.S. Navy computer systems. Top Secret security clearance.

RESEARCH
* Government computer security files.
* Systems network investigation.
* Software investigation.
* Personal interviewing.
* Telephone investigation.

SURVEILLANCE
* Military intelligence evidence gathering.
* Computer security issues evidence gathering.
* Video, network, recording, and photographic techniques.
* Documentation of research.

EXPERIENCE

June 1982– July 1996: Computer Security Analyst, U.S. Navy
May 1972–June 1982: Military Police Officer, U.S. Navy
June 1970–May 1972: Computer Security Analyst,
                     University of California, Berkeley, CA

EDUCATION

Bachelor of Science in Computer Science
University of California, Berkeley, CA, 1970

References available on request.

COMPUTER TECHNOLOGY/REPAIR

LOUISE DESOLA

7352 Mt. Elbrus Ridge
Brooklyn, NY 11234
(212) 555-9007
ldesol@myisp.com

EDUCATION

Associate in Applied Science
Computer Technology and Repair
Brooklyn Community College, 1984

OVERVIEW

Nine years of experience, with increasing responsibilities, as a computer technician, with in-depth exposure to motherboard troubleshooting and repair of PCs and Macs. Heavy network experience and knowledge of Unix operating systems. Focus on data and voice installation. Certification in PDS systems and Fiber. Two years' PC maintenance experience in a Novell Network environment. Seeking a position on an MIS team as a computer repair technician.

ABILITIES

Hardware:

- Provide liaison between manufacturers and users on warranty services backing installations of more than $1 million in value.
- Perform diagnostics on PCs and peripheral equipment to troubleshoot problems—down to the component level.
- Install/upgrade PC components such as network cards, memory chips, disk drives, modems, and CD-ROM drives.
- Configure PC memory and network drivers.
- Coordinate cabling/wiring projects.
- Place and monitor service calls for equipment repair.
- Expedite licensing issues.
- Maintain and repair PC and Macintosh computer systems.
- Maintain and repair Novell Network computer systems.
- Maintain and repair PDS, Fiber, and Unix operating systems.
- Configure and support systems, and inventory equipment.

Software:

- Microsoft Windows, WordPerfect, Paradox, Lotus 1-2-3, Excel, Lotus Freelance, and Harvard Graphics.

EMPLOYMENT

June 1985–Present:

Computer Repair Technician,
MIS Analysis Systems, Inc.
New York, New York

July 1984–June 1985:

Computer Repair Technician,
Coral Gardens Computer Store
Coral Gardens, Florida

References on request.

Jim Patton

766 Sands Road • Biloxi, MI 22000 • (814) 555-7312 • Fax (814) 555-7301 • jpatt@myisp.com

OBJECTIVE
A position with a mortgage banking firm as a database manager or WAN systems manager.

SOFTWARE
Databases in Datatrieve, Fortran, Paradox, Excel, and Unix.

HARDWARE
PC, Novell environment, and VAX/VMS/DCL.

DATABASE MANAGEMENT EXPERIENCE

October 1988–1997
FIRESTONE MORTGAGE BANKING, INC., Biloxi, MI
WAN Systems Manager/Database Manager
- Responsible for managing the technical databases utilizing WAN systems within the mortgage banking department of a large financial corporation.
- Retrieved databases containing technical, financial, and analytical operations, and disseminated information.
- Managed LAN databases.
- Utilized MS-DOS operating systems, multiple network technologies, and PC-based toolsets.
- Managed databases in a multiple-site PC-LAN environment.
- Managed remote access and remote LAN databases.
- Utilized various hardware platforms to retrieve and upgrade data.
- Hands-on experience in a Unix client-server environment.
- Improved productivity in a high-volume records management environment.
- Searched financial, legal, technical, and business databases. Supplied clients with packaged information.
- Utilized competitive intelligence database retrieval techniques.
- Disseminated the latest information for mortgage banking clients.

EDUCATION
Associate in Science Degrees:
1) Records Management, 1986
2) Computer Science and Information Systems, 1988
Biloxi Community College, Biloxi, MI

References available on request.

DATA ENTRY OPERATIONS

JOAN EBEKSON

442 Mt. Abernathy Court
Darby, PA 21123
(214) 555-9977

EDUCATION

Certificate in Data Entry Operations
Midfair Adult Continuing Education Division
Darby Community College District, 1992
(Certificate at 12,000 KPH)

Certificate in Desktop Publishing/Word Processing
Midfair Adult Continuing Education Division
Darby Community College District, 1991
(Certificate at 60 WPM)

OVERVIEW

Two years of increasingly responsible data entry experience testing at 12,000 keystrokes per hour. Mainframe computer experience. Seeking a permanent, full-time position during daytime hours as a data entry operator.

ABILITIES

Hardware:
- Operated mainframe computers.
- Entered data at tested 12,000 keystrokes per hour.
- Operated PC's for data tracking and word processing.
- Operated ten-key adding machine.

Software:
- Managed mailing lists using Microsoft Windows, WordPerfect, Paradox, Lotus 1-2-3, Excel, Lotus Freelance, PageMaker, dBase, and Microsoft Publisher.
- Keyboarded correspondence at 60 WPM using WordPerfect.
- Expedited numeric and clerical duties using spreadsheets.
- Entered and tracked orders using dBase.

EMPLOYMENT

June 1992–Present: Data Entry Operator, Mailing List Management, Inc., Darby, PA.

May 1991–June 1992: Order Entry Clerk, Greene Software Development Co., Inc., Darby, PA.

DESKTOP/ELECTRONIC PUBLISHING

VICTORIA PRESTON

6834 Linden Street
San Diego, CA 92115
(619) 555-1387 • Fax (619) 555-1383
vprest@myisp.com

– EDUCATION –

Associate in Applied Science
Desktop Publishing/Office Information Systems
Miramar College, San Diego, CA, 1992

Certificate in Commercial Art
San Diego City College, 1994

– OVERVIEW –

Four years of assignments as a desktop publisher with increasing responsibilities utilizing PC and Macintosh. Focus on electronic publishing text layout and graphics design of software manuals and training materials. Two years' experience using Imagesetter, Linotronic, and Selectset. Seeking a position as a desktop publisher designing text and graphics in the electronic publishing industry.

– SOFTWARE –

- Design text, graphics, slides, and multimedia presentations using CorelDraw!, MS Publisher, Lotus Freelance, PowerPoint, PageMaker, PhotoShop, and WordPerfect.
- Design multimedia presentation graphics using QuarkXPress, Adobe Illustrator, PhotoShop, and Freehand software on the Mac.
- Computer tracing from original art.
- Create color separations and slides.
- Convert WordPerfect for Windows text and graphics to Ventura Publisher or Aldus PageMaker text and graphics.

– HARDWARE –

- Macintosh and PCs; color or B & W scanners; color, laser, or inkjet printers.
- Operate Imagesetter. Knowledge of Linotronic and Selectset.

– EMPLOYMENT –

June 1994–Present: Desktop Publisher, Electra Software Manual Corporation, San Diego, CA.

August 1990–June 1994: Desktop Publisher, Courseware Textbooks, Inc., Miramar, CA.

References and portfolio on request.

DESKTOP VIDEO/ANIMATION/SPECIAL EFFECTS

Kyle A. Redding

909 Butterworth Drive, El Cajon, CA 92121 • (619) 555-7854 • Fax (619) 555-7811 • kredd@myisp.com

Job Overview

Corporate desktop video, animation, and special effects producer covering the computer industry seeks a multimedia creative position with an ad agency or video/multimedia production company utilizing computer graphics design. Six years' experience in creating special effects using Video Toaster and Genlock peripherals. Winner of 1993 Frank Award for best animation for cable TV commercials created on a personal computer. Experienced with video cameras and editing equipment.

Hardware

- PC and Macintosh
- Genlock peripherals
- JVL broadcast and industrial quality video cameras
- VHS video conversion
- Videotape editing using a variety of equipment

Corporate Animation Employment

1992–1994: Desktop Video Producer, Multimedia Infomercial and Animation Production Company, Inc., El Cajon, CA.

1991–1992: Desktop Animation Creative Director, Computer Productions (Ad Agency), El Cajon, CA.

1989–1991: Special Effects Designer/Producer, Barstow Video Productions, Inc., New Orleans, LA.

Professional Associations

- Computer Graphics SIGGRAPH of ACM
- International Society of Animators

Education

A.S., Computer Graphics Video
Grossmont College, El Cajon, CA, June 1994.

References and video portfolio on request.

DIGITAL SPECIAL EFFECTS/IMAGE MANIPULATION

Ariadne Abbot
7799 Cable Court • Los Angeles, CA 90028 • (213) 555-9734 • Fax (213) 555-9797

JOB TITLE: DIGITAL TECHNOLOGIES SPECIAL EFFECTS PRODUCTION

SPECIAL EFFECTS:
- Created cutting-edge computer and video technologies to create exotic visual effects.
- Produced own multimedia entertainment and education products for a variety of electronic media.
- Translated sounds and images into computer code to alter the way films, television programs, and advertisements are produced.
- Created next-generation video games, animated films, simulator rides, and computer software programs.
- Established an in-house digital special effects company at Interactive Television Corp. in Los Angeles.
- Created mechanical and animated characters for films.
- Developed a library of digital images.
- Marketed digital effects-based characters.
- Built an interactive animation system and other creative tools that enabled movie directors to directly manipulate the actions in an animated scene, saving the company $900,000 in creative expenses during 1993.
- Expanded computing operations into special effects to build alliances between the software and entertainment companies. Interactive Television Corp. and Smorth Inc. of Hollywood.
- Located cable TV partners for a variety of firms entering the interactive TV arena.
- Developed special effects image manipulation.

EXPERIENCE:
June 1992–October 1997:
Digital Special Effects and Image Manipulation Producer, Interactive Television Corporation, Los Angeles, CA.

EDUCATION: Master of Fine Arts, Animation and Special Effects
University of California, Los Angeles, CA, 1992
Bachelor of Science, Computer Science, Fine Arts Minor
University of California, Los Angeles, CA, 1985

References and portfolio on request.

DOCUMENT PRODUCTION MANAGEMENT

Thera Ellis

1756 West First St.
Rowe, IA 30206
(310) 555-0977
Fax (310) 555-0909

GOAL

Communications document production manager's position in an engineering consulting firm.

HIGHLIGHTS OF QUALIFICATIONS

— Knowledgeable in all phases of document production.
— Experienced in managing a staff of 20 reprographics personnel.
— Excellent word-processing, editing, and graphic design skills.
— Planned and scheduled production of proposals, reports, and studies in a time-sensitive, high-volume environment, using internal resources and outside services efficiently.
— Optimized use of hardware and software.
— Developed and maintained quality- and cost-control systems.
— Interfaced with corporate professionals at all levels in a variety of specialties.
— Managed cutting-edge document production technologies.
— Developed realistic budgets to control costs.

RELATED EXPERIENCE

1982–Present:
Crowe Engineering Consulting, Inc., Rowe, IA.
Fifteen years' experience, with increasing responsibilities, in document production positions with one firm. Successfully managed document production teams generating high-quality products under tight deadlines. Excellent communications skills.

EDUCATION AND SPECIALIZED TRAINING

Bachelor of Arts Degree,
Major in Creative Studies: English, with writing emphasis,
and graphic design/commercial art
Rowe Liberal Arts College
Rowe, IA, June 1982

References on request.

DRAFTING/MEDICAL (COMPUTER AIDED)

Mai Ling Chan
410 Newton Street
Washington, DC 30206
(202) 555-0977
maich@myisp.com

OVERVIEW
CADD project manager and senior medical designer/draftswoman with five years' medical design and OSHPD procedure experience seeks immediate opening using knowledge of computer-aided drafting.

QUALIFICATIONS

* Knowledgeable in all phases of computer-aided drafting.
* Utilized virtual reality computer technology to draft and design 3-D medical simulations.
* Experienced in drafting building drawings, construction, drainage, street improvement, site development plans.
* Use intergraph, PC, pencil, ink, Leroy pins, and templates.
* AutoCAD software experience and graphic design skills as an AutoCAD drafter in medical and engineering model simulation for Medical Drafting Specialists, Washington, DC.
* Planned and scheduled production of blueprints, designs, and drawings in a time-sensitive, high-volume environment, using internal resources and outside services efficiently for medical, architectural, and engineering drafting projects.
* Developed and maintained quality- and cost-control systems and computed realistic budgets.
* Interfaced with corporate professionals at all levels.

RELATED EXPERIENCE
1991–Present:
Senior Medical Designer/Drafter, Medical Drafting Specialists, Inc.,
Washington, DC

Six years' experience in progressively responsible medical and engineering drafting/design projects with one firm. Successfully used AutoCAD software to draft and design high-quality blueprints and designs under tight deadline pressure. Excellent communications skills. Successfully trained staff in OSHPD procedure while working on medical drafting projects.
Naturalized U.S. citizen from Taiwan.

EDUCATION
Associate in Science Degree,
Architectural Computer-Aided Design and Drafting
Taiwan Junior College, Taiwan, 1990

REFERENCES ON REQUEST.

DRAFTING/ENGINEERING (COMPUTER AIDED)

James B. Marstoni
918 Bard Street
Buffalo, NY 02122
(716) 555-0977
Fax (716) 555-0922

FOCUS
Systems engineering drafter specializing in production and development of instrumentation systems drawings, designs, and blueprints seeks a position as an intermediate drafter.

OVERVIEW
Seven years' experience using computers to create and modify engineering drawings according to military and government standards. Experience in drafting TACTS/ACMI range instrumentation systems for an instrumentation production firm.

QUALIFICATIONS
- Knowledgeable in all phases of computer-aided drafting, including CADDS 4X and AutoCAD software. Familiar with wireframes and E/M assemblies. Strong CADKEY skills.
- Created and modified engineering drawings in compliance with IAW MIL-STDs.
- Generated and incorporated engineering change orders.
- Seven years' electro/mechanical drafting experience.
- Experienced in MiniCad software.
- Knowledge of engineering terminology.
- Knowledge of government military standards (MIL-STDs), military specifications, and basic math.
- Ability to read and understand engineering drawings, sketches, schematics, blueprints.
- Skilled with scanning equipment.

RELATED EXPERIENCE
1990–Present:
Intermediate Drafter, Instrumentation Systems, Inc., Buffalo, NY.

EDUCATION
A.S., Drafting
Buffalo Community College, 1990

REFERENCES ON REQUEST.

FASHION DESIGN/SOFTWARE

Fasulya Zakia Hanny

171 Lyon Street
New York, NY 10122
(212) 555-0977 • Fax (212) 555-2931
fhann@myisp.com

OVERVIEW

Consumer production fashion and textile designer/software stylist seeks a senior designer's position. Experienced in developing lines for home furnishings and gifts apparel industry. Fashion design utilizing computer software includes heavy experience designing infant to preteen clothing for child clothing manufacturer. Experienced in computer grading and production.

EXPERIENCE

Eight years' experience using computers to create and modify children's clothing and textiles. Developed 11 lines for home furnishings, six lines for gifts apparel, and 20 lines for individual infant to preteen clothing for one children's clothing manufacturer. Extensive computer experience for designing, styling, grading, and production tracking.

ABILITIES

- Knowledgeable in all phases of fashion design and styling software.
- Utilized and modified grading and production software.
- Generated and incorporated design change orders.
- Five years' experience designing and styling home furnishings and textiles.
- Three years' children's clothing design experience.
- Knowledge of garment industry terminology.
- Knowledge of grading and production standards.
- Designing patterns with software.
- Sewing samples from sketches.

RELATED EMPLOYMENT

1989–Present:
Designer/Stylist, Gregory Garment and Home Furnishing Design Industries, Inc., New York, NY.

EDUCATION

A.S., Fashion Design
Fashion Institute of Technology
New York, New York, 1989

References available upon request.

INFORMATION SERVICES/SYSTEMS ANALYSIS

Jim Thompson
1900 Glendale Drive
Brooklyn, NY 11230
(718) 555-9087

OVERVIEW: Professional systems analyst in the health care industry seeks position interacting with all levels of personnel.

PROGRAMMING LANGUAGES: COBOL, ASSM.

SOFTWARE/HARDWARE SYSTEMS ANALYSIS EXPERIENCE:

- Seven years' experience in two multi-institutional health care systems consulting firms performing the following applications using superior analytical and project management skills:
  - Modified and upgraded installed systems.
  - Adhered to QA and systems management control disciplines.
  - Managed internal/external resources, work products, and project time schedules.
  - Oversaw application design, development, and maintenance in compliance with IS standards.
  - Performed application coding and system tailoring.
  - Maintained and administered databases.
  - Informed users on the status of enhancements, releases, and alternate solutions.
  - Conducted project meetings.
  - Maintained complete documentation of project materials.
  - Developed, implemented, and maintained applications.
  - Analyzed systems. Programmed computers.
  - Structured and implemented systems designs.

EMPLOYMENT:
August 1991–Present:
Information Services Systems Analyst, Berg Healthcare Services, Flushing, NY.
June 1989–August 1991:
Information Services Systems Analyst, Sands Hospital Systems, Brooklyn, NY.

EDUCATION: Master of Science
Computer Science and Systems Analysis
Brooklyn College, Brooklyn, NY, 1989

References on request.

INTERACTIVE DESIGN

Skye Owis
PO Box 4333   San Diego, CA 92164   (619) 555-3087

OVERVIEW: Independent interactive multimedia computer game, entertainment, instructional designer working in the following platforms: CD-ROM, CD-I, 3DO, interactive broadcast television production and development, interactive feature film production, videodisc players scriptwriting and design, and writing instructional material for interactive multimedia learning as entertainment materials. Computer game designs emphasize learning values.

CREATIVE EXPERIENCE:
- Wrote documentary films for training.
- Wrote instructional plan book known as a bible for three feature films and animation.
- Wrote interactive multimedia mystery novel series.
- Designed interface and whole package with interlocking branches of several suspense novels turned into interactive multimedia computer games.
- Wrote comic books and animation series.
- Hired and trained coauthors to write scripts for computer game companies.
- Wrote character-driven stories and scripts for computer games, three-dimensional optical technologies, and new interactive broadcast television productions
- Developed interactive designs and scripts for videodisc players using new interactive language flow charts and 3-D thinking strategies.
- Wrote and designed books and stories for CD-ROM.

EMPLOYMENT:
June 1993–Present:
    Independent Computer Game Designer/Writer,
    Three Dimensional Optical Animation and Multimedia, Inc.,
    San Diego, CA.
January 1983–June 1993:
    Cartridge computer game designer and scriptwriter,
    Learning As Entertainment Corporation,
    San Diego, CA.

EDUCATION:
    Master of Arts degree,
    English (creative writing emphasis),
    San Diego State University
    San Diego, CA, December 1982

REFERENCES AND PORTFOLIO ON REQUEST.

INTERACTIVE FICTION WRITING

Anne Antonis

1756 First Weston Drive
Edmonton, Alberta, Canada T6K 4C6
(403) 555-8764 • Fax (403) 555-8709
aanton@myisp.com

OVERVIEW:

Novelist/Scriptwriter seeks staff or freelance position as a computer interactive multimedia fiction writer for a software manufacturer. Telecommuting preferred.

FICTION WRITING EXPERIENCE:

1992–Present: *Magazine of Ancient Historical Fiction*:
Author of 12 short stories on CD-ROM and CD-I laser disc.

1990–1992:   Interactive computer game script, *The Adventures of Dr. Chuan*, and seven science fiction suspense novels.
Thorndine & Co., Inc. Publishing, New York, NY.
Each project sold over 60,000 copies annually since 1990.

1985–1990:   Two novels: *Time Traveling Buccaneers* and *Bellydancer-Nun-Psychiatrist*,
Science Fiction Suspense Press, Inc.
Toronto, Canada, 1986, 1987

SOFTWARE EXPERIENCE:

Wrote book on applications software uses for home-based business owners, published by Ole & Lane, NY, 1985.

Wrote video script training teachers in the operation of the Eric computer system for educational research, Edmonton Education Department, Media Center, 1978.

EDUCATION:

M.A., English (Scriptwriting Emphasis),
University of Alberta, Edmonton, December 1979

B.S., English Education
University of Alberta, Edmonton, October 1974

LIST OF ADDITIONAL PUBLISHED WORKS ATTACHED

REFERENCES ON REQUEST

INTERACTIVE RESUME WRITING

TSIPKE SURA MERIMDERSKI

10 Echo Dr. • San Leandro, CA 92124
(619) 555-1234
tsipkemerimderxxx.com

OBJECTIVE: To obtain a position as a computer graphic artist/multimedia technician in which I may utilize my talents in writing/designing interactive resumes and Webmaster portfolios for the Web.

WEB FORMATTING SKILLS: My previous position provided extensive experience on various PC systems and use of my organizational and people skills to coordinate more than 20 field personnel. While a student at Multimedia College I prepared a news layout utilizing QuarkXPress and Adobe Illustrator, a 60-second commercial using Adobe Premiere, various pieces of artwork using Adobe Photoshop and 323 interactive resumes using Director for clients of a resume writing company where I worked part time.

OVERVIEW: I write a monthly article for an instructional newsletter about interactive resume writing. I have published a short story; perform volunteer work with the Poway Performing Arts Company; consulted on interior design projects; serve as Vice President of the Board of Directors at my synagogue; chair the Sanctuary Remodeling Committee; and sing with the 1910 Wolskowisk Klezmer choir and the San Diego Civic Chorale.

EDUCATION:

Multimedia College	Multimedia Technology Certificate	1997
San Leandro State Univ.	Adult Education Teaching Credential	1995
San Leandro State Univ.	BA – Creative Writing	1978

EXPERIENCE:

Real Estate Trusts Corp.   1991–present
Position: Executive Secretary. Responsibilities include complete secretarial and administrative duties. Position supports Chief Operating Officer. Extensive work on numerous PC systems required. Coordinate travel plans and meeting facilities for management conferences. Interface with facilities management to maintain office and environment in a professional manner. Prepare and maintain monthly and quarterly incentive reports for 61 account executives and regional managers.

Canadian National Mortgage Company   1989–1991
Position: Audit Administrator/Funder. Closed and funded residential loans in accordance with FHLMC guidelines. Developed and maintained post-funding audit procedures. Worked closely with department heads in setting up office files, systems, and procedures for a new Vancouver office. Established contact with media and formulated advertising campaign.

SUMMARY: I am a self-initiator, detail oriented and motivated to see projects on which I work completed as thoroughly and professionally as possible. I have excellent verbal and written communication skills and I am a skilled project manager. I write interactive resumes for the World Wide Web for secondary income. I am computer literate on both Mac and PC systems and enjoy working alone. I am willing to telecommute or work at a telecenter, meeting new challenges. I welcome the opportunity to expand my interactive resume writing skills by working for a human resource corporation.

Anna Kutkowski

29 Vera Place
San Diego, CA 92111
(619) 555-1237
annakutkowski@palm.org

INTERNET/INTRANET PRODUCTS GROUP SOFTWARE ENGINEER
Seeking environment with extensive phones.

EXPERIENCE:

1994–1996   RENARD CO., San Diego
Information management in library automation.

Developed products for the Internet in a UNIX Sun Solaris environment using HTML, CGI, JAVA, C language, 4GL development tools.

Interfaced to RDBMs, WWW developing for client/server environments.

Two years' direct experience with Internet security issues.

Two years' experience with Oracle and full-text retrieval engines.

Supported database applications for a computer library automation corporation.

Troubleshooting expertise strong in Windows, DOS, Novell, database maintenance.

Extensive telecommunications experience.

EDUCATION:

B.S. Computer Information Systems, San Diego State University, 1994

Courses in Network Administration, 1996, at Network Institute, San Diego, focusing on network and system administration. Trained in techniques of maintaining and upgrading heterogeneous network environments. Knowledge of BSCS with Routers, Hubs, Gateways, Modems, CSU/DSU, multipole UNIX and Windows operating systems and Internet/intranet.

ADDITIONAL COMPUTER APPLICATIONS EXPERIENCE:

Specialize in convergence of technologies applications with heavy experience in embedded micro, GPS, cell and RF technology, Windows and DOS applications.

Knowledge also of the following software and systems: Unix Administrator, Visual Basic, Visual C++, MS Access, Windows NT Administrator, Novell 3x, 4x, Windows, HelpDes/Tech Support HW/PC Support, C language.

References on request.

MARKETING COMMUNICATIONS/COMPUTER PRESENTATION GRAPHICS

Michael Levine
33 Bright Boulevard
Far Rockaway, NY
(718) 555-7375 • Fax (718) 555-7340
mlevi@myisp.com

GOAL
Marketing communications coordinator specializing in computer presentation graphics seeks a position with a leading document imaging company.

OVERVIEW
Five years' marketing experience as a communications coordinator in a high-tech industry specializing in computer presentation graphics and document imaging. Excellent communication and organizational skills. Computer literate with PC hardware and applications software. Self-motivated. Three years' experience as a marketing proposal writer and representative for a hand-held computer products corporation. Specialized in trade show planning, sales demonstrations, and advertising.

ACHIEVEMENTS
- Coordinated collateral development and trade show participation.
- Developed corporate presentations.
- Maintained press relations.
- Disseminated all marketing communications and computer presentation graphics imaging.
- Wrote marketing proposals.
- Acted as manufacturer's representative.
- Planned trade shows and demonstrated equipment on sites.
- Supported manufacturer's representatives in VAR and OEM sales networks.

EMPLOYMENT
1990–Present: Marketing Communications Coordinator and Computer Graphics Presentations Software Publicist
Document Imaging, Inc., New York, NY.

1988–1990: Marketing Representative and Proposal Writer
Systems Corporation, New York, NY.

EDUCATION
B.A., Communications, marketing minor,
New York University, NY, 1988

References on request.

MARKETING MANAGEMENT

Xandra Tyler
899 Brink Blvd. • Newport Beach • CA 90023
(714) 555-0998

OVERVIEW
Four years of experience as a computer sales and marketing manager. In-depth exposure to business and financial software. One year in customer and territory development; two years in personnel recruitment and training; and one year in office management, budgeting, and advertising. Strong sales, problem-solving, coordinating, organizing, planning, and verbal communications skills.

DIRECT SALES EXPERIENCE
° Trained sales staff in cold calling, canvassing, telemarketing, and retail sales of personal computers.
° Surpassed sales quotas in first six months of employment.
° Won four saleswoman-of-the-month awards, one for each year worked.
° Recruited, hired, and trained computer sales force.
° Designed forecasts, budgets, and expense controls.
° Wrote marketing brochures and direct marketing letters.
° Coordinated and worked end user/dealer trade shows.
° Improved customer service, tripling gross annual sales during first year of employment.

PRODUCT DEVELOPMENT
° Developed new product line, including system definition, pricing, and implementation plans.
° Budgeted vertical products within specific time frameworks.
° Organized and trained sales staff in computer sales and marketing strategies.
° Gave four national annual computer graphics presentations to executives, dealers, and sales staff, utilizing public speaking skills.
° Monitored the performance of a national sales staff through field trips throughout the United States, China, Japan, and Malaysia. Traveled 60 percent of the time.

EMPLOYMENT
June 1989–Present:
Marketing and Sales Manager, Cost Effective Computers, Inc.,
Newport Beach, CA.

EDUCATION
Bachelor of Science Degree, Marketing
California State University, Irvine, CA, 1989

References available upon request.

Robert B. Dyne
898 Warsaw St.
Goldsboro, NC 25730
(919) 555-0975

JOB OBJECTIVE
Registered medical records technician (A.R.T.) with degree and certification seeks a position as a medical records software manufacturer's representative presenting medical records software to hospitals. Willing to travel nationally.

OVERVIEW
One year of experience using medical records technology software for coding and records administration in the medical records department of a large, general hospital.

QUALIFICATIONS
Accredited Medical Records Technician (A.R.T). Knowledge of coding of diseases, retrieval, preparation for legal procedures with medical records, tumor registry, insurance coding, medical terminology, physiology and anatomy, medical records software, records management, databases, spreadsheets, statistical typing, word processing with WordPerfect, and medical transcription.

RELATED EXPERIENCE
1993–Present: Medical Records Technician, St. Michael's Hospital, Goldsboro, NC.
1980–1993: Medical Transcriptionist, St. Michael's Hospital, Goldsboro, NC.

EDUCATION AND SPECIALIZED TRAINING
Associate in Science Degree, Medical Records Technology
Goldsboro Community College, Goldsboro, NC, 1993
A.R.T. Certification, 1993

Certificate in Medical Transcription
Goldsboro Community College, Goldsboro, NC, 1980

REFERENCES ON REQUEST

Tatiana Kutkowsky

2616 Clareina Blvd. / La Jolla, CA 92037 / (619) 555-1419

JOB OVERVIEW

Certified Medical Transcriptionist seeks a position with a health care systems company, medical office, or hospital using radiology medical terminology. Prefer to telecommute.

SOFTWARE

WordPerfect, Microsoft Word, dBase, Lotus 1-2-3, and medical transcription software, including medical terminology spelling and grammar checking software dictionaries on PC or Macintosh.

MEDICAL TRANSCRIPTION EXPERIENCE

October 1988–1993
Radiologic Surgery Clinic, La Jolla, CA

RESPONSIBILITIES

- Used medical transcription software on an IBM computer to accurately transcribe medical treatment and procedures from recordings on magnetic tape cassettes.
- Utilized practical knowledge of medical terminology, anatomy, physiology, internal organization of medical reports, medical report standards and requirements, and the medicolegal significance of medical transcripts.
- Transcribed medical histories, physicals, consultations, operative reports, discharge summaries, referral letters, and documentation in radiology subspecialties.
- Typed 90 words per minute (on a PC) with no errors from the spoken word. (Recent certificate attached.) Excellent auditory skills.
- Proofread and edited for accuracy of medical records.
- Used a variety of equipment to transcribe in many different types of medical settings, including hospitals and offices.

EDUCATION

Certificate in Medical Transcription and Medical Office Administration (one-year program)
Mesa Community College
San Diego, CA, 1988

References on request.

Rabina Diades
9880 Serendipity Road
Seattle, WA 95023
(206) 555-0498 • Fax (206) 555-0444
rdiad@myisp.com

OVERVIEW

Four years of experience as a midi synthesizer music composer, multimedia desktop publisher and video producer specializing in color separations and computer presentation graphics. Seeking a position as a multimedia designer/producer using graphics, music, video, and text.

ABILITIES

* Improved customer service, increasing gross annual sales during first year of employment by $850,000.
* Utilized DigitalMedia Studio desktop video publishing system combining hardware and software to provide 24-bit, full screen, full motion, 30-frame-per-second digital editing and production for the Macintosh.
* Utilized desktop publishing software for color separation.
* Designed multimedia shows using midi synthesizer music, Roland synthesizers, and PC animation programs for technical trade show presentation graphics.
* Produced multimedia videos for electronics trade shows.
* Composed background music for courseware design in multimedia training productions for computer trade shows.
* Designed multimedia budgets, forecasts, and expense controls to meet production/promotion requirements.
* Coordinated and worked end user/dealer trade shows.

PRODUCT DEVELOPMENT

* Developed new video product line, including multimedia system definition, pricing, and implementation plans.
* Budgeted vertical products within specific time frameworks.

EMPLOYMENT
June 1989–Present: Multimedia Producer/Designer, Multimedia Presentation Graphics, Inc., Seattle, WA.

EDUCATION

B.S., Computerized Music Composition
University of Washington, Seattle, 1993

A.S., Desktop Publishing/Desktop Video
Seattle Community College, 1989

References on request.

Jan Ronald Wagner

P.O. Box 8976
6134 Via Canada Del Osito
Rancho Santa Fe, CA 92067-8976
Phone/Fax: (619) 756-0953   Pager: (619) 531-6924
wagnerjr@adnc.com

The Multimedia 500

(Please ask for a disk of this game, which is my interactive resume.)

Objective

To obtain a creative position in a multimedia environment that utilizes my computer and business background, as well as my extensive experience as a television producer and writer.

Summary

Creative, multitalented media professional and businessman, with more than 10 years experience in writing and producing for television. *Key strengths* include:
- a thorough understanding of customer objectives, including customer service.
- a proven ability to consistently deliver projects on time and within budget.
- fosters an atmosphere that invites creative input from the entire production team.
- a quick study who is conscientious, organized, and detail-oriented.
- possesses a working knowledge of Photoshop, Director, QuarkXPress, Illustrator, Premiere, Sound Edit 16, Word, WordPerfect, IST business software, PageMill & the Internet.
- cross platform computer experience (Macintosh, Windows, and Unix).
- more than 3 years as owner and operator of a parts supply business.

Employment Highlights

Mobile Electric Supply, San Diego, CA	Owner & operator	1992–96
KUSI TV, San Diego, CA	Television Writer/Producer	1991–92
S.D. County Office of Education, S.D., CA	TV Writer/Producer/Director/Editor	1986–87
Western Video & Film, San Diego, CA	TV Writer/Producer/Director	1985–86
The Brick, San Diego, CA & Alberta, Canada	Broadcast Advertising Manager	1984–85
Allarcom Ltd., Edmonton, Alberta, Canada	TV Writer/Producer	1980–84
CFCN TV, Lethbridge, Alberta, Canada	TV Writer/Producer	1979–80

Education

Foundation College, San Diego, CA   1996
    Multimedia Technology Certificate (cumulative Grade Point Average – 4.0)
    Web Page Design Certificate

San Diego State University, San Diego, CA   1991
    Completed coursework for Masters in Television Production

Southern Alberta Institute of Technology, Calgary, Alberta, Canada   1979
    Honors Diploma – Television, Stage & Radio Arts (TV Writing & Production)
    • awarded 2 scholarships for high achievement

University of Calgary, Calgary, Alberta, Canada   1977
    Bachelor of Arts Degree – History Major

Television production demo tape, portfolio, and interactive resume available upon request.

NETWORK SYSTEMS ENGINEERING

Kendall Kewn
996 Bedford Hwy.
Atlanta, GA 25730
(819) 555-0125

OVERVIEW
Certified Novell Network Engineer in Novell Network services seeks a position as a network systems engineer designing, implementing, installing, troubleshooting, maintaining, and modifying local area networks. Knowledge of network services.

EXPERIENCE
Two years' experience using Novell Netware, 3-Com networks, D-Link peer-to-peer networks, Artisoft LANtastic networks, TCP/IP, Unix, and Apple etal network. Support Netware Lite and LANtastic networks. LAN-to-LAN and home-to-LAN with modem systems installed and supported in a variety of locations.

QUALIFICATIONS
° Design, install, maintain, troubleshoot, and repair computer systems and peripherals.
° Supervise in the process of configuration, assembly, and testing of computer systems.
° Provide training for technicians and field service personnel.
° Assist in sales presentations.
° Evaluate new products.
° Design circuits.
° Provide customized hardware and software solutions to fit customer's requirements.
° Familiar with many bus technologies, network topologies, and protocols.
° Six years' experience maintaining telephone equipment and devices.

RELATED EMPLOYMENT
<u>1991–Present:</u>   Network Systems Engineer
Greystone LAN Corporation, Atlanta, GA.
<u>1985–1991:</u>   Network Systems Engineer and Systems Analyst,
Nevada Bell Telephone Company, Reno, NV.

EDUCATION
B.S., Computer Science and Electronics
University of Georgia, Atlanta, GA, 1985

References available upon request.

Victoria Tiffany Meghan

56 First Avenue
Boise, Idaho 80776
(208) 555-1589 • Fax (208) 555-1221
vtimeg@myisp.com

OVERVIEW

Neural networks and fuzzy logic heuristics specialist in biology seeks a research associate or assistant position linking computer programming skills with pharmacology, where both programming skills and biological sciences degree will be utilized.

ABILITIES
* Background in both biology and mathematics.
* Experience in and knowledge of computer programming.
* Interested in animal models to study the disposition of anticancer therapeutics.
* Experience with cell culture related to computing.
* Experience with the use of radioactive materials.
* Knowledge of neural networks applied from biological sciences to computer science and fuzzy logic.

EXPERIENCE
One year of experience as a research assistant in molecular genetics and yeast biology. Knowledge of recombinant DNA techniques, growth maintenance, DNA transfer, and identification of recombinants.
Computer programming with mathematical models using neural network and fuzzy logic principles to apply biological research. Focus on animal models and computing.

EMPLOYMENT
1992–Present:
Research Assistant, General Networks Corporation, Boise, Idaho.
1987–1992:
Computer Programmer, Genetic Engineering Corporation, Boise, Idaho.

EDUCATION
Bachelor of Science with special major in Biology and Mathematics
(minor in Computer Science)
University of Idaho, Boise, ID, 1992

References on request.

Robert Dalle
26 Reina Blvd. • El Cajon, CA 92121 • (619) 555-1889

OVERVIEW
Computer numeric control (CNC) technician in computer industrial technology seeks a position in computerized manufacturing, specializing in robotics technology.

ABILITIES
- CNC machine operator able to program computers to manufacture parts.
- Computer programmer.
- Drafter.
- Basic mathematics and physics knowledge.
- Developed computer-aided manufacturing software.
- Obtained maximum productivity from machines.

EXPERIENCE
One year of experience as a computer numeric control operator for one of the world's largest manufacturers of arc welding products and robots and a major producer of electric motors and thermal cutting equipment. Realized maximum potential of computerized equipment by training technicians in CNC operation. One year of prior experience as a computer programmer and machinist for same firm.

EMPLOYMENT

1993–Present: **CNC Operator and Robotics Technician**
Sands Electric Motor Company, El Cajon, CA.

1991–1993: **Computer Programmer and Machinist**
Sands Electric Motor Company, El Cajon, CA.

EDUCATION
Associate in Science
Computer-Aided Manufacturing Technology
Center for Applied Competitive Technologies
San Diego City College
San Diego, CA, 1991

Associate in Science
Computer Science and Information Systems
San Diego City College
San Diego, CA, 1989

References upon request.

PERSONNEL MANAGEMENT

ESTHER SANCHEZ
9998 Sweetwater Blvd.
Chicago, IL 60636
(312) 555-9575
esanch@myisp.com

OVERVIEW Human resource manager seeks a personnel management position in a sophisticated, fast-paced electronic technology environment.

RELATED EXPERIENCE Five years' experience in human resources in a high-volume manufacturing environment with two years in a supervisory position. Fluent in English and Spanish. Previous personal computer experience includes numerous spreadsheet and word-processing packages. Former trainer in industrial psychology.

RESPONSIBILITIES Managed the human resources department, which included the following responsibilities:
— Recruitment.
— Salary and benefits administration.
— Training and development.
— Employee services.
— Recognition and safety program management.

EMPLOYMENT

1989–Present: **Personnel and Human Resources Manager**
Computercorps, Inc., Chicago, IL

1986–1989: **Bilingual (English/Spanish) Trainer in Industrial Psychology**
Computer College, San Juan, Puerto Rico

1980–1986: **Bilingual Personnel Clerk**
Personnel Department
University of Chicago Medical Center, Chicago, IL

EDUCATION B.A., Industrial Relations Psychology/Personnel Management
University of Chicago
Chicago, IL, 1980

REFERENCES ON REQUEST

Mereet deCordoba

111 Lemon Drive • Key West, FL 30398 • (305) 555-9589 • mdecord@myisp.com

OVERVIEW

Diverse programmer and hardware/software systems administrator seeks a position with a product or service-based corporation.

SOFTWARE/HARDWARE

Knowledge of PCs, Lantastic, Novell, dBaseIV+, C, EDI, DOS, and Unix. FoxPro/Windows multiuser. FoxBASE/Macintosh multiuser. SQL and Windows software.

ABILITIES

- Program.
- Manage all systems.
- Train users.
- Maintain and repair equipment.
- Write software user manuals.
- Team player.

EXPERIENCE

FoxPro Windows: Three years' experience programming FoxPro multiuser. Three years' experience programming with SQL and Windows software. Unix: Three years' experience supporting PC-based Unix with strong customer service skills. Two years' experience with FoxBASE Macintosh computer programming. Two years' experience programming with FoxBASE multiuser. Two years' experience in technical writing: software user manuals.

EMPLOYMENT

1992–Present: **Computer Programmer and Systems Administrator**
Control Inc., Key West, FL

1989–1992: **Computer Programmer and Technical Writer**
Hawley Computers, Inc., Key West, FL

EDUCATION

Bachelor of Science Degree
Computer Science/Programming
University of Miami, Miami, FL 1989
Certificate in Technical Writing, 1987

QUALITY/REGULATORY ASSURANCE

JAMES VINCENTE

890 Foxgrove Lane
Philadelphia, PA 17898
(215) 555-8764

JOB OVERVIEW: Seeking a position as director of quality and regulatory affairs. Twenty-four years' experience in regulatory compliance overseeing strategic regulatory affairs quality control. Reported directly to the CEO in one of the nation's largest electronics firms.

EXPERIENCE:

1989–Present: **Director, Quality and Regulatory Affairs**
Quality and Configuration Manager: Managed Class II critical devices and supporting disposables. In-depth understanding of and experience with current GMPs, SMDA of 1990, and 510 (k) submissions, including DMR and DHR content/management. Configured software.

1983–1989: **Senior Manager in Medical Device Quality Control**
Managed complex, software-driven, electromechanical products.

1973–1983: **Quality Control Technician**
Quality inspector of hearing aids. Electronic circuit knowledge. Hands-on soldering, troubleshooting, and problem solving.

EMPLOYMENT:

1989–Present: **Director, Quality and Regulatory Affairs**
Infusion Med-Instruments, Inc., Philadelphia, PA.

1983–1989: **Senior Manager, Medical Device Quality Control**
Star Medical Instruments, Inc., Philadelphia, PA.

1973–1983: **Quality Control Technician**
Serendipity Hearing Aids, Inc., Philadelphia, PA.

EDUCATION: Associate in Sciences Degree, Quality Control and Assurance
Philadelphia Technical College, Philadelphia, PA, 1973

References upon request.

ROBOTICS TECHNOLOGY

MARTIN MOSS
23 Bloomfield Street
Dearborn, MI 48128
(313) 555-3899 • Fax (313) 555-1234
mmoss@myisp.com

OVERVIEW

Robotics technician position wanted installing, troubleshooting, and repairing robots. Specialist in robot applications and maintenance.

EMPLOYMENT
1984–1993

<u>AUTOMATED COMPUTERS, INC.</u>, Dearborn, Michigan
Robot Repair Technician
Installed, diagnosed, maintained, and repaired robots and robotic systems in factories where robots lift heavy loads.
- Interfaced with welding engineers and industrial designers to troubleshoot and solve problems.
- Utilized robotics software systems to operate, control, and repair robots.
- Diagnosed computer problems for builders and users of robots.
- Trained electricians and mechanics to repair robots on-site in factories.
- Repaired robot-related automated factory equipment and computers used to control robots.
- Repaired defense robots used by the military.

1980–1984

<u>U.S. NAVY</u>   Stationed at Long Beach, CA
Underwater Robotics Technician
- Maintained, diagnosed, and repaired underwater robots while serving in the Navy. Trained in the Navy's extensive underwater robotics programs.

EDUCATION

Bachelor of Science Degree
Robotics and Manufacturing Technology
Northrup University
Los Angeles, CA 1984

Associate in Sciences Degree
Industrial Technology
Henry Ford Community College
Dearborn, MI 1980

MEMBERSHIP

Robotics International of the Society of Manufacturing Engineers, Dearborn, MI.

The Robotics Institute, Pittsburgh, PA.

REFERENCES ON REQUEST.

JEANNE D'ARCY
561 Orange Avenue
Nashville, TN 45138
(615) 555-9589 • Fax (615) 555-9221

CAREER GOAL

Field sales representative seeks an assigned territory selling hardware and software multimedia products for the personal computer.

ACHIEVEMENTS

- Marketed professional development seminars to dealers that resulted in a 50 percent increase in sales.
- Designed new market penetration and sales to computer manufacturing industry, thereby securing an agreement for the largest dollar volume contract in present company's history.
- 250 percent of sales quota 1992
- 175 percent of sales quota in 1991
- 188 percent of sales quota in 1990
- Established tenth company office, expanding business beyond tenth year projections by 260 percent.
- Obtained the first marketing program with Fortune 500 companies, generating a 75 percent increase in new revenue base.
- Created and implemented multimedia market by establishing relationships with major chain reseller stores.
- Provided information interface between company and customers.
- Attended user group meetings and industry events.
- Directed sales of personal computers and peripheral products.

EMPLOYMENT

1984–Present: Field Sales Representative
Multimedia Marketing, Inc.
Nashville, TN

1980–1984: Sales Manager
Computer Events, Inc.
Nashville, TN.

1975–1980: Field Sales Representative,
Marketshare Corp.,
Baton Rouge, LA.

EDUCATION

Bachelor of Business Administration Degree
Marketing Management
University of Tennessee
Nashville, TN, June 1975

REFERENCES ON REQUEST

June Langst

60 Elmwood Place
Rockville, MD 20854
(301) 555-8960 Fax (301) 555-2213
jlang@myisp.com

JOB OBJECTIVE:

To find a challenging scientific programming position that utilizes my master's degree in mathematics.

EXPERIENCE:

Computer security analyst with 20 years' experience in computer research toward developing better security systems. Expertise in scientific computer programming and mathematical analysis. Specialist in designing mathematical models for security problem interpretation and solution. Knowledge of operations research and development.

SOFTWARE:

FORTRAN, PL/1, C, C++, Assembly, Pascal.
Lisp, DEC. Neural Networks, Fuzzy Logic, Artificial Intelligence applications software, heuristics.

HARDWARE:

Cray Supercomputers and PCs.
VAX-11/750 and above, PDP, DGM600, CDC, MODCOMP.

ACCOMPLISHMENTS:

* Created a study resulting in higher assurance of computer security.
* Designed a relational database to analyze classified military security computer operating system requirements using operations research statistical techniques.
* Developed mathematical models specializing in research development.
* Presented statistical breakdowns for survey questionnaire.

EMPLOYMENT:

    1977–Present: **Security Analyst Programmer**,
                           Data Security Dynamics, Inc.,
                           Rockville, MD

EDUCATION:

Master of Science Degree in Mathematics
Johns Hopkins University, Baltimore, MD, 1977

Bachelor of Science Degree in Mathematics
Johns Hopkins University, Baltimore, MD, 1975

References available upon request.

SOFTWARE ENGINEERING

BARRY MINTON
8990 Santa Cruz Blvd.
Santa Cruz, CA 95143
(408) 555-9889
bmint@myisp.com

OVERVIEW: Software engineer experienced in system definition seeks a challenging opportunity to utilize applications development, data communications, graphics, relational databases, and systems engineering in project management.

ACHIEVEMENTS:
* Prepared detailed technical documentation.
* Made oral presentations to customers and company management.
* Developed software within DOD and commercial environments.
* Designed software.
* Implemented, tested, documented, and integrated COTS/GOTS.

SOFTWARE: Unix, C language, Unix workstations, Program Design Language (PDL), GUI. Macintosh software: Think C, MPW, MacApp, Tool Box, and CodeWarrior.

HARDWARE: PC and Macintosh.

ANALYSIS AND DESIGN:
Structured analysis and design utilizing RDBMS (e.g., Sybase), CASE tools, and DOD-Std-2167A.

SECURITY CLEARANCE:
Top Secret. Eligible for access to classified information.

EXPERIENCE: Seven years' experience in a commercial environment. Experience in all areas of development (functional specifications, design, program specifications, programming, and testing).

EMPLOYMENT: 1990–Present: Software Engineer,
Government Software Engineering, Inc., Cambria, CA.

EDUCATION: Bachelor of Science Degree
Computer Science
University of California, Santa Cruz, CA, 1990

REFERENCES: On request

SOFTWARE TALENT AGENTING

Marcia Destinee Whisper
1744 Bright Blvd., Eugene, OR 98254
(503) 555-9432 • Fax (503) 555-9221
mwhis@myisp.com

CAREER GOAL   SOFTWARE TALENT AGENT STAFF POSITION

SOFTWARE EXPERIENCE

- **Wrote book on software talent agenting** for public relations agency owners, published by West & West, Marketing Promotions Press, London, England, 1990.
- **Weekly national newspaper columnist** for *The Talent Agent's News* (for owners of software talent agencies).

SOFTWARE AGENTING EXPERIENCE

- 1987–Present: Account Executive, Dynamic Software Talent Agency Inc., Eugene, OR.

Ten years' experience operating a software talent agency for absentee owner with over 150 clients. Specialist in marketing and promoting patented and copyrighted software for independent software designers, manufacturers, and consultants.

ABILITIES

- Find software designers for leading manufacturers.
- Package software created by independent contractors.
- Recruit software talent for software firms.
- Copyright and patent software for designers.
- Refer software designers and engineers to jobs.
- Consult and counsel software talent seeking markets.
- Create promotions, publicity, ad campaigns, marketing programs, and press kits for software designers, writers, artists, or manufacturers.
- Train software designers in packaging, distributing, marketing, and selling their software.
- Track software audiences for market research.
- Research software markets and create mailing lists.
- Locate publishers and producers for software writers, multimedia or video artists, and software designers.

EDUCATION

Master of Arts in English (Writing emphasis)
University of Oregon, Eugene, OR, December 1986

REFERENCES UPON REQUEST

SOFTWARE TEST MANAGER

ROBERT A. SHELDON

876 Rayna Lane (303) 555-1999 • Fax (303) 555-1231
Chicago, IL 60603 rshel@myisp.com

OVERVIEW
Software test manager seeks an innovative intrapreneurial environment in which to develop products, create market acceptance, provide hands-on leadership, and to develop software test methods from the ground up.

RESPONSIBILITIES
- Selected and implemented test methods.
- Determined and controlled test environments.
- Wrote software test suites.
- Documented test results.
- Managed the testing of new products.
- Implemented systems around a client/server model on a PC under Windows and OS/2.
- Verified designs of complex software products.
- Developed software test plans.
- Prepared test procedures.
- Documented test results.

EXPERIENCE
Two years' software engineering development experience managing the following software testing procedures:
- Tested voice annotation software and toolkits that connect data and phone networks to provide multimedia services (voice and data) to the desktop personal computer.
- Connected local area networks (LAN) to wide area networks (WAN).
- Implemented systems using client/server models on customized VME-based servers operating under VxWorks and UNIX.
- Tested tools and methods using knowledge of automated regression.

RELATED EMPLOYMENT
June 1991–Present Software Test Manager
Innovative Software Corporation, Chicago, IL.

EDUCATION
Bachelor of Science degree,
Computer Science and Information Systems
University of Chicago, Chicago IL, 1991

REFERENCES AVAILABLE UPON REQUEST.

SOFTWARE MANUAL WRITING

SALLY TUCKER
971 Sunshine Lane
Chicago, IL 60603
(303) 555-1589 ◦ Fax (303) 555-1554
stuck@myisp.com

CAREER GOAL
Software user manual writer seeks a creatively technical environment in which to develop, write, and edit software user manuals from the ground up.

RESPONSIBILITIES
c Planned software user manuals to meet the needs of users.
◦ Organized and transcribed interview notes from programmers and software designers.
◦ Increased the number of potential software customers by making complex steps easier to understand.
◦ Documented use of manuals by novice users.
◦ Designed software user manuals.
◦ Wrote user manuals to make software more marketable.
◦ Reduced the amount of after-sale support required by dealers by making the manuals easy to use.
◦ Tracked sales increase in manuals from dealers.
◦ Reduced the number of technical support personnel publishers had to hire, and saved the company $50,000 through improved manuals.

EXPERIENCE
Two years' software user manual writing/editing experience managing the following procedures:
◦ Planned the revision of COBOL and other software manuals.
◦ Determined audience and training requirements.
◦ Organized and outlined manuals by researching operation of the programs.
Progressively detailed each draft of manuals.
◦ Coordinated programmers with other writers and illustrators to plan the software design and the manual together.

RELATED EMPLOYMENT
June 1991–Present: Software User Manual Writer
                       Kyleberg and Stetson Computer Training Corporation
                       Chicago, IL.

EDUCATION
Bachelor of Science Degree
English Education
New York University, NY, 1991

REFERENCES ON REQUEST.

MARINA SABRET

2432 Elysian Glen
Palo Alto, CA 94587
(415) 555-1875 • Fax (415) 555-1808
msabr@myisp.com

OVERVIEW: Systems analyst will provide sales and technical support for your online report viewing software.

EXPERIENCE: Ten years' experience in training system administrators and end users at customer sites in the operation of MVS/CICS-based application.
IBM mainframe systems analyst and programmer with knowledge of JCL. Traveled throughout the United States.

DUTIES: Performed analysis, evaluation, architecture definition, trade-off studies, customer presentation and interface, proposal preparation and generation.

HARDWARE: Imagery Intelligence Processing Systems. Open systems POSIX compliant client server architecture. Two-bit workstations.

SOFTWARE: Unix/C software and communications protocols.
GUI, relational DBMS (Sybase); CASE Tools, DOD-Std-2167A.

EMPLOYMENT:
- **1988–Present:** Systems Analyst and Trainer, Info-Development, Palo Alto, CA.
- **1986–1988:** Programmer and Systems Analyst, Training Systems, Inc., San Francisco, CA.
- **1983–1986:** Systems Analyst/Systems Engineer, Image Systems, Berkeley, CA.

EDUCATION: Bachelor of Science Degree
Computer Science
California State University,
San Francisco, CA, 1983

REFERENCES ON REQUEST

SYSTEMS ENGINEERING

Louise Mendoza
1995 Ward Ave./Austin, TX 78754
(512) 555-5921
lmendo@myisp.com

OVERVIEW:
Systems engineer experienced in weather systems analysis and design seeks a challenging opportunity to perform system requirements in hardware and software integration.

ACHIEVEMENTS:
- Performed functional decomposition.
- Made/bought analyses.
- Performed COTS component trade-off studies and selections.
- Designed and executed time and sizing studies.
- Conducted reliability, availability, and maintainability analyses.
- Integrated software and hardware.
- Provided vendor/subcontractor coordination.
- Prepared technical proposals.
- Made oral presentations to customers and company management.
- Presented oral and written design reviews.

SOFTWARE/HARDWARE:
C computer language, UNIX and MS-DOS. PCs and LAN/WAN technologies.

SYSTEMS ENGINEERING:
Systems engineering requirements analysis. Integration and testing of distributed workstation-based systems. Knowledge of automated weather systems. Familiar with military standards, DOD engineering drawings and lists. Experience with communications protocols, (X.25/ADCCP).

EXPERIENCE:
Four years' experience in a commercial environment. Experience in all areas of development (functional specifications, design, program specifications, programming, and testing).

EMPLOYMENT:
1989–Present: **Systems Engineer,** Great Weather Systems Engineering Inc., Austin, TX, 1989

EDUCATION:
Bachelor of Science Degree
Electrical Engineering and Computer Science
University of Texas, Austin, TX, 1989

REFERENCES:
Upon Request.

TAPE LIBRARIAN

Zachary Westland
895 Plains Ave.
St. Louis, MO 63100
(314) 555-3971

JOB OVERVIEW: Tape librarian experienced in legal and news source on-line services and database retrieval/searching, seeks position with timeshare data transmission firm.

EXPERIENCE:

1983–Present: Reference and Source Tape Librarian

- Serviced database companies by providing them with a way to transmit their data.
- Created abstracts of articles, placing them on-line within timesharing computer services to be accessed by computer users.
- Transmitted data by modem and fax as well as by tape, audio, and videoconferencing.
- Stored reports and records, and maintained archives and database tapes/disks.
- Maintained on-line services offering database producers a network to reach users.
- Compiled and wrote a directory of on-line databases.
- Organized and maintained tapes of legal abstracts, contest and sweepstakes entries, academic research article abstracts, electronic news sheets, and dissertation abstracts.
- Managed numerical and textual reference databases and referred users to primary sources.
- Transmitted both reference and source data. Created channels for transmission.
- Managed reference and source databases.

EMPLOYMENT:

1989–Present: Tape Librarian
Computer Bank Tape Library
St. Louis, MO.

1983–1989: Tape Librarian
Cranshaw Legal Library
St. Louis, MO.

EDUCATION: B.A., Public History
University of Kansas, Kansas City, MO, 1983

REFERENCES ON REQUEST

TECHNICAL ILLUSTRATION

TILLIE FOSTER

(614) 555-1453 · Fax (614) 555-1422
tfost@myisp.com

7780 Pine Road
Columbus, OH 43231

OVERVIEW

Technical illustrator seeks permanent position in the computer industry. Excellent training in technical illustration, drafting, engineering graphics, architectural illustration, computer-aided drafting and design, industrial design, and presentation graphics. Expertise in computer applications of technical illustration on Cadds 4X, Macintosh, and PC.

COMPETENCIES

- Advanced technical illustration methods.
- Architectural drafting and advanced design.
- Assembly drawing.
- Airbrush.
- Basic blueprint reading.
- Computer-aided design and computer applications in drafting and technical illustration (advanced).
- Dimensioning and tolerancing.
- Electronic design and illustration.
- Engineering graphics.
- Engineering design.
- Industrial design. Developed complex concepts in graphic arts.
- PCB (circuit board) design (advanced).
- Presentation graphics.

SOFTWARE/HARDWARE

Presentation graphics on Macintosh using Adobe Illustrator, Freehand, and Quark software. AutoCAD, MiniCad, and CorelDraw! software on the PC. Technical illustration on Cadds 4X.

EMPLOYMENT

June 1995–Present: Technical Illustration Intern, Site Engineering, Inc., Columbus, OH.

EDUCATION

Associate in Arts Degree
Technical Illustration
Columbus Community College, Columbus, OH, 1995

REFERENCES ON REQUEST

Joan Bedford

377 Park Place, Raleigh, NC 27699 (919) 555-9326
jbed@myisp.com Fax (919) 555-9322

TECHNICAL WRITER

Experience

1987–1996: **Wrote two books per year on applications software uses** for home-based business owners, totaling 20 books published by Simon & Schuster, Arco, VGM, and numerous other major career book publishers.

Independent Computer Career Book Writing:
Author of numerous published books on computer graphic design and technical writing careers for major NY career book publishers.

Word Processing and Desktop Publishing:
Owner of a private word-processing, desktop publishing, and technical writing home-based business specializing in computer career information using WordPerfect, CorelDraw!, MS Publisher, and MS Word software on a PC.

1980–1987: **Reporter** and weekly national newspaper columnist for *The Small Business Entrepreneur's News*. Wrote business strategies advice columns and software reviews.

1975–1980: **Wrote three video scripts per year** to train teachers in the operation of the Eric computer system for educational research, and numerous other computer database systems for the Raleigh Education Department, Media Center, as an independent contractor.

Education

Master of Arts Degree in English
New York University, New York, NY
June 1975.

LIST OF PUBLISHED WORKS ATTACHED
REFERENCES ON REQUEST

TECHNICAL TRAINING

Leslie Stephens

78 Green Street
Boston, MA 02114
(617) 555-8317
lsteph@myisp.com

OVERVIEW:
Technical trainer seeks a staff position as a software applications instructor.

EXPERIENCE:
Developed, designed, and presented on-site and in-house training courses for diverse corporate clients in group and tutorial settings and for community college business and computer students.

SOFTWARE:
Word Processing software training:
WordPerfect, Microsoft Word (PC and Macintosh).
Windows and DOS.
Printer techniques for word processing.
Use of scanners in word processing.
Advanced word-processing methods.

Desktop Publishing software training:
PageMaker
MS Publisher
WordPerfect Presentations (presentation graphics software)
MS PowerPoint
Color separation techniques in desktop publishing.
Printer techniques for desktop publishing.
Scanners in desktop publishing.

EMPLOYMENT:
1981–Present:
Software Applications Instructor, Department of Office Education
Boston Community College, Boston, MA.

EDUCATION:
M.A., Business Education
University of Massachusetts, Boston, MA, 1981

References available on request.

VIDEO COMPUTER GAMES DESIGN

Jason Jared

1137 Meridian Street • Denver, CO 80275 • (303) 555-1914 • jjared@myisp.com

GOAL: Computer video games designer specializing in virtual reality simulations seeks staff position with educational, entertainment, or computer games software manufacturer.

EXPERIENCE: Ten years' experience designing computer cartridge video games as a video games artist for entertainment and educational software manufacturers. One year of experience in virtual reality games design.

ACHIEVEMENTS:
- Produced digital multimedia games in simulated virtual reality.
- Created Amiga-based special effects advanced digital multimedia software.
- Converted comic strip characters into 3-D computer games.
- Designed background and character movements.
- Illustrated games software.

HARDWARE: IBM, Virtual Reality Simulation peripherals, and Macintosh.

SOFTWARE: CorelDraw!, Freehand, Quark, PhotoShop, Virtual Reality Simulations, Adobe Illustrator, Tool Box. Advanced animation software for PC and Mac. Harvard Graphics software. Multimedia software.

EMPLOYMENT:

1992–Present: **Computer Video Games Designer,**
Virtual Reality Games Software, Denver, CO.

1990–1992: **Video Games Artist,**
Multimedia Systems, Inc., Denver, CO.

1987–1990: **Special Effects Artist,**
Image Magic Digital Multimedia, Boulder, CO.

EDUCATION: Bachelor of Science Degree
Special Major in Computer Graphics
University of Southern Colorado, Pueblo, CO, 1987

REFERENCES UPON REQUEST.

VIDEOCONFERENCING

Kevin Zimms

1784 Queens Highway
Prairie Village, KS 66200

(913) 555-1114 • Fax (913) 555-1214
kzimms@myisp.com

OVERVIEW: Teleconferencing executive seeks a position utilizing multimedia teleconferencing equipment to motivate, inspire, persuade, and influence the growth of international firms.

EXPERIENCE: Three years' experience selling and marketing electronic satellite network communications services and videoconferencing equipment.

RESPONSIBILITIES:
- Produced video conferences for executives in worldwide corporations utilizing electronic satellite communications to transmit data.
- Planned and created computer conferences, telephone conferences, and video conferences between Pacific Rim nations and the United States.
- Designed video conferences to link colleges with home-based students in 24 states.
- Sold videoconferencing equipment to Fortune 500 corporations, saving the companies a total of $50,000 annually in travel expenses.
- Linked corporations worldwide by telephone, computer, and video cameras via satellite communications.
- Edited all videotape for conferences.

HARDWARE: Knowledge of industrial and broadcast-quality video cameras, Genlock equipment, PC and Macintosh computers, modems, scanners, fax, and electronic satellite communications.

SOFTWARE: WordPerfect, PageMaker, Director, dBase IV, and Lotus 1-2-3.

EMPLOYMENT:

1993–Present: Video conference equipment rental and sales manager, Teleconference Computer Corporation, Prairie Village, KS.

1990–1993: Video conference coordinator, Lawrence Communications, Lawrence, KS.

EDUCATION: Bachelor of Arts Degree, Telecommunications and Film, University of Kansas, Lawrence, KS, June 1990

REFERENCES AVAILABLE ON REQUEST

VIRTUAL REALITY

Karen Leeds

560 Medallion Highway
Gainesville, FL 32600
(904) 555-5310
kleeds@myisp.com

OVERVIEW:
Virtual reality interactive, computer-generated, three-dimensional graphics simulation production position wanted by recent college graduate interested in producing 3-D models for architects, court medical presentations, animation, education, health care training, and entertainment.

EXPERIENCE:
* Created interactive, computer-generated 3-D graphics simulations on military jet fighter pilot training computer games.
* Designed games for active participants in computer-generated world in real time with 360 degrees of action.
* Operated virtual reality equipment, such as Virtuality 1000CS machine, made by Horizons Entertainment in Missouri.
* Operated virtual reality games at demonstrations and trade shows instructing players how to project 3-D images onto a liquid crystal screen using a head visette.
* Adjusted system images and sounds in response to player's movement.
* Designed computer video games.
* Acted as recruiter for an electronic university, training sales managers in virtual reality demonstration and machine monitoring.

HARDWARE:
Virtuality 1000CS machine operation.

EMPLOYMENT:
1996–Present:
Virtual Reality Design Intern, High Tech Simulations, Simulations Inc., Gainesville, FL.

INTERNSHIP:
Completed one-year internship in virtual reality production, design, and sales departments for a high-tech virtual reality training and entertainment corporation.

EDUCATION:
Bachelor of Arts Degree
Special Major in Medical Illustration and Computer Science
University of Florida
Gainesville, FL, June 1996

REFERENCES ON REQUEST

FLAVIA TUC

124 Aerina Lane
Brooklyn, NY 11123
(718) 555-1234 • Fax (718) 555-2212
ftuc@myisp.com

WEB ADVERTISING PRODUCER

QUALIFICATIONS

➤ Ability to plan, organize, and adapt cable television infomercials, ad copy, and commercials to the World Wide Web using graphics, text, and sound effects/music.
➤ Proficient in Macromedia Authorware, Director, and a variety of multimedia authoring software. Self-taught high school graduate who learned software and video on-the-job.
➤ Dynamic public relations representative with strong communications skills sensitive to Internet issues.
➤ Adaptable team player with 10 years of video production and script writing background.

PROFESSIONAL EXPERIENCE

Multimedia and Computer Graphics
➤ Developed multimedia materials using Quark, Illustrator, Photoshop, SoundEdit, Adobe Premiere, and Director.
➤ Knowledge of both PC and Macintosh desktop publishing.
➤ Knowledgeable in navigating the Internet and World Wide Web sites.
➤ Experience with HTML and Perl programming, designing Web pages.
➤ Experience since 1979 in film and video production for documentaries and commercials.
➤ Produced 12 infomercials for cable television stations in the past decade.

Creativity and Developing Internet/Web Infomercials
➤ Designed own Web page with PageMill and HTML.
➤ Designed and marketed business packages.
➤ Designed, created, and marketed 12 infomercials for both the Web and cable television.

Management
➤ Supervised and coordinated video and film crews for San Diego Media, Inc.
➤ Responsible for effective production of infomercials for cable television.
➤ Controlled and maintained inventory for video production.

EMPLOYMENT

1989–1997   Webmercials, Inc., Los Angeles. Produced cable and Web infomercials.
1979–1989   Film and Video Marketing, Inc., Los Angeles. Produced films and videos; ad copywriting.

References upon request

WEB SITE DESIGN AND ADMINISTRATION

ILISEN TERSDOTTIR
1789 BENTAR AVE • LA JOLLA, CA 92037
(619) 555-1236
ettes@kore.com

OBJECTIVE: WEBMASTER/WEB ADMINISTRATOR
To obtain a position as a computer graphic artist/multimedia technician in which I may utilize my detail-oriented talents and skills on the Internet to their highest potential and develop new abilities as a project manager/Webmaster.

COMPUTER SKILLS: My previous position as a Webmaster involved putting up Web pages, designing the art and graphics, and writing the advertising copy. Additionally, it provided extensive experience on various PC systems and use of my organizational and people skills to coordinate more than 100 field personnel. While a student at Webmaster College I prepared a news layout utilizing QuarkXPress and Adobe Illustrator, a 60-second commercial using Adobe Premiere, various pieces of artwork using Adobe Photoshop, and an interactive resume using Director.

HIGHLIGHTS: I write a monthly article for *Web Connection* magazine, and have published a short story on the Internet for Digital Storytellers, Inc. Twice a year I design and supervise the setup of digital storytelling conferences in a variety of cities internationally. In my spare time I write novels for CD-ROMs for three major interactive book publishers and design Web pages for a variety of my clients as a home-based independent contractor.

EDUCATION:

Webmaster College	Multimedia Technology Certificate	1997
San Diego State Univ.	Adult Education Teaching Credential	1996
San Diego State Univ.	B.A. in Creativity Studies	1995

EXPERIENCE:

Bank of Cambria *1995-1997*
Position: Webmaster

Designed and programmed sites and put up Web pages. Wrote advertising copy and advised clients of the bank and executives on the layout and design of advertising Web pages. Created Web shopping mall pages for Bank of Cambria. Coordinated travel plans and meeting facilities for management conferences. Interfaced with facilities management to maintain office and environment in a professional manner. Prepared and maintained monthly and quarterly incentive reports for 75+ account executives and regional managers.

National Mortgage Company *1992-1994*
Position: Audit Administrator/Funder

Closed and funded residential loans in accordance with FHLMC guidelines. Developed and maintained post-funding audit procedures. Worked closely with department heads in setting up office files, systems, and procedures for a new San Diego office. Established contact with media and formulated advertising campaign. At this point I enjoyed working in advertising so much that I decided to write ad copy for the multimedia industry. When the Internet Web browsers became popular in 1995, I trained to be a Webmaster and moved into page design.

References on request

WIRELESS COMMUNICATIONS

James Keystone

1170 Mt. Everest Place • Barrington, IL 60012
(708) 555-9635 • Fax (708) 555-9221
jkeys@myisp.com

OVERVIEW: Corporate telecommunications management position wanted. Wireless transmission executive seeks position building, designing, promoting, or selling global cellular systems.

EXPERIENCE: Two years' experience marketing cellular networks in the United States and overseas to open global links. One year of experience designing, maintaining, and repairing foreign cellular networks.

DUTIES:
- Installed, maintained, and repaired cellular networks and systems for electronic publishing companies in the United States and abroad.
- Marketed distance teaching cellular systems to rural public schools in the United States.
- Sold international wireless telecommunications equipment for multimedia, linking over 50 nations in 1995.
- Retained customers and alleviated customer dissatisfaction in a high-call work environment.
- Worked closely with customer service personnel, financial services, and dealer care departments. Trained staff in customer service skills.

EMPLOYMENT:

1994–Present: **Marketing Manager,**
International Wireless Communications, Inc.,
Barrington, IL.

1993–1994: **Wireless Transmission Technician,**
Global Hotlinks, Inc.,
Barrington, IL.

EDUCATION: Associate in Sciences Degree
Computer Science and Electronics
Chicago Community Technical College
Chicago, IL, 1992

REFERENCES AVAILABLE UPON REQUEST

Irene Hart

1245 Village Street
San Diego, CA 92106
(619) 555-8166 • Fax (619) 555-8349
ihart@myisp.com

OVERVIEW

Word-processing specialist, supervisor, and staff trainer experienced in high-tech document production seeks high-growth corporate environment. Five years' experience in the word-processing department of a computer manufacturer, with increasing responsibilities.

COMPETENCIES

- Advanced level word processing with WordPerfect software on PCs.
- Mail merging, sorting, labeling, custom mailing, and text editing of direct mail marketing material.
- Electronic publishing and data transmission utilizing word-processing and desktop publishing software, including: MS Publisher and PageMaker.
- Statistical keyboarding and integration of tabular material and graphics into wordprocessing documents and desktop publishing software, including spreadsheets and dBase programs.
- Use of software spelling checkers, dictionaries, grammar-checking software, and editing software.
- Record keeping utilizing dBase IV and Lotus 1-2-3.
- Integration of spreadsheets and database programs into word-processing text and/or graphics.
- Experience with laser printers, label printers, fax, scanners, modems, and electronic transmission networks.
- Text entry keyboarding speed of 80 words per minute (certificate holder) using WordPerfect.
- Editing and proofreading of all documents.
- Staff training and supervisory ability.

EMPLOYMENT

1992–Present: Word-Processing Specialist
　　　　　　　　　Lennody Computers, Inc., San Diego, CA.

EDUCATION

Certificate in Word Processing and Desktop Publishing
San Diego City College
San Diego, CA, 1992

REFERENCES ON REQUEST

11
STEERING STRATEGIES

To what companies will you send your résumé? You can find a listing of all the software and hardware companies in the United States or Canada in your public library. Look in the industrial directories under computer hardware, software, or on-line companies. For a quick listing, you can find excellent databases of U.S. software, hardware, and on-line companies on Parson's Technology software, "Address Book for Windows." You could then compile your list using that software.

Address Book for Windows is an expandable database for storing names, addresses, and phone numbers of organizations or individuals and includes the capability to dial the phone numbers automatically. It also contains databases of airlines, motels, and other names, addresses, and phone numbers you'll need for travel or job relocation. You can write for further information to: Parson's Technology, One Parson's Drive, P.O. Box 100, Hiawatha, Iowa, 52233-0100.

Think Small

Are you willing to try new search techniques to interest an employer? Then target smaller companies. As the larger corporations downsize to cut costs, smaller businesses are less likely to lay off as frequently, according to a recent poll taken by the American Management Association (New York).

By the year 2000, Virginia employment trends and labor forecaster Marvin Cetron optimistically predicted that the services industry will employ 88 percent of the American workforce. Cetron stated to Perri Capell, associate editor of the *Wall Street Journal's Managing Your Career* (a college edition of the *National Business Employment Weekly)*, in the 1993 article, "Hiring Demand Shows Signs of Life," that "We'll have a completely different economy, where computerization and literacy will be absolutely essential."

The computerized world economy now focuses on the growth of export trade businesses. Your résumé will have a better chance if sent to divisions of companies that show growth.

Therefore, seek out small to mid-size firms that are growing fast. A good indicator of a healthy company is export volume. For example, Sun Microsystems Inc. of Mountain View, CA, showed a 44 percent growth in exports during 1992.

Check a company's growth rates before mailing your résumé by looking at *Hoover's Handbook of American Business* (Reference Press Inc.).

The handbook charts ten-year sales and earnings growth and total debt ratio for more than 500 major employers, according to Capell's article.

Another reference book you should look through before sending out your résumé is the *Bond Guide* (Standard & Poor's). You can find these reference publications in any major public or college library. The monthly *Bond Guide* is a booklet that rates thousands of corporate bonds based on whether a company can pay principal and interest by the due date. If you see a corporation rated less than BB, think carefully before you send it your résumé.

Professional employment researchers, career consultants, trend forecasters, college counselors, and résumé specialists look at investment analysts' current reports to research financially sound firms. Investigative reporters covering employment trends read computer industry trade journals to get the most timely information for similar research.

Try "Investext." It's a computerized anthology, a CD-ROM database of professional analysts' reports. It's available from Information Access Company, 362 Lakeside Drive, Foster City, CA 94404, 1(800)227-8431.

Investext is available on-line or you can find it on CD-ROM in several major libraries. Information Access Company also offers "The General Business File." This database contains full-text articles taken out of trade magazines as well as full-text stock analysts' reports.

Use trade journals to network with others in your field. Most major public and college libraries maintain a current collection of trade journals listing companies and names of key personnel in management. Read the trade journals' help wanted advertisements. Many trade magazines also run a category for job seekers called positions wanted.

An index of trade journals and industry-oriented magazines, including those for the computer industry, is listed in *Gale's Directory of Publications*. Computer industry professional and business associations are included with other types of associations in *The Encyclopedia of Associations*.

If you are looking for a job in the computer mail order business there are library reference books that list the small to medium-sized high growth companies such as Dell Computer Corporation, a pioneer in the computer mail-order business.

Sometimes, when you can't find such information in your public or college library, you can ask university placement directors for it (a small fee may be charged if you're not a student). Many offer such information sources and databanks to the public as well as to their students.

If you want to obtain the names, addresses, and phone numbers of top executives in major corporations so you can direct your résumé to a particular person in your field, your library may contain *The Greenwich Register* (Hunt-Scanlon Publishing Company). Of course, searching the Internet is often the best way to locate up-to-date information on people to network with and companies you'd like to work for.

By checking these reference books or databases and searching the Internet, you can send your résumé to the company most likely to be hiring in your niche.

As has been emphasized throughout this book, the best way to put your résumé in the right hands is to network. Build a team of business contacts by joining industry groups in your specialization. Track the trends.

12
NEW OPPORTUNITIES WITH THE INTERNET AND THE WORLD WIDE WEB

The Internet and the World Wide Web are creating jobs for computer personnel each day. They are only two aspects of a vast new industry made up of the converging technologies—computer, telephone, and TV.

Jobs related to the Internet include designing Web sites, writing advertising copy for them, accounting, marketing, management, and software engineering using the technology of TCP/IP or other Internet protocols, digital signal processing, Internet systems security analysis, and netcasting (continuous up-to-the-minute news or Web broadcasts on your computer screen). Of course, the growing number of companies that are Internet service providers offers many jobs. Telephone company employees are being trained to service customers as Internet providers themselves.

As the Internet continues to expand, a variety of other jobs will open in customer relations, technical support, repair, sales, and language translations. As more multimedia majors graduate from schools, competition will increase for Internet programmers, software engineers, and Web designers. More and more Webmasters, or designers/administrators of Web sites, will be in demand too. Are you a network administrator with a knowledge of servers, routers, and concentrators? With the convergence of technologies, computer industry employers are seeking people who can identify and respond to systems problems.

The Internet is expected to expand steadily for the next decade, creating new technology jobs—from those who make the routers and switchers to those who design the graphics and animation. Cable companies will soon become Internet providers, creating still more jobs.

When the Web was first becoming popular, the best jobs went to people who were in the business of creating Web browsers. Today, as more corporate investors want to offer the Web on TV, more jobs that combine the skills of a TV producer with a computer programmer and graphic designer or content writer are opening up.

Using a small piece of hardware called a set-top box, TV viewers can access the Web through their TVs. Using a remote control, they can interact with Web sites and do all the things that computer users do when they access the Web. Companies like Sony and Philips are manufacturing these set-top boxes to sell for about $300 each. They are marketing this Internet TV to noncomputing TV viewers. Thus, with the Web on TV, there is going to be a flood of newcomers to the Internet.

Jobs in this emerging field include content writers who know formatting languages such as Java, HTML, and VRML. Skill in these languages is necessary to put up graphics, text, and video on the Web so both computer users and TV viewers with set-top boxes can browse the sites. If you want to learn these skills and languages, look for a college or continuing education course in them or buy some of the current software that lets you teach yourself. New software programs can turn any existing document into a Web page, automatically translating your text into HTML format.

Providers of the Web on TV are looking for content developers and will be offering "channels" to content providers who meet their qualifications. Such people must have training in multimedia, Internet and Web design, and Perl programming, as well as sales and marketing of Internet-related products and services.

FREELANCE WORK

Working in the Internet industry requires that you wear many hats. Writers, editors, and Web site designers or programmers can work for a variety of electronic magazines or book publishers who also offer print versions. If you write, design, or manage information on a freelance basis, the Web is a good place to search for income. Many on-line journalists are asked to write their pieces in HTML. There are hundreds of sites to download tutorials as well as software that will automatically convert your document to HTML format.

Tremendous opportunities are occuring for people who can put up multilingual Web pages using new software such as Accent Software's suite of applications that allows users to access, author, publish, and distribute World Wide Web pages and e-mail on the Internet using any language version of Microsoft Windows, because of the great potential for finding international clients.

If you're freelancing as an artist, photographer, consultant, sales agent, manufacturer's representative, debt collector, literary agent or other type of independent contractor, turn your Web search engines on *consultants* or *consulting, contingency professionals* or *temporary employment*. Or search the title of your profession, such as programmer, analyst, researcher, or contractor.

Freelance work is dramatically increasing for those who can put up Web pages for businesses, individuals, and especially advertising agencies. Web design is found in the marketing departments of corporations or ad agencies, or with independent consultancies who often ally themselves with Internet providers.

Freelancers are needed for Web tracking, or keeping track of how many times an ad at a Web site is visited. Web trackers are the equivalents of air checkers—persons who are hired by ad agencies for their clients to keep tabs on how many times a radio or TV ad is broadcast on the air.

MANAGING THE DEVELOPMENT OF TECHNICAL INFORMATION

Managing the Development of Technical Information is a new job title/category. Workers—both freelancers and telecommuters—with these skills are in great demand on the Web. This field includes writing, teaching, or training on-line, and it encompasses Web design, tracking, advertising, marketing, sales, and artistic work from digital photography to talent management. Check your local area for courses in managing technical information. The University of California offers an extension certificate program in managing the development of technical information.

OTHER EMERGING AREAS

Some job hunting sites on the Web suggest emerging careers such as software talent manager, hypertext on-line journalist, digital photographer's agent, virtual reality Internet designer, or telecommuting pilot (setting up telecommuting stations in employees' homes for government and corporate employers).

Certain publishers are hiring on-line database developers. They are seeking experienced UNIX programmers and database developers for help with high quality text development projects. You need to know Perl programming and how to develop algorithms for word lists in many different languages.

Jobs in the field of large scale text conversion and other editorial tasks are increasing, and the Web is the place to search for these jobs. Much of this work can be performed off-site.

If you have strong sales and marketing skills in addition to Internet expertise, you may want to look into such newly created job areas as creating virtual trade shows on the Internet. (For job hunters, visiting a virtual trade show is an excellent way to showcase their skills or make contacts for interviews.)

Internet sportscasting is creating new jobs for producers, writers, and programmers who specialize in on-line sports producing. Journalists who can design and implement sports and games content for on-line services such as America Online, CompuServe, and the Internet act as project managers of the content development process.

Another emerging technology combines hardware, software, and network support in a product such as Newscatcher, making it possible to receive information from the Internet without wires. This wireless receiver picks up Internet information instantly over a wireless paging network, delivering multimedia news and information to the user (while freeing up phone lines).

YOUR RESUME ON THE WEB

You don't need to know HTML or other formatting languages to put your resume up on the Web. New software is coming on the market every day that can convert your documents into HTML format for putting up your own Web page. Some of these programs are Claris Home Page, Adobe PageMill, Microsoft FrontPage, and Corel WebMaster. Programs such as Myrmidon for the Mac can turn any file into a Web page with just the click of a button or can turn other applications into Web authoring tools. Many programs are on the market with ready-to-use Web graphics too.

In addition to changing resumes, the Web is affecting how interviews are conducted. Today, Web designers and administrators, network engineers, and immersive video content writers are hired on-line faster than they are hired in traditional face-to-face interviews. Naturally, the personal interview is preferred, but there are benefits to on-line interviews, such as reduced travel time.

See Chapter 1 for details on software that helps you job search on the Web.

APPENDIX A

RÉSUMÉ TRACKING FOLLOW-UP WORKSHEET

(Use or copy this form for your files.)

Date _____

Company _____

Name _____

Address _____

_____

_____

_____

Phone _____

Interview _____

Interview Comments: _____

_____

_____

Follow-up Letters _____

_____

Job Offer _____

Referrals _____

Related Information _____

_____

_____

Quarterly Follow-Up _____

_____

Results_____

_____

APPENDIX B

COMPUTER INDUSTRY ASSOCIATIONS

Advertising/Multimedia

Association of Independent Commercial Producers (AICP)
11 East 22nd Street
Fourth Floor
New York, NY 10010
(212) 475-2600
Fax: (212) 475-3910
http://www.aicp.com

International Chain of Industrial and Technical Advertising Agencies
c/o Poppe Tyson
201 Littleton Road
Morris Plains, NJ 07950
(201) 539-0300

Young Professionals Division
c/o Lintas: New York
1 Dag Hammarskjold Plaza
New York, NY 10017
(212) 459-5690
(Jr. professionals in advertising, marketing, and public relations under age 30 or with less than two years' professional experience. Affiliated with Advertising Club of New York.)

Artificial Intelligence

American Association for Artificial Intelligence
445 Burgess Drive
Menlo Park, CA 94025
(415) 328-3123

CD-ROM, CD-Interactive, and Multimedia

Association for the Advancement of Computing in Education
(Publisher of *Ed-Tech Review*)
P.O. Box 2966
Charlottesville, VA 22902
(804) 973-3987

Electronic Artists Group
P.O. Box 580783
Memphis, MN 55458
(612) 331-4289

Interactive Multimedia Association (IMA)
3 Church Circle, Ste. 800
Annapolis, MD 20401
(410) 626-1380

International Interactive Communications Society (IICS)
P.O. Box 1862
Lake Oswego, OR 97035
(503) 649-2065

Multimedia Publishers Group
Advanced Strategies
60 Cutter Mill Rd., Ste. 502
Great Neck, NY 11021
(516) 482-0088

San Francisco-Multimedia Development Group
2601 Mariposa Street
San Francisco, CA 94110
(415) 553-2300
Fax: (415) 553-2403

CD-Interactive Publishing

Optical Publishing Association
P.O. Box 21268
Columbus, OH 43221
(614) 793-9660

Optical Publishing Association
7001 Discovery Blvd. #205
Dublin, OH 43017

Software Publishers Association
1703 M Street NW
Suite 700
Washington, DC 20036
(202) 452-1600

Communications

Computer and Communications Industry Association
666 11th Street NW
Suite 600
Washington, DC 20001
(202) 783-0070

Council of Communications Management
Oak West Office Plaza
17W703 E. Butterfield Road
Oakbrook Terrace, IL 60181
(708) 268-0707

International Communications Association (ICA)
2735 Villa Creek Drive
Suite 200
Dallas, TX 75234-7419
(972) 233-3889
(800) ICA-INFO
Fax: (972) 488-9985
http://www.icanet.com

International Interactive Communications Society (IICS)
P.O. Box 1862
Lake Oswego, OR 97035
(503) 649-2065

Networking Institute
505 Waltham Street
West Newton, MA 02165
(617) 965-3340
Fax: (617) 965-2341
tni@netage.com
http://www.netage.com

Society for Technical Communication
901 N. Stuart Street
Suite 304
Arlington, VA 22203
(703) 522-4114

Computational Linguistics

Association for Computational Linguistics
c/o Priscilla Rasmussen
P.O. Box 6090
Somerset, NJ 08875
(908) 873-3898
Fax: (908) 873-0014

Independent Computer Consultants Association (ICCA)
11131 South Towne Square
Suite F
St. Louis, MO 63123
(314) 892-1675
Fax: (314) 487-1345
70007.1407@compuserve.com
http://www.icca.org
(National network of independent computer consultants for supporting the success of its members in providing professional services. Membership open to individuals, partnerships, and corporations.)

Computer Graphics and Animation

Association for Computing Machinery
1515 Broadway
New York, NY 10036-5701
(212) 869-7440
Fax: (212) 944-1318

World Computer Graphics Association
6121 Lincolnia Road
Suite 302
Alexandria, VA 22312
(703) 642-3050
Fax: (703) 642-1663

Computer Press

Computer Press Association
1260 25th Avenue
San Francisco, CA 94122
(415) 681-5364

Multimedia Publishers Group
Advanced Strategies
60 Cutter Mill Road
Suite 502
Great Neck, NY 11021
(516) 482-0088

Society for Technical Communication
901 N. Stuart Street
Suite 304
Arlington, VA 22203
(703) 522-4114

Software Publishers Association
1703 M Street NW
Suite 700
Washington, DC 20036
(202) 452-1600

Computer Security

International Association for Computer Systems Security
6 Swarthmore Lane
Dix Hills, NY 11746
(516) 499-1616

Data Communications

International Facsimile Association
4023 Lakeview Drive
Lake Havasu City, AZ 86403
(602) 453-3850

Data Entry

Information Systems Audit and Control Association (ISACA)
3701 Algonquin Road
Suite 1010
Rolling Meadows, IL 60008
(847) 253-1545
Fax: (847) 253-1443

Database Management

International Data Base Management Association
10675 Treena Street
Suite 103
San Diego, CA 92131
(619) 578-3152
(800)767-SHOW
(Promotes the database management industry. Conducts hands-on computer workshops and seminars.)

National Center for Automated Information Retrieval
165 E. 72nd Street
Suite 1B
New York, NY 10021
(212) 249-0760

Data Processing

Black Data Processing Associates
Information Technology Thought Leaders
1111 14th Street NW
Suite 70D
Washington, DC 20005
(202) 789-1540

Special Interest Group for Business
Data Processing and Management
c/o Association for Computing Machinery
11 West 42nd Street
New York, NY 10036
(212) 869-7440

Digital Photography

American Society of Media Photographers (ASMP)
14 Washington Road
Suite 502
Princeton Junction, NJ 08550-1033
(609) 799-8300
Fax: (609) 799-2233

Entrepreneurship

Young Entrepreneurs Organization
1321 Duke Street
Suite 300
Alexandria, VA 22314
(703) 519-6700
http://www.yeo.org
(Entrepreneurs under age 40 who have either founded or own a firm with annual gross revenues exceeding $1 million.)

VFEA International Trade Association (VITA)
7825 East Gelding Drive, #104
Scottsdale, AZ 85260-3415
(602) 951-8866
Fax: (602) 951-0720
http://www.vita.com

Games and Simulation (Computer)

International Simulation and Gaming Association
c/o Steven E. Underwood
University of Michigan
2609 Draper Road
Room 208 EPB
Ann Arbor, MI 48109-2140
(313) 764-4333

North American Simulation and Games Association
c/o John delRegato
Pentathlon Institute
P.O. Box 20590
Indianapolis, IN 46220
(317) 782-1553

Hardware

AM/FM International (Computers)
14456 E. Evans Avenue
Aurora, CO 80014
(303) 337-0513

CDLA, The Computer Leasing and Remarketing Association
1200 19th Street NW
Suite 300
Washington, DC 20036-2401

Center for Office Technology (COT)
301 North Kent Street
Suite 102
Alexandria, VA 22314
(703) 684-7760
Fax: (703) 684-4554
ctroftek@erols,com
http://www.cot.org
(National association of employers and manufacturers dedicated to improving the office working environment and promoting informed approaches to issues associated with computers and office technology.)

Computing Technology Industry Association (CompTIA)
450 East 22nd Street
Suite 230
Lombard, IL 60148
(630) 268-1818
Fax: (630) 268-1384
75300.2507@compuserve.com

DDA – Association of the DEC Marketplace
107 South Main Street
Chelsea, MI 48118
(313) 475-8333
Fax: (313) 475-4671
admin@dda.org
http://www.dda.org

Information Technology

Information Industry Liaison Committee
5430 Grosvenor Lane
Suite 200
Bethesda, MD 20814
(301) 564-4505

Information Technology Association of America
1616 N. Fort Meyer Drive
Suite 1300
Arlington, VA 22209
(703) 522-5055

Management/Technology

Association of University Technology Managers
71 East Avenue
Suite S
Norwalk, CT 06851
(203) 852-7168

Music (Computerized)

Computer Musician Coalition
1024 W. Wilcox Avenue
Peoria, IL 61604
(309) 685-4843

International MIDI Association
5316 W. 57th Street
Los Angeles, CA 90056
(213) 649-6434

Networking

International Association of Telecomputer Networks
660 E. Highway 434
Suite A
Winter Springs, FL 32708
(407) 327-7777

Networking Institute
505 Waltham Street
West Newton, MA 02165
(617) 965-3340

Office Information Systems

Society for Information Management
401 N. Michigan Avenue
Chicago, IL 60611-4267
(312) 644-6610

Special Interest Group on Office Information Systems
c/o Prof. Carson Woo
University of British Columbia
Faculty of Commerce
2053 Main Mall
Vancouver, BC, Canada V6T 1Z2

Robotics

American Defense Preparedness Association
2101 Wilson Boulevard
Suite 400
Arlington, VA 22201-3061
(703) 522-1820
(Military artificial intelligence/robotics.)

Robotics Industries Association
P.O. Box 3724
900 Victors Way
Ann Arbor, MI 48106
(313) 994-6088

Robotics International
of the Society of Manufacturing Engineers
P.O. Box 930
Dearborn, MI 48128
(313) 271-1500

Software

Business Software Alliance
1150 18th Street NW
Suite 700
Washington, DC 20036
(202) 872-5500
Fax: (202) 872-5501
software@bsa.org
http://www.bsa.org

Software Publishing

Software Publishers Association
1703 M Street NW
Suite 700
Washington, DC 20036
(202) 452-1600

Technical Illustration

Society for Technical Communication
901 North Stuart Street
Suite 904
Arlington, VA 22203
(703) 522-4114
Fax: (703) 522-2075
stc@stc-va.org
http://www.stc-va.org

Telecommunications

Association of Telemessaging Services International (ATSI)
1200 19th Street NW
Washington, DC 20036-2412
(202) 429-5151
Fax: (202) 223-4579

MultiMedia Telecommunications Association (MMTA)
2500 Wilson Boulevard
Suite 300
Arlington, VA 22201
(703) 907-7472
Fax: (703) 907-7478
http://www.mmta.org
(Affiliated with the Telecommunications Industry Association (TIA), MMTA supports the development of global markets for delivering new technology-based solutions to the business community.)

Satellite Broadcasting and Communications Association
c/o Charles C. Hewitt
225 Reinekers Lane
Suite 600
Alexandria, VA 22314
(703) 549-6990

Society of Telecommunications Consultants
13766 Center Street
Suite 212
Carmel Valley, CA 93924-9693
(408) 659-0110
(800) STC-7670
Fax: (408) 659-0144
stchdq@attmail.com

Telecommunications Industry Forum
c/o Alliance for Telecommunications Industry Solutions
1200 G Street NW
Suite 500
Washington, DC 20005
(202) 434-8844
Fax: (202) 393-5453

Teleconferencing

International Teleconferencing Association (ITCA)
1650 Tysons Boulevard
Suite 200
McLean, VA 22102-3915
(703) 506-3280
(800) 360-4822
Fax: (703) 506-3266

Training

Association for the Advancement of Computing in Education
(Publisher of *Ed-Tech Review*)
P.O. Box 2966
Charlottesville, VA 22902
(804) 973-3987

Center for Computer-Assisted Legal Instruction
229 19th Avenue South
Minneapolis, MN 55455
(612) 625-3419

ICIA Educational Technologies Division
11242 Waples Mill Road
Suite 200
Fairfax, VA 22030-6079

Society for Applied Learning Technology
50 Culpepper Street
Warrenton, VA 22186
(703) 347-0055

Training Media Association
198 Thomas Johnson Drive
Suite 206
Frederick, MD 21702
(301) 662-4268
Fax: (301) 695-7627
http://trainingmedia.org

Videotex

Videotex Industry Association
8403 Colesville Road
Suite 865
Silver Spring, MD 20910-3366
(301) 495-4955

Wireless Communications

National Communications Association
7 Park Avenue
Suite 14-3
New York, NY 10016
(212) 725-0248

The Personal Communications Industry Association
500 Montgomery Street
Suite 700
Alexandria, VA 22314
(703) 739-0300
Fax: (703) 836-1608
(PCs, paging, SMR carriers.)

Women's Associations

Association for Women in Computing
41 Sutter Street
Suite 1006
San Francisco, CA 94104

APPENDIX C

COMPUTER INDUSTRY TRADE PERIODICALS
(Software, Technical & Trade Systems)

ACM Transactions on Computer Systems
ACM Transactions on Database Systems
ACM Transactions on Programming Languages and Systems
Association for Computing Machinery
1515 Broadway, 17th Floor
New York, NY 10036-5701
(212) 869-7440
Fax: (212) 869-0481

ADAPSO
The Computer Software and Services Industry Association
1300 N. 17th Street, Suite 300
Arlington, VA 22209-3899
(703) 522-5055

AEC News Report
AEC Systems Computer Solutions
(Architecture, Engineering, Construction)
365 Willard Avenue, Suite 2K
Newington, CT 06111
(203) 666-1326
Fax: (203) 666-4782

Canadian Datasystems
Maclean Hunter Ltd.
777 Bay Street
Toronto, ON, Canada M5W 1A7
(416) 596-5906

Computer Industry Report
International Data Corporation
5 Speen Street
Framingham, MA 01701
(617) 872-8200

Computer Industry Update
IMR, Inc.
P.O. Box 681
Los Altos, CA 94022
(415) 941-6679

Computerworld
CW Publishing, Inc.
375 Cochituate Road
P.O. Box 9171
Framingham, MA 01701-9171
(617) 879-0700

Computing Reviews
Computing Surveys
Association for Computing Machinery
1515 Broadway, 17th floor
New York, NY 10036-5701
(212) 869-7440
Fax: (212) 944-1318

Datamation
Cahners Publishing Company
275 Washington Street
Newton, MA 02158-1630
(617) 558-4281
Fax: (617) 558-4506
http://www.datamation.com

Datapro Applications Software Solutions
Datapro Research Corporation
1805 Underwood Blvd
Delran, NJ 08075
(609) 764-0100

Dataworld
Faulkner Technical Reports
6560 North Park Drive
Pennsauken, NJ 08109-4374
(609) 662-2070

Dr. Dobb's Journal
Miller Freeman, Inc.
600 Harrison Street
San Francisco, CA 94107
(415) 905-2200
Fax: (415) 905-2232

EDP Weekly
Computer Age
EDP News Services, Inc.
714 Church Street
Alexandria, VA 22314-4202
(703) 739-8500
Fax: (703) 739-8505

High Technology Careers Magazine
Diversity Careers Magazine
Virgual Job Fair Website
Westech ExpoCorp
4701 Patrick Henry Drive
Suite 101
Santa Clara, CA 95054-1847
(408) 970-8800
Fax: (408) 980-5103
http://www.vjf.com
(Information on the changing job market for engineering, computer, and IS/DP professionals, and recruitment products and services.)

The Independent
Independent Computer Consultants Association
P.O. Box 27412
St. Louis, MO 63141
(314) 997-4633

InfoWorld: subsidiary of IDG Communications
155 Bovet Road
Suite 800
San Mateo, CA 94402
(415) 572-7341
Fax: (415) 358-1269

Micro Software Marketing
P.O. Box 380
Congers, NY 10920

MIS Quarterly
University of Minnesota
Carlson Schoool of Management
271 19th Avenue South
Minneapolis, MN 55455
(612) 624-2029
Fax: (612) 624-2056
misq@csom.umn.edu
http://www.misq.org

Software Maintenance News
Software Maintenance Association
56 Bay Street
Suite 400
Staten Island, NY 10301
(718) 816-5522

Software Protection
Law & Technology Press
1112 Ocean Drive
Suite 103
Manhattan Beach, CA 90266
(213) 372-1678

COMPUTER/ELECTRONIC SERVICE

CESN Publications
P.O. Box 428
Peterborough, NH 03458
(603) 924-9457

Electronic Products
645 Stewart Ave.
Garden City, NY 11530
(516) 227-1300

Electronic Publishing
PennWell Publishing Company
10 Tara Boulevard
Suite 500
Nashua, NH 03062-2801
Editorial: (603) 891-0123
Subscriptions: (918) 831-3161

Intertec
Intertec Publishing Corporation
P.O. Box 12901
Overland Park, KS 66212
(913) 888-4664

ISCET Update
International Society of Certified Electronics Technicians
2708 West Berry Street
Fort Worth, TX 76109
(817) 921-9101

Micro Marketworld
174 Concord Street
Suite 21
Peterborough, NH 03458
(603) 924-9471

Modern Electronics
76 N. Broadway
Hicksville, NY 11801
(516) 681-2922

NASD News
National Association of Service Dealers
c/o North American Retail Dealers Association
10 East 22 Street
Lombard, IL 60148
(630) 953-8950
nardahdg@aol.com

NESDA Member Memo and *NESDA Update*
Professional Electronics
National Electronic Sales and Service Dealers
Association (NESDA)
2708 West Berry Street
Fort Worth, TX 76109
(817) 921-9061

Readout
North American Computer Service Association
506 Georgetown Drive
Casselberry, FL 32707
(305) 331-0181

Technical Notebook (Quarterly)
International Society of Certified Electronics Technicians
2708 West Berry Street
Fort Worth, TX 76109
(817) 921-9101

Technician Association News
Electronics Technicians Association, International (ETA)
602 North Jackson
Greencastle, IN 46135
(317) 653-4301
eta@indy.tdsnet.com
http://www.eta-sda.com

COMPUTER MAGAZINES (General, Mass-Market, Computer-User)

Byte
The McGraw-Hill Companies
24 Hartwell Avenue
Lexington, MA 02173
(617) 860-6336
http://www.byte.com

MacUser
Ziff-Davis Publishing Company
P.O. Box 56986
Boulder, CO 80322-6986
(800) 627-2247

MacWEEK
Coastal Associates Publishing
P.O. Box 1766
Riverton, NJ 08077-7366
(609) 461-2100

MACWORLD
Macworld Communications, Inc.
501 Second Street, 5th Floor
San Francisco, CA 94107
(415) 243-0505

PC Magazine
Ziff-Davis Publishing Company
P.O. Box 54093
Boulder, CO 80322-4093
(800) 289-0429

PC WORLD
PC World Communications, Inc.
501 Second Street, #600
San Francisco, CA 94107
(415) 243-0500

COMPUTER GRAPHICS

Computer Artist
Digital Magic
PennWell Publishing Company
10 Tara Boulevard
Suite 500
Nashua, NH 03062-2801
Editorial: (603) 891-0123
Subscriptions: (918) 831-3161

Computer Graphics World
Advanced Technology Group
10 Tara Boulevard
Suite 500
Nashua, NH 03062-2801
Editorial: (603) 891-0123
Subscriptions: (918) 831-3161
Fax: (603) 891-0539

Fast Company
U.S. News & World Report
1290 Avenue of the Americas
Suite 600
New York, NY 10104
Editorial Offices:
77 North Washington Street
Boston, MA 02114
(617) 973-0300

Internet World
Mecklermedia Corporation
11 Ferry Lane West
Westport, CT 06880
(203) 226-6967
(800) 632-5537

MacArtist
MacArtist, Inc.
901 E. Santa Ana Boulevard
Suite 103
Santa Ana, CA 92701
(714) 973-1529

Step-By-Step Design
Step-By-Step Publishing
6000 North Forest Park Drive
Peoria, IL 61614
(309) 688-2300

DESKTOP PUBLISHING/DESKTOP VIDEO

Desktop Communications
International Desktop Communications Ltd.
342 Madison Avenue
Suite 622
New York, NY 10173-0002
(212) 768-7666
Fax: (212) 768-0288

Publish
Integrated Media, Inc.
501 Second Street
Suite 310
San Francisco, CA 94107
(415) 243-0600
(800) 656-7495

MULTIMEDIA, CD-INTERACTIVE, AND CD-ROM

Ed-Tech Review
P.O. Box 2966
Charlottesville, VA 22902
(804) 973-3987

New Media
Hypermedia Communications Inc.
901 Mariner's Island Boulevard
Suite 365
San Mateo, CA 94404
(415) 573-5170

Online User
Online World
462 Danbury Road
Wilton, CT 06897-2126
(203) 761-1466

Web Master
CIO Communications, Inc.
492 Old Connecticut Path
P.O. Box 9208
Framingham, MA 01701
(508) 872-0080

MULTIMEDIA ELECTRONIC MUSIC AND AUDIO

Electronic Musician
Act III
P.O. Box 41094
Nashville, TN 37204
(800) 888-5139

Keyboard
Miller Freeman, Inc.
Box 58528
Boulder, CO 80322-8528
(800) 289-9919

Mix
Act III
P.O. Box 41094
Nashville, TN 37204
(800) 888-5139

Recording Engineer/Producer
Intertec Publishing Corp.
9221 Quivira Road
P.O. Box 12901
Overland Park, KS 66212
(913) 541-6628

VIRTUAL REALITY

PCVR
1706 Sherman Hill Road
Unit A
Laramie, WY 82070
(307) 742-7675

INDEX

Abilities:
  key, 2
  resume, 26–29
    sample, 36
Achievement worksheet, 83–84
Action verb resource, 84–86
Address, 19
Advertisement answering, 42, 45
  sample, 53
Age, 22
Ageism, 107
Artwork, 31
As-needed workers, 119–123
ASCII format, 12
Assessment, self, 16

Basic information worksheet, 61
Benchmarking, 3
Blind ads, 45
Bond Guide, 229
Brainstorming, 21

Career:
  changes, 2–3, 28
  selection, 126–148
CD-ROM, 4
Change:
  in computer industry, 16–18
  responding to, 13–14
Character of Organizations, The, 3
Checklist, 100–103
Chronological:
  employment history worksheet, 71–72
  resumes, 24–25
    sample, 35
Civil service:
  level, 20
  resumes, 12
  retirees, 113–119
Communications, interactive, 4
Commutation, 23
Competency, 5
Competitive edge, 105–106
Compulsive organizations, 5–6
Computer Career Preference Classifier, 131–148
Computer industry:
  changing, 16–18
  emerging areas, 233–234
Conferences, 49–50
Consultants, resume development, 12
Contractors, resume strategies, 119–123
Conventions, 49–50
Cooperative education programs, 112
Courses, relevant, 20, 107
Cover letters, 40–59, 110–111
  advertisement answering, 42, 44–45
    sample, 53
  conferences, 49–50
    sample, 57
  conventions, 49–50
    sample, 57
  employment agency, 48
    sample, 52
  hook questions, 40–41
  information seeking, 47–48
    sample, 55
  informational, 45–47
  professional organizations, 48–49
  samples, 43–44, 52–57
  student strategies, 110–111
  tips, 41
  types, 42
  trade shows, 49–50
    sample, 57
Creative resume, 30–33
  sample, 39
Cultural diversity, resume strategies, 123–125
Customization of resumes, 13

Databases, resume, 10–12
Day-in-the-life worksheet, 70
Disabilities, 22
Discontinuity, job, strategies, 106–108
Diversity, industrial, 16–18
Do What You Are, 129
"Dynamic dozen" traits, 23

Editing, 87–103
  checklist, 100–103
Education, 19–20, 115–116
  worksheet, 65–66
  See also: Training
Employment agency, cover letters, 48
  sample, 52
Employment history:
  discontinuity, 106–108
  highlights, 19
Encyclopedia of Associations, 108, 229
Expanded resume, 29–30
  sample, 37–38
Expertise worksheet, 69
Extrovert personality style, 149–150

Feeling personality style, 157–159
First impression, 5, 15
Follow up letters, 40–59
  sample, 58–59
Foreign languages, 21
Format, resume, 15
Freelance work, 232–233

Gale's Directory of Publications, 229
Gifts Differing, 160
Goals, 16, 20
  clarity, 1–2
Greenwich Register, The, 229
Group fit, 4–5

Hardware competencies, 19
  worksheet, 68
Hiring cycles, 9
Hobbies, 21
Honors, work related, 20
Hook questions, 40–41
Hoover's Handbook of American Business, 228–229
"Hot sheets," 8–9
Hotlines, 8

Immigrants, resume strategies, 123–125
Impulsive organizations, 5–6
Independent contractors, resume strategies, 119–123
Information seeking letters, 47–48
  sample, 55
Informational cover letter, 45–47
Interactive communications, 4
Internet opportunities, 231–234
Interviews, 50
  informational, 6–7
Intrapreneurs, 106
Introduction to Type and Careers, 129
Introvert personality style, 151–152
Intuitive personality style, 152–154
"Investext," 229

Job:
  description, 32
  discontinuity strategies, 106–108
  market, hidden, 8–9
  objectives, worksheet, 67
  search:
    control of, 12–13
    interest, demonstrating, 110
    strategies, 228–230
  selection, 126–148
  titles, changing, 17
Judging personality style, 159–161

Keirsey Temperament Sorter, 108

Letters:
  cover, 40–59
  follow-up, 50–51
Life skills, transferable, 20

Marital status, 22
Middle management, 1
Military service, 21
Modified abilities resume, 29
Myers Briggs Type Indicator, 129

Networking, 6–10
  hidden resources, 8–9
  public speaking, 7–8
  sample letter, 56
  writing, 7
New Directions in Career Planning and the Workplace, 129
Nontraditional resumes, 104–112
  applications, 104–105

Objectives, 33–34
  worksheet, 67
Opportunities, 2–3
Organizational memberships, 21
Organizations, 3–6
  behavior, 3
  benchmarking, 3
  character, 3
  compulsive, 5–6
  impulsive, 5–6
  needs, 4
  traditions, 6
  visioning, 3–4
Outplacement agency, cover letters, 48

Perceiving personality style, 159, 161–162
Personal requirements, worksheet, 73–74
Personality:
  profiles, 163–167
  surveys, 129–148
  types, 149–167
Photographs, 22
Planning the resume, 60–86
Please Understand Me, 129
Portfolios, 31
Positioning: The Battle for Your Mind, 41
Power resume, 14–15
Presentation, 2
Pressure, working under, 13–14
Professional associations, 20–21, 48–49, 108–109
Profit making, 14
Public speaking, 7–8
Publications, 20

References, 23, 116
  worksheet, 75–76
Research, 15
Resumes:
  abilities style, 26–29
    sample, 36
  checklist, 100–103
  chronological style, 24–25
    sample, 35
  components, 19–39
  consultants, 12

creative style, 30–33
  sample, 39
customization, 13
databases, 10–12
distribution, 6–7, 9
editing, 87–103
expanded style, 29–30
  sample, 37–38
format, 15, 19–21
  worksheet, 77–82
information to exclude, 22–23
interactive, 11–12
marketing tool, 21–22
modified abilities style, 29
nontraditional, 104–112
organization, 24
planning, 60–86
power, 14–15
production, software assisted, 11–12
samples, 88–90, 92, 95, 98, 168–227
screening services, 10–11
strategies, 106–125
style, 14, 23–33
World Wide Web, 234
writing, 12–15
Retiree strategies, 113–119

Salary history, 22
Screening services, 10–11
Security clearances, 20
Self assessment, 16
Seminars, planning, 7–8
Sensing personality style, 154–155
Skills, 27, 116
  marketable, 106
  organization, 60–86
  worksheet, 62–63
Slanting resumes, 13
Software:
  competencies, 19
  resume producing, 11–12
  worksheet, 68
Strategies, resume:
  immigrants, 123–125
  independent contractors, 119–123
  job discontinuity, 106–108
  retirees, 113–119
  students, 108–112
  temporary employees, 119–123
Student, resume strategies, 108–112
Success, opportunities for, 2–3

Team:
  spirit, 105
  work, 4–5
Technical information development, management of, 233–234
Technostress, 13
Telecommuting, 112
Telephone, 19
Temporary:
  employees, resume strategies, 119–123
  work, 28
Thinking personality style, 156–157
Titles, job, changing, 17
Trade shows, 49–50
Traditions, reflecting, 6
Training, 19–20, 32–33
  worksheet, 64
Traits, desirable, 23
Tutoring, 110
Type Talk at Work, 156

Verbs, action, resources, 84–86
Visioning companies, 3–4
Volunteering, 110

Work:
  history, 115
    gaps, 26, 106–108
    highlights, 19
  study, 112
Worksheets, 61–84
  achievements, 83–84
  basic information, 61
  chronological employment history, 71–72
  day-in-the-life, 70
  education, 65–66
  expertise, 69
  hardware, 68
  job objective, 67
  personal requirements, 73–74
  references, 75–76
  resume format, 77–82
  skills, 62–63
  software, 68
  training, 64
World Wide Web opportunities, 231–234
Writing:
  publication, 7
  resume, 12–15

ABOUT THE AUTHOR

Anne Hart has written 51 books, numerous scripts, and more than 300 articles, as well as several novels, plays, and screenplays. She enjoys writing about new ways people use the Internet and she specializes in how-to books about creative expression in the newest media and in emerging technologies. Hart also writes about business and contemporary issues, careers, telecommuting, and the relationship of personality type computer communications.

NOTES

NOTES

NOTES

NOTES

NOTES

NOTES